MARGARET HOLZMANN'S
ICONIC
KNIT BLANKETS
AND MORE

30+ Graphic Patterns for Blankets, Pillows, Tops, and Table Runners

MARGARET HOLZMANN

STACKPOLE BOOKS

Essex, Connecticut
Blue Ridge Summit, Pennsylvania

STACKPOLE BOOKS

An imprint of The Globe Pequot Publishing Group, Inc.
64 South Main Street
Essex, CT 06426
www.globepequot.com

Distributed by NATIONAL BOOK NETWORK

Copyright © 2024 by Margaret Holzmann
Illustrations by Margaret Holzmann
Photography by Gerard Holzmann

All rights reserved. No part of this book may be reproduced in any form or by any electronic or mechanical means, including information storage and retrieval systems, without written permission from the publisher, except by a reviewer who may quote passages in a review.

The contents of this book are for personal use only. Patterns herein may be reproduced in limited quantities for such use. Any large-scale commercial reproduction is prohibited without the written consent of the publisher.

We have made every effort to ensure the accuracy and completeness of these instructions. We cannot, however, be responsible for human error, typographical mistakes, or variations in individual work.

British Library Cataloguing in Publication Information available

Library of Congress Cataloging-in-Publication Data

Names: Holzmann, Margaret, author.
Title: Margaret Holzmann's iconic knit blankets and more: 30+ graphic patterns for blankets, pillows, tops, and table runners / Margaret Holzmann.
Other titles: Iconic knit blankets and more
Description: Lanham, MD : an imprint of Globe Pequot, the trade division of The Rowman & Littlefield Publishing Group, Inc., [2024]
Identifiers: LCCN 2024027853 (print) | LCCN 2024027854 (ebook) | ISBN 9780811775724 (paperback) | ISBN 9780811775731 (ebook)
Subjects: LCSH: Knitting—Patterns. | Blankets.
Classification: LCC TT825 .H645 2024 (print) | LCC TT825 (ebook) | DDC 746.43/2041—dc23/eng/20240624
LC record available at https://lccn.loc.gov/2024027853
LC ebook record available at https://lccn.loc.gov/2024027854

∞™ The paper used in this publication meets the minimum requirements of American National Standard for Information Sciences—Permanence of Paper for Printed Library Materials, ANSI/NISO Z39.48-1992.

Contents

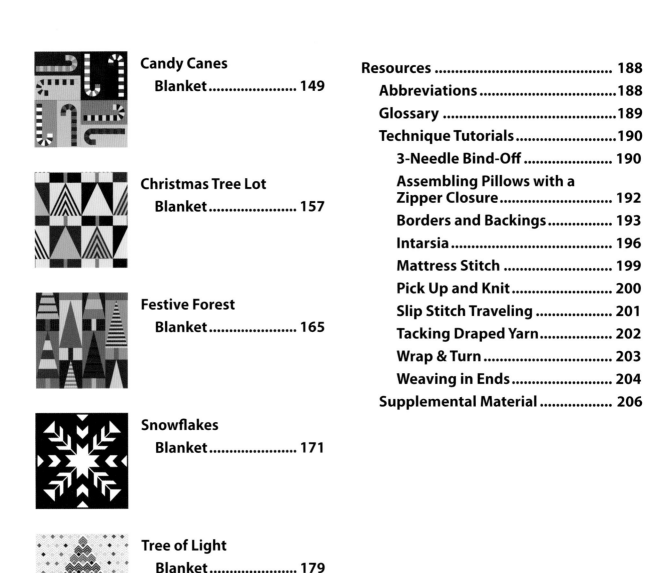

General Notes for All Patterns

1. See page 188 for Abbreviations.

2. See page 189 for a Glossary of techniques with written explanations. An asterisk (*) is appended to entries with associated videos.

3. See page 206 for access to videos and other supplemental materials.

4. Use a 40"/100 cm circular needle (longer is fine) to work Borders. Smaller pieces that may be knitted on straight needles, if desired.

5. When markers (m) are used, slip them when they are encountered unless directions say otherwise. Directions may not say when to slip markers.

6. Use a knitted cast-on (see "Glossary" on page 189). If a CO edge will later have stitches picked up on it, a provisional CO may be substituted.

7. In written instructions, stitch generation, such as pu&k or casting on, counts as Row 1.

8. Pu&k is used in all patterns and therefore is not listed in the "Techniques" section.

9. Instructions may refer to a "garter st ridge," which is created by working a RS knit row and then a WS knit row. One ridge equals two rows.

10. On blankets that use wrap & turn (short rows), when knitting a wrapped stitch, knit only the stitch on the needle. Do not knit wraps and wrapped stitches together. When instructions say: "Knit to <N> sts before end, w&t," the stitch wrapped is N. For instance: "Knit to 3 sts before end, w&t," means to knit to the 3rd stitch from the end of the row, wrap the 3rd stitch from the end, then turn.

11. A gauge is specified for all patterns. Check gauge before starting, changing needle size if needed to obtain gauge. Block gauge swatch if using a natural fiber yarn. Yarn requirements are based on the given gauge. If gauge is different, more or less yarn may be required. Gauge may differ from yarn label because it is calculated over garter stitch, whereas yarn labels use stockinette stitch.

12. Changing to a different yarn weight and needle size will result in a larger or smaller blanket. If using a heavier yarn than called for, add 5 percent to yarn requirements for each 0.5 stitch per inch (2.5 cm) decrease between pattern gauge and gauge of substitute yarn. If using a lighter weight yarn than called for, decrease yarn requirements by 5 percent for each 0.5 stitch per inch (2.5 cm) increase between pattern gauge and gauge of substitute yarn.

13. If a pattern says to "leave a long tail" when cutting yarn but does not specify a length, leave a tail four times the length of the seam to be sewn in that yarn color.

14. When sewing seams, always use a yarn color that matches one of the pieces being sewn.

15. When sewing embellishments on, lift the edge of the embellishment and stitch on the WS of the embellishment and RS of the blanket.

16. To organize yarn while knitting: (1) Place each color in a clear plastic bag and label with the assigned letter for the color, and/or (2) With a hole-puncher, make holes in an index card or cardboard. Label each hole with assigned letter for color, then through each hole, tie on a short strand of matching color yarn.

17. When working wrong side rows with a small number of stitches, purl backward so that work does not need to be frequently turned.

18. For better control when working with a small number of stitches, work on wooden needles.

19. Pattern stitches (illustrated in light green boxes within patterns) are worked back and forth.

20. The Borders of all blankets are started by picking up and knitting stitches on Blanket edges.

21. Blue italic numbers in figures indicate the number of stitches to pu&k on an edge.

22. Where slip stitch crochet is specified, chain stitch embroidery may be substituted.

23. Symbols used in construction figures are:

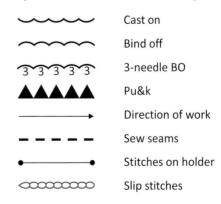

∿∿∿∿∿	Cast on
⌒⌒⌒⌒	Bind off
3 3 3 3	3-needle BO
▲▲▲▲▲	Pu&k
⟶	Direction of work
– – – – –	Sew seams
•———•	Stitches on holder
⧉⧉⧉⧉⧉	Slip stitches

Introduction

The collection of patterns in this book is inspired by an appreciation for the things in my everyday life including: my community, holidays, the ocean, pets, and nature. This collection started when I designed the Safe at Home blanket and published it as an "Indy" pattern. The warm reception and the fun I had knitting it got me excited about designing more blankets that reflect "Life" themes.

The patterns in this book continue my exploration into geometric knitting, which I refer to as "the new colorwork," because it uses under-exploited techniques for shaping and joining to create colorful motifs rather than traditional stranded (Fair Isle) or intarsia. Some blankets contain intarsia but it is used sparingly.

The techniques used include:

Garter stitch - all designs in this collection use only garter stitch, because it has a useful built-in geometry where 1 stitch wide equals 2 rows, making it easy to knit complex shapes. The bumpy surface texture of garter stitch hides stitch maneuvers and less-than-perfect seams. The fabric it produces is denser than stockinette stitch, so it makes a thicker, warmer blanket.

Pick Up and Knit - this useful stitch generation method is used extensively in starting a new piece off the edge of an already completed piece to eliminate sewing.

Shaping - increases and decreases form the basis of geometric knitting. The familiar ones are used, including knit 2 sts together; slip, slip, knit 2 sts together through back loops; and central double decrease.

Wrap & Turn - allows knitting of curved and more complex shapes. Also known as "short rows," one benefit to working this technique in garter stitch is that the wrapped stitch and wrap are not knitted together on the next row, saving time and reducing complexity.

3-needle Bind-Off - is used both for joining individual pieces of a blanket together and for shaping. Its use eliminates all or most sewing in many of the blankets.

Intarsia - is used for small areas when the other methods above just won't do the trick.

Knitting a blanket is a big commitment of time and money. To try out a pattern on a smaller scale using leftover yarns, instructions for a pillow, runner, or other accessory are provided for some of the blankets. These "Try it Out" pages are bordered with dots.

The color schemes for the patterns have been chosen carefully, but they may not reflect your tastes. It can be a lot of fun to explore other color combinations and personalize your blanket. The coloring pages, available online, will allow you to experiment with and plan out your own color ideas. Many of the designs, such as Flower Show, depicted below, make excellent stash busters. For the best results, select high-contrast colors for adjacent pieces.

Instructional videos for techniques used in this book are available to purchasers. Suggested videos for each blanket design are listed on page 207. For access to coloring pages and videos see "Supplemental Material" on page 206.

Patterns are organized alphabetically by name, except for the holiday blankets, which are found together at the end of the book.

CAMP ALONG

Head for the woods, the mountains, or the desert with a blanket of colorful campers.

TECHNIQUES

3-needle BO, wrap & turn, intarsia

SIZES

Small (Large): 40 x 56.5"/102 x 144 cm (54.5 x 75.5"/144 x 192 cm)

There are specific videos for all steps in this pattern. See page 207 for the link to videos.

YARN

Cascade Yarns 220 Superwash, worsted (100% superwash wool; 220 yds/200 m; 3.5 oz/100 g):

Pattern color ID	Color swatch	Color ID	Color name	Color description	# Balls for Size	
					Small	Large
A		817	Ecru	off-white	4	6
B		296	Myrtle Heather	dark forest green	1	2
C		864	Christmas Green	true green	1	2
D		905	Celery	muted medium green	1	1
E		887	Wasabi	bright yellow-green	1	2
F		250	Laurel Green	light mint green	1	2
G		313	Rich Brown	dark brown	1	1
H		908	Magenta	deep red	1	1
I		837	Berry Pink	very bright pink	1	1
J		838	Rose Petal	medium pink	1	1
K		854	Navy	navy	1	1
L		252	Celestial	royal blue	1	2
M		204	Smoke Blue	muted medium blue	1	2
N		279	Sterling Blue	light blue	1	2
O		907	Tangerine Heather	orange	1	1
P		345	Autumn Sunset	peach	1	2
Q		289	Cream Puff	light peach	1	1
R		263	Gold Fusion	yellow-gold	0	1
S		820	Lemon	medium yellow	1	2

NEEDLES

(2) US Size 7/4.5 mm 40"/100 cm circular needles, 1 straight or circular US Size 9/5.5 mm for 3-needle BO

NOTIONS

Tapestry needle, removable stitch markers, stitch holders

Gauge

18 sts x 36 rows = 4"/10 cm in garter st

Notes

- The blanket is composed of two Blocks: Campers and Trees. Blocks are sewn into horizontal Strips, which are joined modularly with "sashing" Strips.

- Instructions are for size Small with changes for Large in parentheses.

- The term "ridge" refers to two rows of knitting that create a ridge-like feature on the surface of the knitting. A ridge is formed by a row of knitting on the RS followed by a row of knitting on the WS. A knitted CO counts as a row of knitting on the RS. Therefore, a knitted CO followed by a row of knitting is the first ridge.

- All shapes have written instructions and most have charts. Because of the length of the pattern, charts are placed close to their related written instructions rather than at the end of the pattern. Chart Symbols are defined on page 7.

- When casting on, use a knitted CO.

- When working wrap & turn, do not knit wraps and wrapped sts together on next row.

- If no specific marker handling is given, then slip markers when encountered.

Overview of Pattern

This pattern is organized into these sections:

- Layouts: Block counts, types and colors used for a small and large version of the blanket.
- Camper Block Instructions (Left, Right, Top, Door, and Frame pieces)
- Tree Block Instructions
- Sashing/Assembly
- Borders
- Finishing

Layouts

Make Blocks in quantities and color schemes shown in Figure 2 (3).

In Figure 2 (3), the colors for **Camper Blocks** are specified in this format:

(<C1><C2><C3>)[<D1><D2>] FC {<W1><W2>} (<T1><T2>)<H>

where the color abbreviations (shown in Figure 1) are defined as:

Camper Color 1 (C1) – CO and 1st stripe
Camper Color 2 (C2) – 2nd stripe
Camper Color 3 (C3) – 3rd stripe
Door Color 1 (D1) – main color for door
Door Color 2 (D2) – door's window
Frame Color (FC) – framing pieces
Window Color 1 (W1) – window shade
Window Color 2 (W2) – window glass
Tire Color 1 (T1) – outer tire
Tire Color 2 (T2) – inner (hub) tire
Hitch Color (HC) – color for hitch

In Figure 2 (3), the colors for **Tree Blocks** are specified in format <FC><BC><TC> by these abbreviations:

Frame Color (FC)
Branches Color (BC)
Trunk Color (TC)

CAMPER BLOCK INSTRUCTIONS

Camper Blocks come in four shapes that differ only in the shape of the "Top" part as shown in Figure 4. The name of the Camper is derived from the shape of its Top. In Figures 2 and 3, the shape of the Top is specified in the top left corner of each Camper Block.

See Figure 5 for an overview of Camper Block construction. The "Flat" style Camper is shown in Figure 5, but all Campers are worked in these steps.

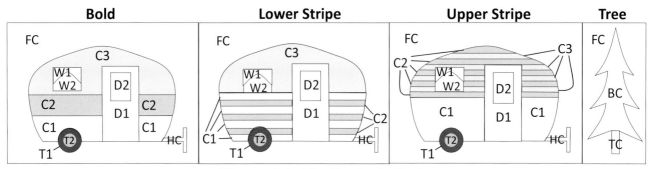

Figure 1: Color Identification for Blocks

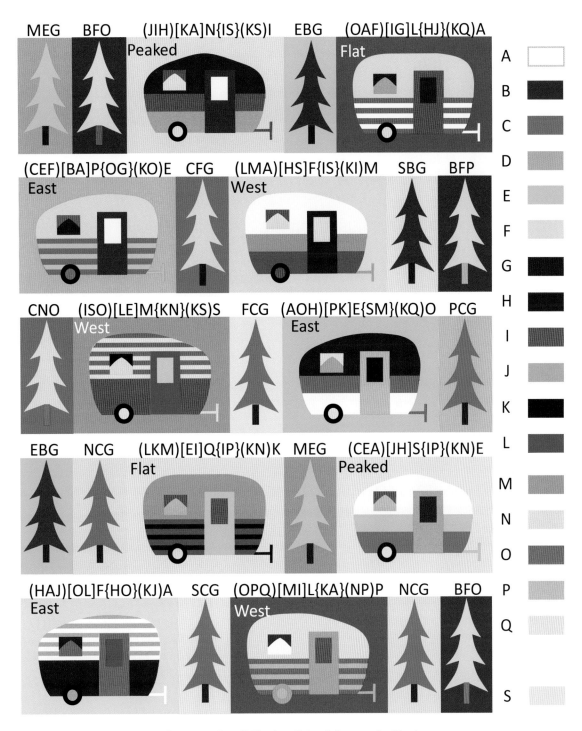

Figure 2: Small Blanket Color Schemes for Blocks

Figure 3: Large Blanket Color Schemes for Blocks

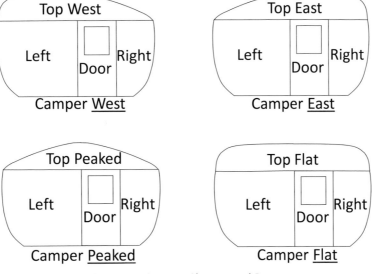

Figure 4: Camper Shapes and Parts

Steps

1–3   The Camper is worked from bottom to top, in this order: 1) Left, 2) Right, 3) Top. Stitches on the Left are on a holder while the Right is worked.

4   The Door is picked up and knitted on the edges of previously completed pieces.

5–8   Four Corners are worked next, from stitches picked up and knitted from the Camper edge.

9   Continuing with the stitches of the Corners, the Upper Frame is worked.

10   The Lower Frame is then worked from stitches picked up and knitted on the bottom of the Upper Frame and Camper pieces.

11–13   Embellishments, shown in brown, are worked after the Block is complete. The Window uses intarsia and is sewn on, the Tire is worked flat and sewn on, and the Hitch is created with crochet or embroidered slip stitch.

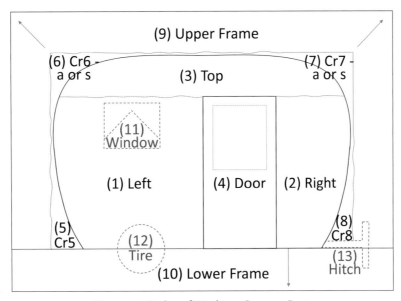

Figure 5: Order of Working Camper Parts

Campers are 58 rows (29 ridges) in height. The striping styles are named as follows: Bold, Lower Stripe, and Upper Stripe, specified in Figure 6. All color changes are made at the beg of RS (odd-numbered) rows. Use Color 1 (C1) for the cast on and initial stripe, Color 2 (C2) is the second color, and Color 3 (C3) for the third color.

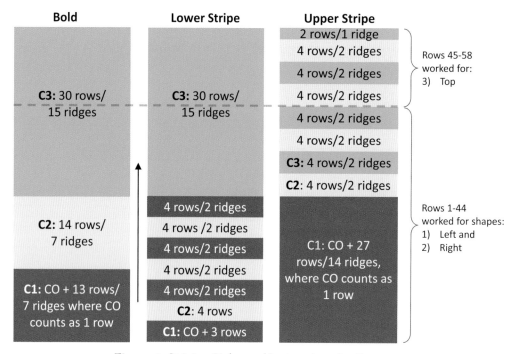

Figure 6: Striping Styles and Instructions for Campers

Upper Stripe

Lower Stripe

Bold Stripe

The Instructions for each Block part, numbered 1–13, are as follows. Charts are provided for some shapes.

(1) LEFT

Notes:

- See Figure 6 for color changes for Camper, and Figure 2 (3) for Block quantities, color schemes, and Camper styles.

- When working stripes, carry yarns between uses and cut after last use.

- This shape is 44 rows in height and therefore ends before the Striping sequence (in Figure 6) is complete.

  With C1, CO 17 sts. (*Note:* This counts as Row 1.)

  Work [Left]. Place 22 sts on holder. Cut all yarns.

Left – 17 sts inc'ing to 23 sts dec'ing to 22 sts

Row 2 and all even (WS) rows to 40: Knit.
Row 3: Knit to last st, kf&b – 1 st inc'd; 18 sts.
Rows 5, 7, and 9: Rep [Row 3] 3 times – 3 sts inc'd; 21 sts.
Row 11: Knit.
Row 13: Rep [Row 3] – 1 st inc'd; 22 sts.
Rows 15, 17, 19, and 21: Knit.
Row 23: Rep [Row 3] – 1 st inc'd; 23 sts.
Rows 25, 27, 29, 31, 33, 35, 37, 39, and 41: Knit.
Row 42: BO 1, knit to end – 1 st dec'd; 22 sts.
Rows 43 & 44: Knit.

Left - Camper

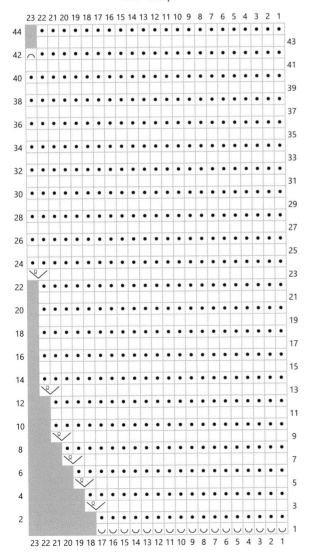

CHART SYMBOLS

☐	RS: knit	•	WS: knit
╱	k2tog	╲	ssk
▲	pu&k	⋀	central double decrease (cdd)
⏚	join	⌒	bind off
⌣	cast on	⧖	kf&b
⊂	RS: w&t	⊃	WS: w&t

Left Bold Stripe version
(ignore Tire - that comes later)

(2) Right

See "Notes" for Left shape.

With C1, CO 6 sts. Work [Right]. Leave sts on needle.

Right - Camper

Right (Bold Stripe Version)

Right (Bold Stripe Version)

Right – 6 sts inc'ing to 12 sts dec'ing to 11 sts

Row 2 and all even (WS) rows to 44: Knit.
Row 3: Kf&b, knit to end – 1 st inc'd; 7 sts.
Rows 5, 7, and 9: Rep [Row 3] – 3 sts inc'd; 10 sts.
Row 11: Knit.
Row 13: Rep [Row 3] – 1 st inc'd; 11 sts.
Rows 15, 17, 19, and 21: Knit.
Row 23: Rep [Row 3] – 1 st inc'd; 12 sts.
Rows 25, 27, 29, 31, 33, 35, 37, 39, and 41: Knit.
Row 43: BO 1, knit to end – 1 st dec'd; 11 sts.

(3) Top

The Top is a continuation of the Left and Right shapes, so row numbering continues at Row 45. Continue established striping specified in Figure 6.

Row 45 (set up, RS): With RS of **Right** facing, k11. Turn and CO 11 sts. Turn and with RS of **Left** facing, knit 22 sts off holder – 44 sts.

Work [Top <shape>] for Camper.

Top West

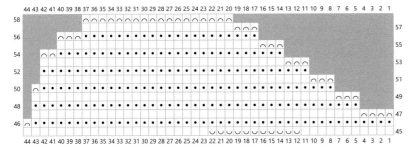

Top Peaked

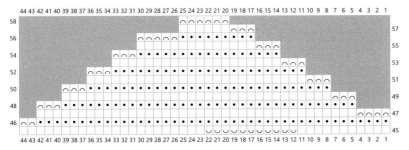

Top East

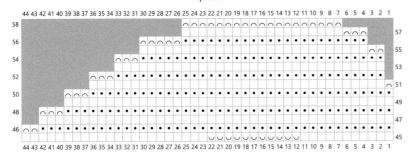

Top Flat

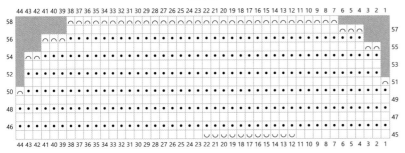

Top West (TW) – 44 sts dec'ing to 0 sts

Row 46 (WS): BO 1, knit to end – 43 sts.
Row 47 (RS): BO 4, knit to end – 39 sts.
Row 48: Knit.
Row 49: BO 3, knit to end – 36 sts.
Row 50: BO 1, knit to end – 35 sts.
Row 51: BO 3, knit to end – 32 sts.
Row 52: Knit.
Row 53: BO 3, knit to end – 29 sts.
Row 54: BO 2, knit to end – 27 sts.
Rows 55–57: Rep [Row 53] 3 times – 9 sts dec'd; 18 sts.
Row 58: BO rem sts.

Top Peaked (TP) – 44 sts dec'ing to 0 sts

Row 46 (WS): BO 2, knit to end – 42 sts.
Row 47 (RS): BO 4, knit to end – 38 sts.
Row 48: BO 3, knit to end – 35 sts.
Rows 49–55: Rep [Row 48] 7 times – 21 sts dec'd; 14 sts.
Row 56: BO 5, knit to end – 9 sts.
Row 57: BO 3, knit to end – 6 sts.
Row 58: BO rem sts

Top East (TE)– 44 sts dec'ing to 0 sts

Row 46 (WS): BO 2, knit to end – 42 sts.
Row 47 (RS): Knit.
Row 48: BO 3, knit to end – 39 sts.
Row 49: Knit.
Row 50: BO 3, knit to end – 36 sts.
Row 51: BO 1, knit to end – 35 sts.
Row 52: BO 3, knit to end – 32 sts.
Row 53: Knit.
Row 54: BO 3, knit to end – 29 sts.
Row 55: BO 2, knit to end – 27 sts.
Row 56: BO 5, knit to end – 22 sts.
Row 57: BO 3, knit to end – 19 sts.
Row 58: BO rem sts.

Top Flat (TF)– 44 sts dec'ing to 0 sts

Rows 46 (WS)-49 (RS): Knit.
Row 50: BO 1, knit to end – 43 sts.
Row 51: BO 1, knit to end – 42 sts.
Rows 52–53: Knit.
Row 54: BO 2, knit to end – 40 sts.
Row 55: BO 2, knit to end – 38 sts.
Row 56: BO 3, knit to end – 35 sts.
Row 57: BO 3, knit to end – 32 sts.
Row 58: BO rem sts.

(4) DOOR

The Door is constructed in 3 steps, labeled A, B, and C in Figure 7. Stitch counts are specified after each row where they change, as follows: <total sts>; <# sts from beg of row to m1>-<#sts bet m1 and m2>-<#sts bet m2 and end of row>.

Note: There are no charts for the Door pieces.

A) Door Frame

With Door Color 1 (D1), and starting at the red triangle in Figure 7, Step A, pu&k 22 sts (1 st per garter st ridge) to next corner, pm (m1), pu&k 11 sts (1 st per CO st) bet "m1" and "m2," pm (m2), and pu&k 22 sts (1 st per garter st ridge) from m2 to end of edge – 55 sts.

Rows 2–4: Work [YS, Rows 2–4] – 4 sts dec'd; 51 sts (21–9–21). Do not cut D1.

B) Window

Place first 11 sts on holder. Place last 11 sts on separate holder – 29 sts (10–9–10).

Rows 5–10: With D2, rep [YS, Rows 3 & 4] 3 times – 12 sts dec'd; 17 sts (7–3–7).
Row 11: Knit to 2 sts bef m, ssk, rm, cdd, rm, k2tog, knit to end – 4 sts dec'd; 13 sts (6–1–6).
Row 12 (WS): K5, k2tog. Rotate needles so that RS of work is together and needle tips are parallel. With larger needle, 3-needle BO rem 12 sts. Cut yarn and insert through rem loop on needle. Pull to tighten and fasten off.

C) Lower Door

Row 5 (RS): With D1 still attached from Step A, and RS of work facing, knit 11 sts off holder on left-lower side of door opening, pm, then pu&k 7 sts (1 st per garter st ridge) from blue triangle at bottom-left corner of Window, in Figure 7, Step C, to bottom-right corner of Window, then knit 11 sts off holder on right-lower side of door opening – 29 sts (11–7–11).
Row 6 (WS): Knit.
Rows 7–10: Work [YS, Rows 3 & 4] twice – 8 sts dec'd; 21 sts (9–3–9).
Row 11: Knit to 2 sts bef m, ssk, rm, cdd, rm, k2tog, knit to end – 4 sts dec'd; 17 sts (8–1–8).
Row 12 (WS): K7, k2tog. Rotate needles so that RS of work is together and needle tips are parallel. With larger needle, 3-needle BO rem 16 sts. Cut yarn and insert through rem loop on needle. Pull to tighten and fasten off.

Y-Square (YS)
Row 2 (WS): Knit. **Row 3 (RS):** *Knit to 2 sts bef m, ssk, sm, k2tog; rep from * once more, knit to end – 4 sts dec'd. **Row 4:** Knit.

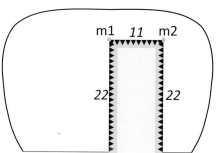

A) Door Frame: m1 & m2 are markers. Numbers in italics are pu&k st counts

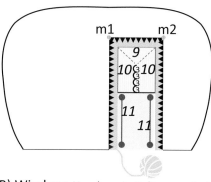

B) Window: Numbers in italics are starting st counts. Blue lines are sts on holders.

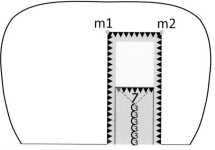

C) Lower Door: Number in italics is pu&k st count for lower edge of Window.

Figure 7: Door Construction

(5) – (8) Corners

Four Corner shapes are worked around the edges of the Camper, to turn it into a rectangular shape.

Pm (m2) on the top edge of Camper just above the left-top corner of the Door (green dashed line in Figure 8). Pm on the edge of the Camper between ridges 14 and 15 on both the Right (m3) and Left (m1) pieces of the Camper (brown dashed lines in Figure 8 on page 14).

Starting at red triangle at bottom-right corner of Camper and using the matching Camper style in Figure 8 for stitch counts, pu&k 16 sts to m3, 31 sts (West or Peaked) or 33 sts (East or Flat) bet m3 and m2, 31 sts (East or Peaked) or 33 (West or Flat) bet m2 and m1, and 16 sts bet m1 and the bottom-left corner of the Camper. Do not remove m's.

Tip: If stitch counts are a little off, adjust on the next (WS) row using k2tog for decreases and kf&b for increases. Plan out where these are to be worked and use markers as reminders.

Figure 9 on page 14 specifies the Corner shapes to be worked per Camper style.

Over the 16 sts bet the end of the row and m1, work [Cr1].

Over the sts bet m1 and m2, work [Cr2s] (East or Peaked) or [Cr2a] (West or Flat).

Over the sts bet m2 and m3, work [Cr3s] (West or Peaked) or [Cr3a] (East or Flat).

Over the sts bet m3 and the beg of the row, work [Cr4].

Corner (Cr1) – 16 sts dec'ing to 15 sts

Row 2 (WS): K9, w&t.
Row 3 (RS): Knit.
Row 4: K6, w&t.
Row 5: Knit to last 2 sts, ssk – 1 st dec'd; 15 sts.
Row 6: K2, w&t.
Rows 7 & 8: Knit.

Corner 2 Angled (Cr2a) – 33 sts inc'ing to 35 sts

Row 2 (WS): K20, w&t.
Row 3 (RS): K12, w&t.
Row 4: K10, w&t.
Row 5: K3, kf&b, k2, w&t – 1 st inc'd; 34 sts.
Row 6: K5, w&t.
Row 7: K1, kf&b, w&t – 1 st inc'd; 35 sts
Row 8: Knit.

Corner 2 Sloped (Cr2s) – 31 sts inc'ing to 35 sts

Row 2 (WS): K23, w&t.
Row 3 (RS): K6, kf&b, k11, w&t – 1 st inc'd; 32 sts.
Row 4: K16, w&t.
Row 5: K6, kf&b, k7, w&t – 1 st inc'd; 33 sts.
Row 6: K12, w&t.
Row 7: K6, kf&b, k4, w&t – 1 st inc'd; 34 sts.
Row 8: K9, w&t.
Row 9: K6, kf&b, k1, w&t – 1 st inc'd; 35 sts.
Row 10: K6, w&t.
Row 11: K5, w&t.
Row 12: K2, w&t.
Row 13: K1, w&t.
Row 14: Knit.

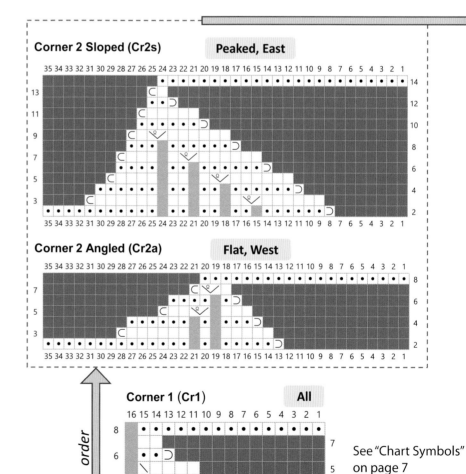

See "Chart Symbols" on page 7

<table>
<tr><td>

Corner 3 Sloped (Cr3s) – 31 sts inc'ing to 35 sts

Row 2 (WS): K26, w&t.
Row 3 (RS): K12, kf&b, k4, w&t – 1 st inc'd; 32 sts.
Row 4: K16, w&t.
Row 5: K8, kf&b, k4, w&t – 1 st inc'd; 33 sts.
Row 6: K13, w&t.
Row 7: K5, kf&b, k4, w&t – 1 st inc'd; 34 sts.
Row 8: K10, w&t.
Row 9: K2, kf&b, k4, w&t – 1 st inc'd; 35 sts.
Row 10: K7, w&t.
Row 11: K4, w&t.
Row 12: K3, w&t.
Row 13: K1, w&t.
Row 14: Knit to m3.

</td><td>

Corner 3 Angled (Cr3a) – 33 sts inc'ing to 35 sts

Row 2 (WS): K28, w&t.
Row 3 (RS): K13, w&t.
Row 4: Knit to 4 sts bef prev wrap, w&t.
Row 5: K4, kf&b, k2, w&t – 1 st inc'd; 34 sts.
Row 6: Rep Row 4.
Row 7: K1, kf&b, w&t – 1 st inc'd; 35 sts
Row 8: Knit.

Corner (Cr4) – 16 sts dec'ing to 15 sts

Row 2 and even (WS) rows to 8: Knit.
Row 3 (RS): K9, w&t.
Row 5: K2tog, k4, w&t – 1 st dec'd; 15 sts.
Rows 7: K2, w&t.

</td></tr>
</table>

(9) Upper Frame

Rm's. Pm on the 29th st from the beg of the row, and on the 29th st from end of the row. Confirm st counts shown in Figure 10. Work [UF]. Cut yarn and fasten off, leaving 40"/100 cm tail.

Upper Frame (UF) – 100 sts inc'ing to 124 sts

Row 1 (RS): *Knit to marked st, kyok; rep from * once more, knit to end – 4 sts inc'd; 104 sts.
Row 2 (WS): Knit. Advance m's to ridge just completed, placing each around the center st of the kyok.
Rows 3–12: Rep [Rows 1 & 2] 5 times – 20 sts inc'd; 124 sts.
Rm's. BO loosely.

(10) Lower Frame

Using FC, and starting at the red triangle in Figure 11, pu&k 54 sts along the lower edge of the Block. The numbers in italics indicate how to distribute these sts. Knit 11 rows. BO loosely.

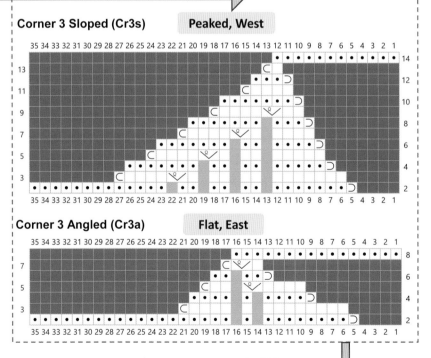

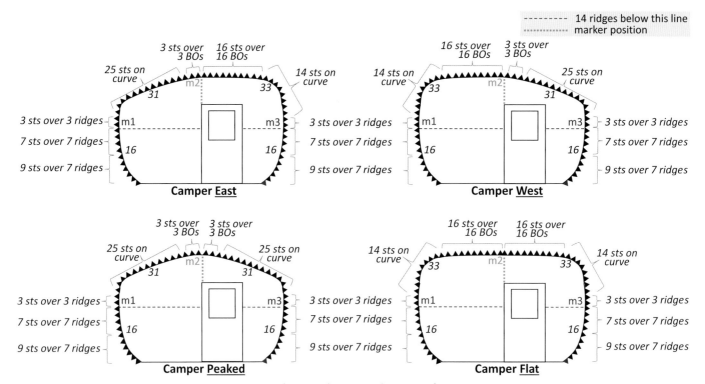

Figure 8: Pick Up and Knit Stitch Counts for Corners

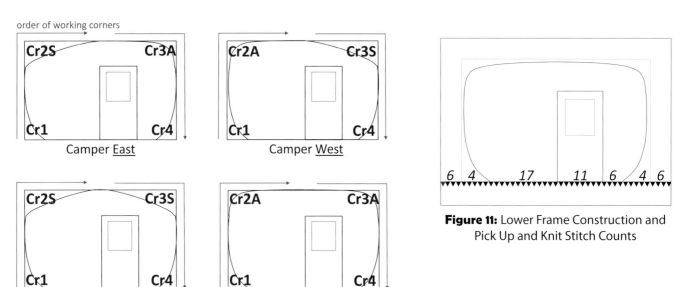

Figure 9: Corner Construction

Figure 11: Lower Frame Construction and Pick Up and Knit Stitch Counts

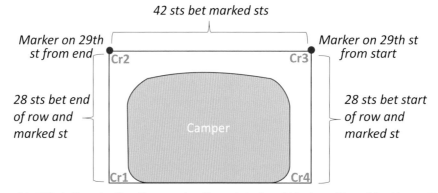

Figure 10: Stitch Counts after Corners Are Completed and Markers Placed for Upper Frame

(11) WINDOW

The window is worked separately using Intarsia and sewn on. Use written instructions or chart.

With W1, leaving a long tail of 10"/25 cm, CO 5 sts, with W2, CO an additional 2 sts – 7 sts.

Work [Window].

With long tails of matching color, sew window to Camper at location in Figure 5, making stitches near the edge of the Window on the WS and on the RS of the Camper.

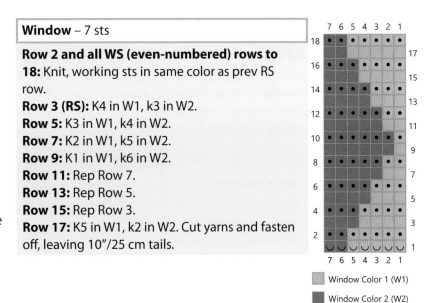

Window – 7 sts
Row 2 and all WS (even-numbered) rows to 18: Knit, working sts in same color as prev RS row.
Row 3 (RS): K4 in W1, k3 in W2.
Row 5: K3 in W1, k4 in W2.
Row 7: K2 in W1, k5 in W2.
Row 9: K1 in W1, k6 in W2.
Row 11: Rep Row 7.
Row 13: Rep Row 5.
Row 15: Rep Row 3.
Row 17: K5 in W1, k2 in W2. Cut yarns and fasten off, leaving 10"/25 cm tails.

Window Color 1 (W1)

Window Color 2 (W2)

(12) TIRE

With T1, leaving 12"/30 cm tail, CO 24 sts. Work [Tire].

Using long tails of matching color and mattress stitch, sew open seam. Tie same color yarns together on WS of work. With long tails of T1, sew Tire to Block at location shown in Figure 5, taking stitches on the WS of the Tire near the edge and on the RS of the Camper Block.

Tire – 24 sts dec'ing to 6 sts
Row 2 (WS): Knit.
Row 3 (RS): *K2tog, k2; rep from * 5 more times – 6 sts dec'd; 18 sts. Cut T1. Attach T2.
Row 5: *K2tog, k1; rep from * 5 more times – 6 sts dec'd; 12 sts.
Row 6: Knit.
Rows 7: K2tog 6 times – 6 sts dec'd; 6 sts.
Row 8: Knit.

(13) TRAILER HITCH See Figure 12.

The Hitch is worked with slip stitch crochet or embroidery chain stitch.

Cut 24"/60 cm of yarn of color HC. Make 6 slip sts from right-bottom corner of Camper from **a** to **b**, working parallel to the bottom edge of the Block. At **b**, pull yarn strand through to RS, then back to the WS catching the last sl st loop. Pull yarn to RS at **c** and make 5 sl sts vertically from **c** to **d**. Pull yarn strand through RS, then back to WS of work, catching last sl st loop. Fasten off on WS.

Weave in ends.

Figure 12: Hitch Location and Construction

TREE BLOCK INSTRUCTIONS

See Figure 2 (3) for quantities of Tree Blocks to make and colors. A Tree Block is constructed in 4 Sections: Top, Center 1, Center 2, and Bottom. There are 11 construction steps, identified in Figure 13.

Top

With FC, CO 19 sts (counts as Row 1).

Row 2 (WS): K9, place these 9 sts on holder for TFE; k1, place this st on m or safety pin; knit to end of row – 9 sts rem on needle.

(1) Top Frame West (TFW) see Figure 14

With 9 sts on needle, work [TF], working *Decrease Row* as: Knit to last 2 sts, ssk.

(2) Top Frame East (TFE) see Figure 14

Transfer 9 sts from holder to needle, and with RS facing, and a separate strand of FC, work [TF], working *Decrease Row* as: K2tog, knit to end.

Top Frame (TF) – 9 sts dec'ing to 3 sts

Rows 3–6: Knit.
Row 7: *Decrease Row* – 1 st dec'd; 8 sts.
Rows 8–12: Knit.
Rows 13–18: Rep [Rows 7–12] – 1 st dec'd; 7 sts.
Row 19: Rep Row 7 – 1 st dec'd; 6 sts.
Rows 20–22: Knit.
Rows 23–26: Rep [Rows 19–22] – 1 st dec'd; 5 sts.
Row 27: Rep Row 7 – 1 st dec'd; 4 sts.
Row 28: Knit.
Rows 29 & 30: Rep [Rows 27 & 28] – 1 st dec'd; 3 sts.
Place rem 3 sts on stitch marker. Do not cut yarn.

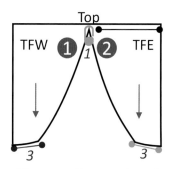

Figure 14: Construction of TFW (1) and TFE (2)

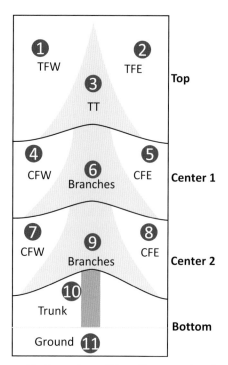

Figure 13: Overview of Tree Construction Steps

Key for Tree Construction Figures
●———● *Sts on holder*
🮲 *St on marker*
〰 *Yarn draped from end of a shape to start of next shape*

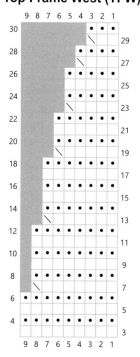

Top Frame East (TFE)   Top Frame West (TFW)

(3) Tree Top (TT) see Figure 15

With BC, working on the RS and starting at the red triangle on the bottom-right corner of TFW, pu&k 16 sts along the curved edge of Top Frame West, knit 1 st off the stitch marker, then pu&k 16 sts along the curved edge of Top Frame East. Work [TT].

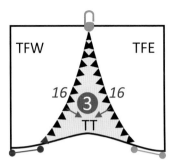

Figure 15: Construction of Tree Top (TT) (3)

Tree Top (TT) – 33 sts dec'ing to 1 st

Row 2 (WS): K13, *k2, k2tog. Rotate needles so tips are parallel, and RS of work tog, then perform 3-needle BO twice (5 sts dec'd)*, slip rem st on 3rd needle to R needle, rotate needles back to their original positions and on WS, knit to end of the row – 6 sts dec'd; 27 sts.

Note 1: Instructions bet * and * are represented by the large "X" symbol in the chart.

Note 2: After completing 3-needle BO, there will be 14 sts on front needle and 13 sts on back needle.

Row 3 (RS): K2tog, knit to last 2 sts, ssk – 2 sts dec'd; 25 sts.

Row 4: K2tog, k7, *k2, k2tog. Rotate needles, bringing RS of work together and tips parallel. 3-needle BO twice (5 sts dec'd), slip rem st on 3rd needle to R needle, rotate needles back to their original positions, and on WS knit to last 2 sts, ssk – 8 sts dec'd; 17 sts.

Note: After completing 3-needle BO there will be 9 sts on front needle and 9 sts on back needle.

On RS, pm after 9th st.

Row 5: K2tog, knit to 2 sts bef m, rm, cdd, pm, knit to last 2 sts, ssk – 4 sts dec'd; 13 sts.

Row 6: Rep Row 3 – 2 sts dec'd; 11 sts.

Row 7: Rep Row 5 – 4 sts dec'd; 7 sts.

Row 8: Knit.

Row 9: Rep Row 5 – 4 sts dec'd; 3 sts.

Row 10: Cdd – 2 sts dec'd; 1 st.

Enlarge loop, insert the skein through, and tighten. Do not cut yarn.

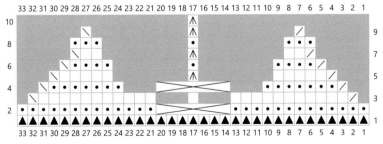

K2, k2tog. Rotate needles so tips are parallel, and RS of work tog, then perform 3-needle BO twice.

CENTER 1 see Figure 16

(4) Center Frame West (CFW)

Transfer 3 rem sts from prev TFW to needle. Beg on RS.

Row 1 (RS): With yarn still attached at **b**, knit 3 transferred sts then starting at red triangle, pu&k 5 sts on lower edge of Tree Top (3) from **a** to **c** – 8 sts. Work [CFW].

(5) Center Frame East (CFE)

Drape FC (still attached) from **f** to **e** as shown in Figure 16.

Row 1 (RS): Pu&k 5 sts from **e** to **f** while simultaneously weaving in draped yarn. Knit 3 sts from holder – 8 sts. Work [CFE].

Center Frame East (CFE)

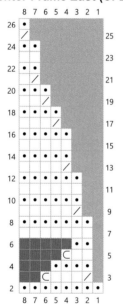

Center Frame West (CFW)

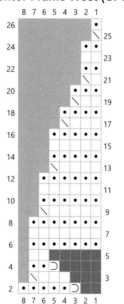

CFW – 8 sts dec'ing to 1 st

Row 2 (WS): K5, w&t.
Row 3 (RS): Knit to last 2 sts, ssk – 1 st dec'd; 7 sts.
Row 4: K2, w&t.
Rows 5–8: Knit.
Row 9: Knit to last 2 sts, ssk – 1 st dec'd; 6 sts.
Rows 10–12: Knit.
Row 13: Rep Row 9 – 1 st dec'd; 5 sts.
Rows 14–16: Knit.
Row 17: Knit to last 2 sts, ssk – 1 st dec'd; 4 sts.
Row 18: Knit.
Rows 19–22: Rep [Rows 17 & 18] twice – 2 sts dec'd; 2 sts.
Rows 23 & 24: Knit.
Rows 25 & 26: Rep [Rows 17 & 18] – 1 st dec'd; 1 st. Place rem st on st marker.

CFE – 8 sts dec'ing to 1 st

Row 2 (WS): Knit.
Row 3 (RS): K2tog, k3, w&t – 1 st dec'd; 7 sts.
Row 4: Knit.
Row 5: K2, w&t.
Rows 6–8: Knit.
Row 9: K2tog, knit to end – 1 st dec'd; 6 sts.
Rows 10–12: Knit.
Row 13: K2tog, knit to end – 1 st dec'd; 5 sts.
Rows 14–16: Knit.
Row 17: K2tog, knit to end – 1 st dec'd; 4 sts.
Row 18: Knit.
Rows 19–22: Rep [Rows 17 & 18] twice – 2 sts dec'd; 2 sts.
Rows 23 & 24: Knit.
Rows 25 & 26: Rep [Rows 17 & 18] – 1 st dec'd; 1 st.
Place rem st on stitch marker.

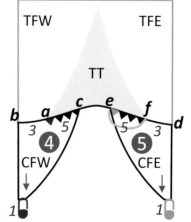

Figure 16: Construction of CFW (4) and CFE (5)

(6) Branches see Figure 17

Drape yarn from **g** to **h**.

Row 1 (RS): With BC, starting at the red triangle, pu&k 13 sts along curved edge of CFW while simultaneously weaving draped yarn, pm, pu&k 5 sts from **c** to **e**, pm, pu&k 13 sts from **e** to bottom of curved edge on CFE – 31 sts. Work [Branches].

Branches - 31 sts dec'ing to 1 st
Row 2 (WS): Knit. **Row 3 (RS):** K2tog, knit to 2 sts bef m, ssk, sm, k2tog, k1, ssk, sm, k2tog, knit to last 2 sts, ssk – 6 sts dec'd; 25 sts. **Row 4:** K2tog, knit to last 2 sts, ssk – 2 sts dec'd; 23 sts. **Row 5:** K2tog, knit to 2 sts bef m, ssk, rm's, cdd, pm, k2tog, knit to last 2 sts, ssk – 6 sts dec'd; 17 sts. **Row 6:** Knit. **Row 7:** K2tog, knit to 2 sts bef m, rm, cdd, pm knit to last 2 sts, ssk – 4 sts dec'd; 13 sts. **Row 8:** Rep Row 4 – 2 sts dec'd; 11 sts. **Row 9:** Rep Row 7 – 4 sts dec'd; 7 sts. **Row 10:** Knit. **Row 11:** Rep Row 7 – 4 sts dec'd; 3 sts. **Row 12:** Rm, cdd – 2 sts dec'd; 1 st. Enlarge rem loop on needle, insert skein through and tighten.

Branches

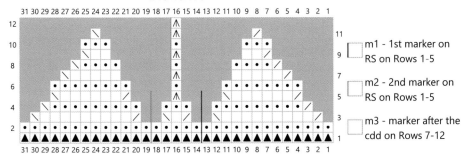

m1 - 1st marker on RS on Rows 1-5

m2 - 2nd marker on RS on Rows 1-5

m3 - marker after the cdd on Rows 7-12

CENTER 2

(7) Center Frame West (CFW) see Figure 18, top

Transfer 1 rem st from prev CFW to needle. Beg on RS.

Row 1 (RS): Knit 1 transferred st at **k**, then starting at red triangle, pu&k 7 sts on lower edge of Branches (6) from **i** to **j** – 8 sts. Work [CFW].

(8) Center Frame East (CFE) see Figure 18, top

On RS, drape yarn from prev CFE from **l** to **m**, pu&k 7 sts from **m** to **l** while simultaneously weaving draped yarn, knit 1 st from marker at **l**. Work [CFE]. Cut yarn.

(9) Branches see Figure 18, bottom

Drape yarn from **o** to **p**, then starting at red triangle at **p**, pu&k 13 sts on curved edge of CFW to **j** while simultaneously weaving in draped yarn, pm, pu&k 5 sts from **j** to **m**, pm, pu&k 13 sts from **m** to end of curved edge of CFE at **r** – 31 sts. Work [Branches].

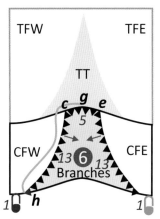

Figure 17: Branch Construction (6)

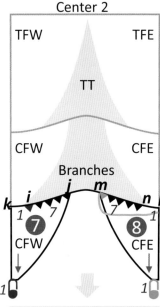

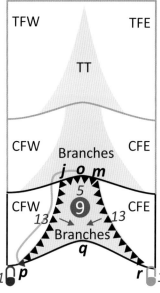

Figure 18: Construction of CFW (7), CFE (8), and Branches (9)

Bottom

(10) Trunk see Figure 19

Starting on RS, drape BC yarn from *q* to *s*, knit 1 st on stitch marker at *s*, then pu&k 9 sts along bottom edge of Branches (9), from *s* to *q* while simultaneously weaving draped yarn. Pu&k 8 sts from *q* to *t*, then knit st 1 on st marker at *t* – 19 sts. *Note*: Make sure that 10th stitch on the needle is centered on the edge at *q*. Cut BC.

Transfer the 19 sts, one-by-one, to the other needle. Onto the same needle with the 19 sts, with FC from CFW (7), at *s*, CO 4 sts – 23 sts on needle (19 in BC and the last 4 in FC). Work [Trunk].

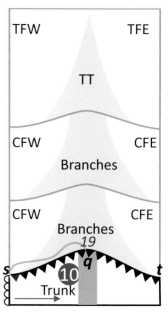

Figure 19: Construction of Trunk (10)

Trunk – 23 sts dec'ing to 0 sts

Notes:

- Join is worked over last st of FC (or TC) and first st of BC as follows: Slip last st of FC (or TC) kwise, slip first st of BC kwise, k2tog-tbl, turn.
- On all RS rows, stitch counts resulting from the row are given, with individual counts for FC (or TC) sts formatted as follows: <n> sts dec'd/inc'd; <total sts> (<FC (or TC sts)>,<BC sts>).

Row 2 (RS): Knit to last st of FC, Join – 1 st dec'd; 22 sts (18, 4).

Row 3: Knit.

Rows 4–7: Rep [Rows 2 & 3] twice – 2 sts dec'd; 20 sts (16, 4).

Row 8: Knit to last 2 sts of FC, kfb, Join – 20 sts (15, 5).

Row 9: Knit.

Rows 10–16: Rep [Rows 2–8] – 3 sts dec'd; 17 sts (11, 6).

Row 17: Knit.

Drop FC but do not cut. Cont with Trunk Color (TC).

Row 18: With TC, knit to last st of FC, Join – 1 st dec'd; 16 sts (10, 6).

Row 19: Knit.

Rows 20–23: Rep Rows [18 & 19] twice – 2 sts dec'd; 14 sts (8, 6).

Cut Trunk Color (TC).

Row 24: Drape FC loosely, and with FC, knit to last st of TC, Join – 1 st dec'd; 13 sts (7, 6).

Row 25: Knit.

Row 26: Knit to last 3 sts of FC, ssk, Join – 2 sts dec'd; 11 sts (6, 5).

Row 27: Knit.

Row 28: Rep Row 2 – 1 st dec'd; 10 sts (5, 5).

Row 29: Knit.

Rows 30–33: Rep [Rows 28 & 29] twice – 2 sts dec'd; 8 sts (3, 5).

Rows 34–38: Rep [Rows 26–30] – 4 sts dec'd; 4 sts (0, 4).

Row 39: BO loosely. Enlarge rem loop on needle, insert skein through loop and tighten.

Trunk

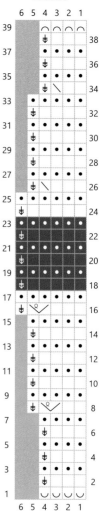

(11) Ground see Figure 20

Drape FC yarn still attached after CFE from **v** to **u,** and with FC, pu&k 19 sts from **u** to **v** while simultaneously weaving draped yarn.

Knit 5 rows. BO loosely. Cut FC, leaving 25"/80 cm tail.

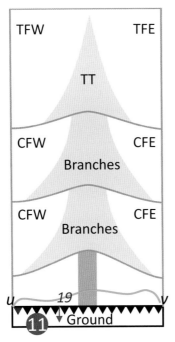

Figure 20: Construction of Ground (11)

ASSEMBLY

Lay out the completed Strips of Campers and Trees as shown in Figure 2 (3).

With long tails from Blocks and mattress stitch, sew together Blocks, aligning corners, to form 5 (7) horizontal Strips.

JOINING OF STRIPS

Between each pair of adjacent Strips work in color A as follows:

Upper Strip Sashing

With a circular needle and starting at bottom-right corner of the Upper Strip, *pu&k 165 (238) sts (54 sts per Camper, and 19 sts per Tree) to end of Strip. Knit 5 rows. Leave sts on needle.* Cut yarn.

Lower Strip Sashing

With 2nd circular needle and starting at top-left corner of Strip, rep bet * and * of Upper Strip Sashing. Do not cut yarn.

Joining

With Lower Strip behind, arrange Strips with RS together and with the needle tips of the 1st and 2nd circular needles parallel. With larger 3rd needle, 3-needle BO all sts. Cut yarn and fasten off.

BORDERS

RIGHT BORDER

With A, and starting at lower-right corner of blanket, pu&k 229 (323) sts (41 sts per Camper or Tree Block and 6 sts per Sashing/Join). *Note:* Pu&k counts as Row 1.

Row 2 (WS): Knit.
Rows 3–12: Work [Border] 5 times – 10 sts inc'd; 239 (333) sts. Cut A leaving 12"/30 cm tail. Attach D.
Rows 13–24: Work [Border] 3 times – 6 sts inc'd; 245 (339) sts. BO loosely. Cut yarn leaving 12"/30 cm tail.

Border
Row 1: Kf&b, knit to last st, kf&b – 2 sts inc'd. **Row 2:** Knit. Rep Rows 1 & 2 for patt.

TOP BORDER

With A, and starting at upper-right corner of blanket, pu&k 165 (238) sts (54 sts per Camper, 19 sts per Tree).

Rep [Rows 2–24] of Right Border – 16 sts inc'd; 181 (254) sts. BO loosely. Cut yarn leaving 12"/30 cm tail.

LEFT BORDER

Rep as for Right Border, starting pu&k at upper-left corner of blanket.

BOTTOM BORDER

Rep as for Top Border, starting pu&k at lower-left corner of blanket. Sew open seams at corner with matching yarn tails and mattress stitch, matching color transitions and corners.

FINISHING

Weave in ends.

Make a Camp Along pillow to try out the pattern!

There are specific videos for all steps in this pattern. See page 207 for the link to videos.

This pillow is worked by making one Camper Block and one Tree Block, sewing them together, then adding a mitered border. See the blanket pattern for yarn colors, needle sizes, equipment, gauge, notes, and Camper and Tree Block instructions.

SIZE

12 x 20"/25 x 50 cm Pillow Cover

SUPPLIES

12 x 20"/25 x 50 cm "lumbar" pillow form
20"/50 cm zipper
Sewing thread matching yarn color A
Sewing needle and safety pins

PILLOW FRONT

Yarn Requirements

The yarn requirements for working the front side only are:

S: Camper's 1st stripe of (C1), Border's 5th stripe - 45 yds/41 m
R: Camper's 2nd stripe (C2) - 30 yds/27 m
O: Camper's 3rd/top-most stripe (C3) - 50 yds/46 m
H: Camper's main door (D1) - 20 yds/18 m
J: Camper door's window (D2) - 10 yds/9 m
M: Camper's framing/background (FC) - 90 yds/82 m
L: Camper's window shade (W1) and Border's 2nd stripe - 18 yds/17 m
J: Camper's window glass (W2) - 3 yds/3 m
K: Camper's outer tire (T1) and Border's 1st stripe - 18 yds/17 m
I: Camper's inner (hub) tire (T2) - 1 yd/1 m
O: Camper's hitch (HC) - 1 yd/1 m
E: Tree's frame/background (FC) - 40 yds/37 m
B: Tree's foliage - 40 yds/37 m
G: Tree's trunk color - 1 yd/1 m
N: Border's 3rd stripe - 15 yds/14 m
D: Border's 4th stripe - 15 yds/14 m
A: Border's 6th stripe - 16 yds/15 m

Illustration of Camp Along Pillow

Instructions

Make a Camper Block, following Bold Stripe instructions (see "Camper Block Instructions" on page 2), in colors from Figure 21.

Make a Tree Block (see "Tree Block Instructions" on page 16) in colors from Figure 21.

Assemble Pillow Front

See Figure 22.

With long tails from Blocks and mattress stitch, sew together the Camper and Tree Blocks along red dashed line, aligning corners.

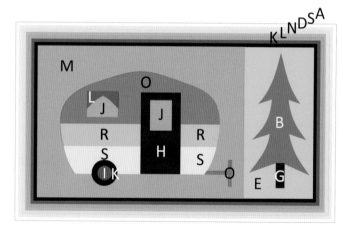

Figure 21: Pillow Colors

Borders

The borders are mitered and are worked so that there are only two open seams to finish.

Right-Top Border

With K and circular needle, starting at bottom-right corner of Tree Block, pu&k 41 sts along right edge of Tree Block to top-right corner, pm, pu&k 73 sts along top edge of pillow (19 on Tree Block and 54 on Camper Block) – 114 sts. Work [DMB].

Left-Bottom Border

With K and circular needle, starting at the top-left corner of the Camper Block, pu&k 41 sts along left edge to bottom-left corner, pm, pu&k 73 sts along bottom edge of pillow (54 on Camper Block and 19 on the Tree Block) – 114 sts. Work [DMB].

Double Mitered Border (DMB) – 114 sts inc'ing to 134 sts

Note 1: Pu&k counts as Row 1.
Note 2: When cutting yarn, leave an 8"/20 cm tail for sewing. To prevent loose end stitches, tie adjacent pairs of cut yarns together.
Row 2 (WS): Cont with K, knit.
Cut K.
Row 3 (RS): With L, kf&b, knit to 1 st bef m, kf&b, sm, kf&b, knit to last st, kf&b – 4 sts inc'd; 118 sts.
Row 4: Knit.
Cut L.
Rows 5 & 6: With N, rep [Rows 3 & 4] – 4 sts inc'd; 122 sts.
Cut N.
Rows 7 & 8: With D, rep [Rows 3 & 4] – 4 sts inc'd; 126 sts.
Cut D.
Rows 9 & 10: With S, rep [Rows 3 & 4] – 4 sts inc'd; 130 sts.
Cut S.
Rows 11 & 12: With A, rep [Rows 3 & 4] – 4 sts inc'd; 134 sts. BO loosely.

PILLOW BACK

Either repeat the Pillow Front (yarn amounts for the Pillow Front should be doubled), or work a plain garter stitch back (instructions below).

Yarn Requirements

250 yds/229 m of O

Instructions

CO 85 sts.
Knit 105 rows (53 ridges).
BO loosely.

PILLOW FRONT/BACK ASSEMBLY

See "Assembling Pillows with a Zipper Closure" on page 192.

Figure 22: Pillow Front Assembly and Border Seams

Design Variations and Ideas

Work a solid color Camper, work the Camper in a color changing yarn, or make up your own striping pattern.

For a Pillow Back variation or for a Pillow Cover with only Trees, make 4 Tree Blocks and sew them together along their long edges, then apply the Borders as you would to the Pillow Front. Use the same background color for the Tree Blocks or different colors. Note: The width of a Tree Block is one-third the width of a Camper Block, so 4 Tree Blocks is the same width as the Camper Block and the Tree Block together.

COPYCATS

**Worked in strips that are knitted together,
these colorful cats will captivate you with their bright hues.**

TECHNIQUES

3-needle BO, wrap & turn

SIZES

Small (Large): 41 x 43"/104 x 109 cm (51 x 64"/130 x 163 cm)

YARN

Valley Yarns, Valley Superwash, worsted (100% extra fine merino; 97 yds/88 m; 1.76 oz/50 g):

Pattern color ID	Color swatch	Color ID	Color name	Color description	# Skeins for Size	
					Small	Large
A		261	Natural	off-white	1	2
B		301	Whisper	light gray	1	2
C		200	Steel Grey	dark gray	1	2
D		220	Black	black	12	19
E		023	Soft Yellow	light yellow	1	2
F		300	Golden Era	gold/strong yellow	2	3
G		307	Coral Corale	coral	1	3
H		302	Sriracha	orange-red	2	3
I		304	Manic Panic	fuchsia	2	3
J		320	Plum	plum	2	3
K		694	Spring Leaf	light green	1	3
L		563	Ice Blue	light blue	1	2
M		502	Blue	med blue	1	3
N		522	Teal	aqua	2	3

NEEDLES

(2) US 7/4.5 mm, minimum 40"/100 cm length circular needles, and an extra larger needle for 3-needle BO

NOTIONS

Stitch markers, removable markers (minimum of 12 in each of 2 different colors), tapestry needle

GAUGE

19 sts x 38 rows = 4"/10 cm in garter stitch

NOTES

- The blanket is worked in vertical Strips from bottom to top. The cat uses simple shaping and some wrap & turn in the ear area.

- Strips are joined by working pick up and knit on the vertical edges of adjacent Strips, using wrap & turn to fill in divots along edges, then working 3-needle BO to join.

- Stitches for the Borders are generated using pick up and knit.

- Charts are provided for all Cat Base and part-Cat shapes, and begin on page 34.

- In pattern stitches, Row 1 is the stitch generation (CO or pu&k, whichever applies).

- Before beginning, see "Single Crochet for Edging" on page 189 and "Wrap & Turn (W&T)" on page 203.

- Some shapes require knitting many consecutive rows straight (with no increases or decreases). To aid in counting progress, before starting the first RS row, place a marker around a stitch just below the needle, then after WS rows, count the number of completed ridges from the marker to determine the number of rows that have been worked, recalling that 2 rows equals 1 ridge.

SPECIAL ABBREVIATIONS

Letters A, B, C . . . N: refer to yarn colors; **BT:** Big Triangle; **CC:** Cat Color; **EB:** Even Base; **EC:** Even Cat; **EG:** Ear Gap; **LE:** Left Ear; **OB:** Odd Base; **OC:** Odd Cat; **RE:** Right Ear; **ST:** Small Triangle, **Tl:** Tail, **Tr:** Triangle.

BLANKET INSTRUCTIONS

Each Strip starts with a Base piece and then 5 or 6 (8 or 9) cats. Cat 1 is worked after the Base, then Cat 2, Cat 3, etc. A cast-on is performed to start the Base, and sts are pu&k along the top and side edges of completed pieces to start the next Cat.

The Cat Color (CC) of each cat is provided in Figure 1. Sts for the next cat are generated by pu&k on the prev cat.

The even-numbered Strips have 9 cats. The 9th cat is only partially worked in the border color to blend in with the Borders.

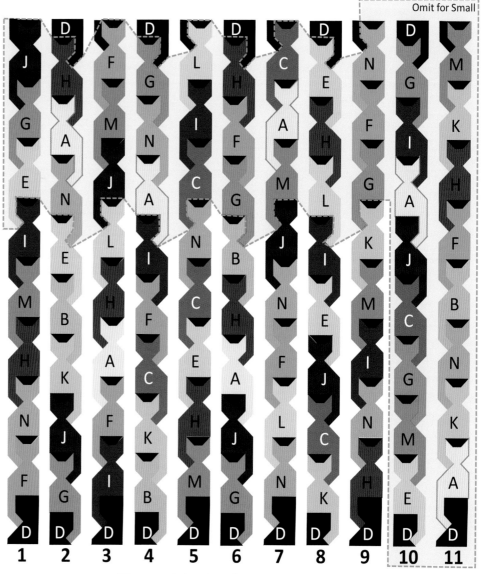

Figure 1: Color chart for Bases, Cats, and Tails

STRIP 1 See Figure 2 for construction

Base With D, CO 20 sts. Work [OB]. Cut yarn, fasten off.

Cat 1

Row 1: With CC for Cat, on RS, beg at magenta triangle, pu&k 15 sts to next corner, pm, 10 sts from red triangle to next corner, pm, 7 sts from green triangle to next corner, pm, and 5 sts from blue triangle on the beg of next edge – 37 sts.

Odd Base (OB) – 20 sts, dec'ing to 10 sts, inc'ing to 15 sts

Rows 2–8: Knit.
Row 9: Knit to last 2 sts, ssk – 1 st dec'd; 19 sts.
Row 10: Knit.
Rows 11–28: Rep [Rows 9 & 10] 9 times; 9 sts dec'd. 10 sts.
Row 29: Knit to last st, kf&b – 1 st inc'd; 11 sts.
Row 30: Knit.
Rows 31–38: Rep [Rows 29 & 30] 4 times – 4 sts inc'd; 15 sts.
Rows: 39–58: Knit. BO loosely.

Odd Cat (OC) – 37 sts, dec'ing to 5 sts, inc'ing to 15 sts

Row 2 and even-numbered rows (WS) to 8: Knit.
Row 3: *Knit to 1 st bef m, kf&b, sm, kf&b; rep from * once more, knit to 2 sts bef m, ssk, sm, k2tog, knit to end – 2 sts inc'd; 39 sts.
Row 5: Knit to 1 st bef m, kf&b, sm, kf&b, knit to 2 sts bef 3rd m, ssk, k2tog, knit to end.
Row 7: Rep Row 3 – 2 sts inc'd; 41 sts.
Row 9: Knit to 1 st bef m, kfbf, rm, kf&b, knit to 2 sts bef 3rd m, ssk, rm, k2tog – 1 st inc'd; 42 sts.
Row 10: BO 22 sts loosely; knit to end – 22 sts dec'd; 20 sts.
Rows 11–20: Knit.
Row 21: Knit to last 2 sts, ssk – 1 st dec'd; 19 sts.
Row 22: Knit.
Rows 23–30: Rep [Rows 21 & 22] 4 times – 4 sts dec'd; 15 sts.
Row 31: K2tog, knit to last 2 sts, ssk – 2 sts dec'd; 13 sts.
Row 32: Knit.
Rows 33–40: Rep [Rows 31 & 32] 4 times – 8 sts dec'd; 5 sts.
Row 41: Kf&b, knit to last st, kf&b – 2 sts inc'd; 7 sts.
Row 42: Knit.
Rows 43–50: Rep [Rows 41 & 42] 4 times – 8 sts inc'd; 15 sts.
Rows 51–60: Knit.

Work [OC]. Turn and with a knitted CO, CO 5 sts. Work [Ears]. Cut CC. With D, work [EG]. Cut D.

Cats 2–5 (8) Work as for Cat 1, picking up and knitting sts on edges of prev completed cat.

Tail With D, on RS, starting at red triangle at top-left corner of Cat 5 (8), pu&k: 10 sts to next corner, pm, 7 sts from green triangle to next corner, pm, then 5 sts from the blue triangle on the beg of next edge – 22 sts. Work [Tl]. Cut yarn and fasten off.

Tail (Tl) – 22 sts dec'ing to 0 sts

Row 2 and even-numbered WS rows to 10: Knit.
Row 3: Kf&b, knit to 1 st bef m, kf&b, kf&b, knit to 2 sts bef m, ssk, k2tog, knit to end; 1 st inc'd; 23 sts.
Row 5: Kf&b, knit to 2 sts bef 2nd m, ssk, k2tog, knit to end – 1 st dec'd; 22 sts.
Row 7: Rep Row 3 – 1 st inc'd; 23 sts.
Row 9: Rep Row 5 – 1 st dec'd; 22 sts. BO loosely.

STRIPS 3, 5, 7, 9, (AND 11)

Work as for Strip 1.

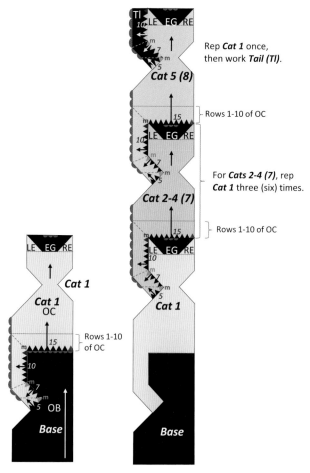

Rep *Cat 1* once, then work *Tail (Tl)*.

Rows 1-10 of OC

For *Cats 2-4 (7)*, rep *Cat 1* three (six) times.

Rows 1-10 of OC

Rows 1-10 of OC

Base and Cat 1   Cats 2-5 (8) and Tail (Tl)

Figure 2: Strip Construction - Odd Numbered

STRIP 2 See Figure 3 for construction

Base With D, CO 13 sts. Work [EB]. Cut yarn and fasten off.

Even Base (EB) – 13 sts, dec'ing to 10 sts, inc'ing to 15 sts

Row 2 (WS): Knit.
Row 3 (RS): K2tog, knit to end – 1 st dec'd; 12 sts.
Row 4: Knit.
Rows 5–8: Rep [Rows 3 & 4] twice – 2 sts dec'd; 10 sts
Row 9: Kf&b, knit to end – 1 st inc'd; 11 sts.
Row 10: Knit.
Rows 11–18: Rep [Rows 9 & 10] 4 times – 4 inc'd; 15 sts.
Rows 19–38: Knit all rows. BO loosely.

Cat 1 With CC for Cat, on RS and beg at magenta triangle on prev shape, pu&k 5 sts to corner, pm, pu&k 7 sts from red triangle to next corner, pm, 10 sts from green triangle to next corner, pm, and 15 sts from blue triangle – 37 sts.

Work [EC]. Turn and with a knitted CO, CO 5 sts.

Work [Ears]. Cut CC.

With D, work [EG]. Cut D.

Cats 2–5 (8) Work as for Cat 1, picking up and knitting sts on edges of previously completed cat.

Cat 6 (9) Work as for Cat 1, BO after completion of Row 20 of the EC pattern stitch.

STRIPS 4, 6, 8 (AND 10) Work as for Strip 2

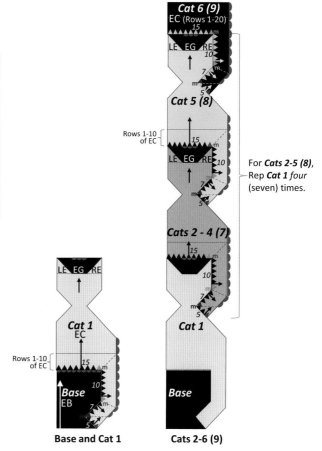

Figure 3: Strip Construction - Even Numbered

Even Cat (EC) – 37 sts, dec'ing to 5 sts, inc'ing to 15 sts

Row 2 and even-numbered (WS) rows to 10: Knit.
Row 3: Knit to 2 st bef m, ssk, sm, k2tog, *knit to 1 st bef m, kf&b, kf&b; rep from * once more, knit to end – 2 sts inc'd; 39 sts.
Row 5: Knit to 2 sts bef m, ssk, sm, k2tog, knit to 1 st bef 3rd m, kf&b, sm, kf&b, knit to end.
Row 7: Rep Row 3 – 2 sts inc'd; 41 sts.
Row 9: Ssk, sm, k2tog, knit to 1 st bef 3rd m, kf&b, sm, kfbf, knit to end – 1 st inc'd; 42 sts. Rm's.
Row 11 (RS): BO 22 sts, knit to end – 20 sts.
Rows 12–20: Knit.
Row 21: K2tog, knit to end – 1 st dec'd; 19 sts.

Row 22: Knit.
Rows 23–30: Rep [Rows 21 & 22] 4 times –15 sts.
Row 31: K2tog, knit to last 2 sts, ssk – 2 sts dec'd; 13 sts.
Row 32: Knit.
Rows 33–40: Rep [Rows 31 & 32] 4 times – 8 sts dec'd; 5 sts
Row 41: Kf&b, knit to last st, kf&b – 2 inc'd; 7 sts.
Row 42: Knit.
Rows 43–50: Rep [Rows 41 & 42] 4 times – 8 sts inc'd; 15 sts.
Rows 51–60: Knit.

Ear Gap (EG) – 19 sts dec'ing to 0 sts

Row 1: K7, pm, k5, pm, knit to end.
Rows 2, 4, 6, & 8: Knit.
Row 3 (RS): K2tog, *knit to 2 sts bef m, ssk, k2tog; rep from * once more, knit to last 2 sts, ssk – 6 sts dec'd; 13 sts.
Row 5: K2tog, knit to 2 sts bef m, ssk, rm, knit to next m, rm, k2tog, knit to last 2 sts, ssk – 4 dec'd; 9 sts.
Row 7: Cdd, k3, cdd – 4 sts dec'd; 5 sts.
BO loosely.

Ears (RE & LE) – 20 sts, inc'ing to 22 sts, dec'ing to 19 sts

Row 1 (RS): K8, w&t.
Row 2: K6, w&t.
Rows 3 & 4: Knit to 1 st bef prev wrap, w&t.
Row 5: Sl2, k2tog, p2sso, k13, CO 5 sts – 2 sts inc'd; 22 sts.
Row 6 (WS): K8, w&t.
Row 7: K6 (to 2 sts from end of row), w&t.
Row 8: K5 (to 1 st bef prev wrap), w&t.
Row 9: Sl2, k2tog, p2sso, w&t – 3 sts dec'd; 19 sts.
Row 10 (WS): Knit.

VERTICAL JOINING

Instructions are for joining Strips 1 and 2, 3 and 4, 5 and 6, 7 and 8, (9 and 10), forming "units" of two Strips of cats. Units are combined by working joins bet Strips 2 and 3, 4 and 5, 6 and 7, 8 and 9, (10 and 11). This assembly order permits working with the smallest pieces for as long as possible. However, Strips may be joined as soon as they are completed. That is, they may be joined in this order: 1 and 2, then (1, 2) and 3, then (1, 2, 3) and 4, etc.

Odd to Even Join see left side of Figure 4

For each of these Strip pairs, 1 and 2, 3 and 4, 5 and 6, 7 and 8, (9 and 10), work Steps 1, 2, and 3 below to join pairs into 2–Strip units. The odd-numbered Strip is on the Left, and the even-numbered Strip is on the Right.

1) Prep Left (odd-numbered) Strip

On RS of the Left (odd-numbered) Strip, with D and the 1st circular needle, and starting at the red triangle on the bottom-right corner of the Strip, pu&k 203 (308) sts along the right edge of the Strip, generating the number of sts per shape specified in blue italics, and placing colored marker pairs bet sets of sts as indicated by the small orange and green pairs of circles.

Note: Use two different colored markers or markers of different styles to represent the orange marker pairs and green marker pairs.

Next Row (WS): On WS, *knit to next orange m, work [Tr] bet orange m's, and cont on WS, knit to next green m, work [Tr] bet green m's; rep from *, ending after last pair of green markers, knit to end. Leave 203 (308) sts on 1st circular needle. Starting at the top of the Strip, and with RS facing, remove the 1st m encountered of each orange pair and each green pair. Cut D.

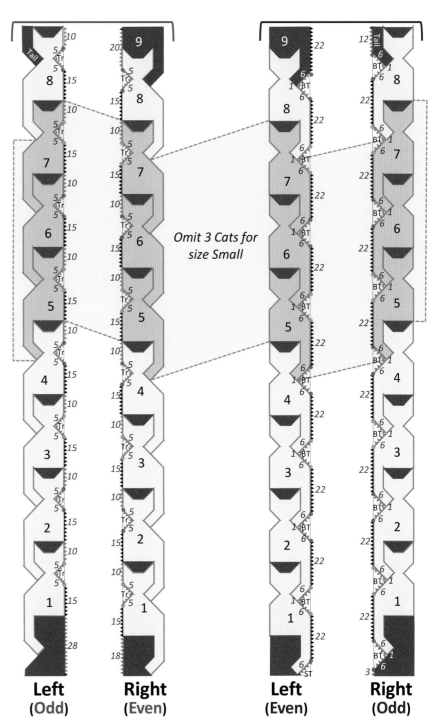

Figure 4: Strip Join

Triangle (Tr) – 10 sts	
Row 2 (WS): K6, w&t.	**Row 7:** K6, w&t.
Row 3 (RS): K2, w&t.	**Row 8:** K7, w&t.
Row 4: K3, w&t.	**Row 9:** K8, w&t.
Row 5: K4, w&t.	**Row 10 (WS):** K9.
Row 6: K5, w&t.	

2) Prep Right (even-numbered) Strip

On RS of Right Strip (even-numbered Strip), with D, and 2nd circular needle, starting at the red triangle at the top-left corner of the Strip, pu&k 203 (308) sts along the left edge of the Strip, generating the number of sts per shape specified in blue italics, and placing colored pairs of m's bet sets of sts as indicated by the small orange and green pairs of circles.

Next Row (WS): *On WS, knit to next green m, work [Tr] bet green m's, and cont on WS, knit to next orange m, work [Tr] bet orange m's; rep from *, ending after last pair of orange markers, knit to end. Leave 203 (308) sts on 2nd circular needle. Starting at the top of the Strip, and with RS facing, remove 2nd m encountered of each orange and green pair.

3) Join

Bring two circular needles parallel with RS together (touching) and WS facing outward, and the Left Strip nearest and Right Strip in back.

With D still attached to the Right Strip, and the 3rd needle, 3-needle BO all sts. Cut yarn and insert through rem loop and tighten. Fasten off securely.

Note: Markers still on the needles are used to check alignment during the 3-needle BO and can be removed when encountered during BO. If BO is out of alignment, perform a decrease on the front or back needle (whichever has too many sts) by inserting the Right needle kwise through the next 2 sts on the needle when binding off.

Big Triangle (BT); 13 sts

Row 2 (WS): K7, w&t.
Row 3 (RS): K1, w&t.
Row 4: K2, w&t.
Row 5: K3, w&t.
Rows 6–13: Cont as established, knitting 1 more stitch per row before the w&t. The last 2 wraps are performed on the last stitch before the marker.
Row 14 (WS): Knit.

Small Triangle (ST); 10 sts dec'ing to 6 sts

Row 2 and all even-numbered (WS) rows to 10: Knit.
Row 3 (RS): K2tog, k7, w&t – 1 st dec'd; 9 sts.
Row 5: K2tog, k5, w&t – 1 st dec'd; 8 sts.
Row 7: K2tog, k3, w&t – 1 st dec'd; 7 sts.
Row 9: K2tog, k1, w&t.
Cut yarn and fasten off.

Even to Odd Join see right side of Figure 4

Join these pairs of Strips: 2 and 3, 4 and 5, 6 and 7, 8 and 9 (10 and 11) (*Note*: Strip 11 is not part of a unit). The even-numbered Strip is on the Left, and the odd-numbered Strip is on the Right. For each of these Strip pairs, work Steps 1, 2, and 3 below.

1) Prep Left Strip

On RS of the Left (even-numbered) Strip, with D and the 1st circular needle, and starting at the red triangle at the bottom-right corner of Strip, pu&k 203 (308) sts along right edge of the Strip, generating the number of sts per shape specified in blue italics, and placing colored marker pairs bet sets of sts as indicated by the small orange and green pairs of circles.

Next Row (WS): On WS, *knit to next orange marker, work [BT] bet orange markers, and cont on WS, knit to next green m, work [BT] bet green m's; rep from *, ending after last pair of green markers, knit to orange m (i.e., to last 6 sts), work [ST]. Leave 203 (308) sts on needle. Starting at top of the Strip, remove the 2nd m encountered of each orange and green m pair. Cut D.

2) Prep Right Strip

With 2nd circular needle, working on RS of the Right (odd-numbered) Strip, and starting at the red triangle at the top-left corner of the Strip, pu&k 203 (308) sts along the left edge of the Strip, generating the number of sts per shape specified in blue italics, and placing colored marker pairs bet sets of sts as indicated by the small orange and green pairs of circles.

Next Row (WS): On WS, *knit to next orange marker, work [BT] bet orange markers, and cont on WS, knit to next green m, work [BT] bet green m's; rep from *, ending after last pair of green markers, knit to next orange marker, work [BT] bet orange markers, knit to end. Leave 203 (308) sts on needle. Starting at top of the Strip, remove the 2nd m of each orange and green m pair.

3) Join

Work as for Join of Strips 1 and 2.

BORDERS

See Figure 5 for construction.

RIGHT BORDER

With D, on the Right edge of Strip 9 (11), work Odd to Even Join, Step 1) Prep Left Strip, then knit 12 rows. BO loosely.

LEFT BORDER

With D, on the Left edge of Strip 1, work Even to Odd Join, Step 2) Prep Right Strip, then knit 12 rows. BO loosely.

TOP BORDER

With D, and starting at right-top corner of Right Border, pu&k 7 sts on left (short) edge of Border, 196 (240) sts across the 9 (11) Strips (20 sts per Strip, and 2 sts per Join), and 7 sts on the short edge of the Left Border; 210 (254) sts. Knit 11 rows. BO loosely.

BOTTOM BORDER

Work as for Top Border, starting pu&k on bottom left corner of Left Border.

FINISHING

Weave in ends.

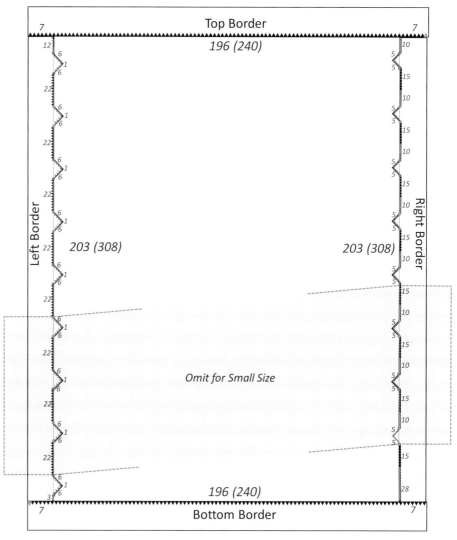

Figure 5: Border Construction

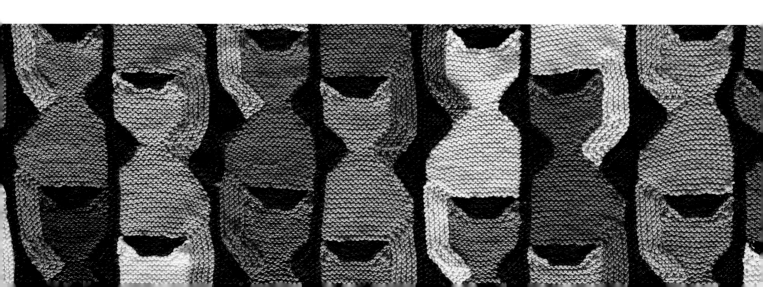

CHARTS

CHART SYMBOLS

☐ RS: knit (k)	• WS: knit (k)
▲ RS: pick up and knit (pu&k)	⟍ RS: knit into front, back (kf&b)
⟍ RS: knit into front, back, front (kfbf)	╱ RS: knit 2 together (k2tog)
RS: slip knitwise, slip knitwise, ⟍ knit slipped sts tog thru back loops (ssk)	⋀ RS: central double decrease (cdd)
Ⓐ RS: sl2, k2tog, p2sso	Ⲥ RS: w&t
Ↄ WS: w&t	ᴗ cast on
⌒ bind off (BO)	■ stitches not worked on this row
☐ marker (m)	☐ marker (m)
☐ marker (m)	▨ no stitch

Odd Base (OB)

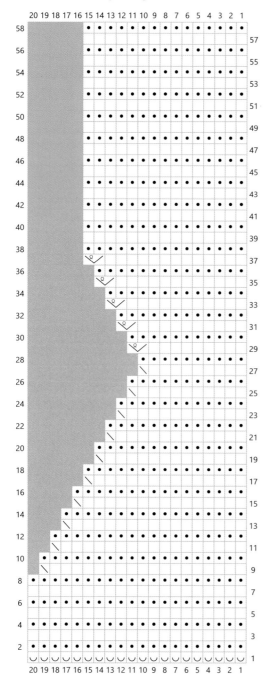

Even Base (EB)

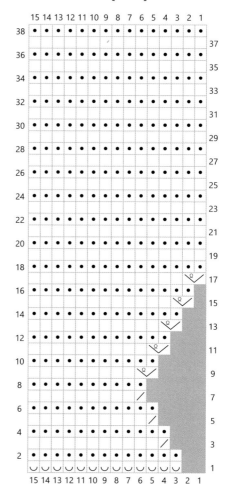

Odd Cat (OC)

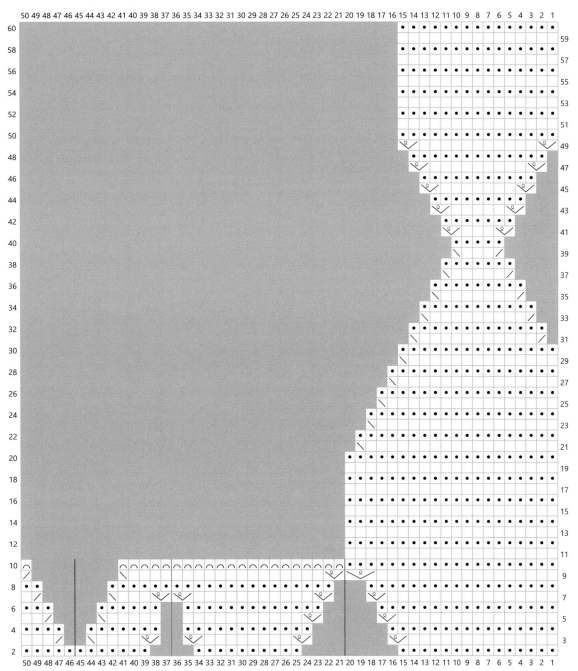

Even Cat (EC)

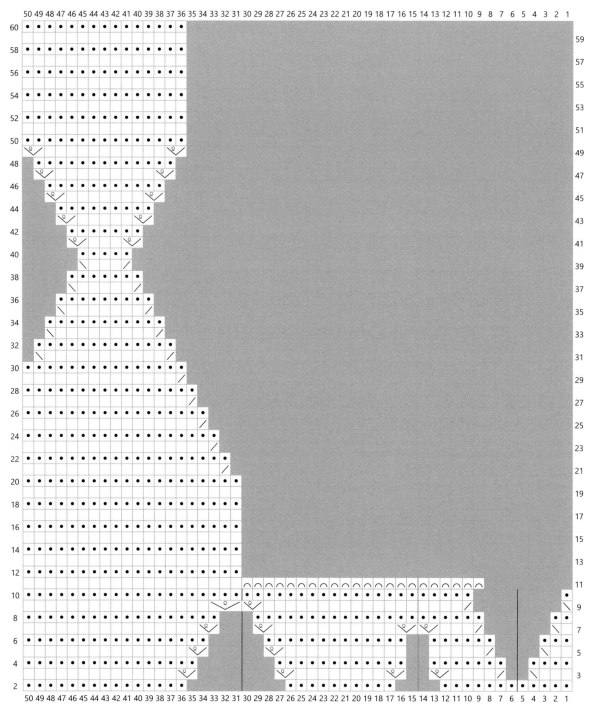

See "Chart Symbols" on page 34

Ears (RE and LE)

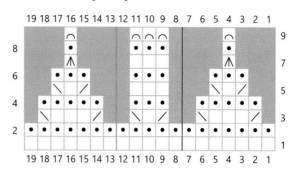

last WS row (Row 60) of cat, then, turn and CO 5

Ear Gap (EG)

Big Triangle (BT)

Triangle (Tr)

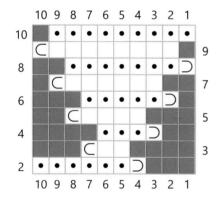

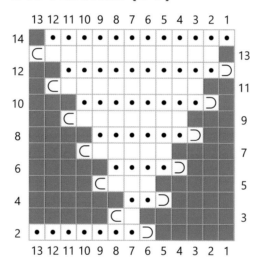

Small Triangle (ST)

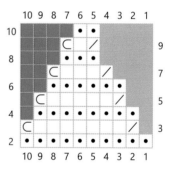

Tail (Tl)

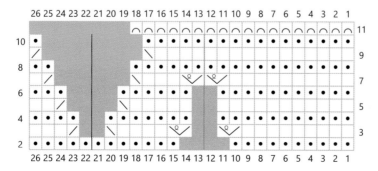

Make a Copycats pillow to try out the pattern!

This pillow is worked in 4 short Strips of 2 or 3 cats, joining the Strips, then picking up and knitting a Right and Left Border. See the blanket pattern for yarn colors, needle size, equipment, gauge, and notes.

SIZE

21"/53 cm square Pillow Cover

SUPPLIES

22"/55 cm square pillow form
22"/55 cm zipper
Sewing thread matching yarn color D
Sewing needle and safety pins

PILLOW FRONT

Yarn Requirements

The yarn requirements for working the front side only are:

A, B, F, G, H, I, J, M: 35 yds/32 m of each for full Cats
D: 180 yds/165 m for Bases, Ear Gaps, Joining, and part-cat pieces.

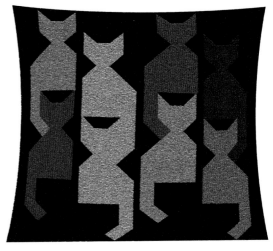

Illustration of Copycats Pillow

INSTRUCTIONS

Strips 1 and 3

Using colors specified for Strip in Figure 6, work as for "Strip 1" on page 28, working only these pieces: Base (OB), Cat 1, Cat 2, and Tail.

Strips 2 and 4

Using colors specified for Strip in Figure 6, work as for "Strip 2" on page 29, working only these pieces: Base (EB), Cat 1, Cat 2, and Cat 6 (9).

Joining of Strips

Odd to Even Joins (Strips 1 and 2, and Strips 3 and 4)

Work as for "Vertical Joining" - "Odd to Even Join" on page 30, referring to the left side of Figure 7 for construction and stitch counts. *Note:* The pu&k generates 98 stitches.

Even to Odd Joins (Strips 2 and 3)

Work as for "Vertical Joining" - "Even to Odd Join" on page 31, referring to the right side of Figure 7 for construction and stitch counts. *Note:* The pu&k generates 98 sts.

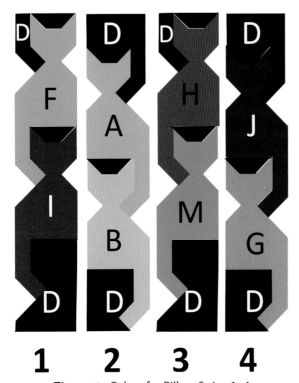

Figure 6: Colors for Pillow Strips 1–4

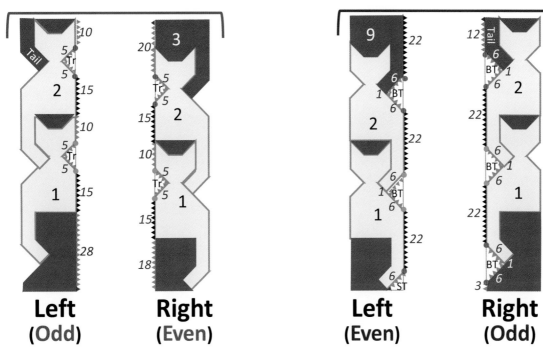

Left
(Odd)

Right
(Even)

Left
(Even)

Right
(Odd)

Figure 8: Strip Joining for Pillow

BORDERS

See Figure 8.

Right Border

With D, on the Right edge of Strip 4, work Even to Odd Join, Step 1) Prep Left Strip, then knit 12 rows. BO loosely.

Figure 7: Borders for Pillow

Left Border

With D, on the Left edge of Strip 1, work Even to Odd Join, Step 2) Prep Right Strip, then knit 12 rows. BO loosely.

PILLOW BACK

Either repeat the Pillow Front (yarn amounts for the Pillow Front should be doubled), or work a plain garter stitch back (instructions below).

Yarn Requirements

500 yds/457 m of D

Instructions

With D, CO 98 sts. Knit 197 rows (99 ridges). BO loosely.

PILLOW FRONT/BACK ASSEMBLY

See "Assembling Pillows with a Zipper Closure" on page 192.

FLOWER SHOW

Express your love of flowers by making this bright, retro blanket in one of three Color Stories: Summertime, Succulent, or Spring Bouquet.

TECHNIQUES

Sewing, wrap & turn, 3-needle BO, crochet (slip stitch)

SIZE

62"/157 cm square

YARN

Jaggerspun Yarns, Mousam Falls, Aran (100% superwash wool; 187 yds/171 m; 3.5 oz/100 g):

Pattern color ID	Color swatch	Color name	Color description	# Hanks for Color Palette		
				Summertime	**Succulent**	**Spring Bouquet**
A		Crème/Ecru	off-white	2	3	3
B		Admiral	dark blue	3	4	
C		French Blue	medium blue	2	3	
D		Plum	deep purple	2		
E		Aster	pale purple	2		
F		Cardinal	red	2		3
G		Fuchsia	hot pink	2		3
H		Cassis	medium pink	2		3
I		Persimmon	orange	2	3	3
J		Chrome	strong yellow	2		
K		Lemon	pale yellow	2	2	4
L		Artichoke	pale green	6	6	6
M		Tourmaline	dark green	2	3	3
N		Jade	blue green	2	3	3

NEEDLES

US Size 7/4.5 mm 40"/100 cm circular needle, US 10/6 mm straight needle for 3-needle BO

NOTIONS

Removable stitch markers, tapestry needle, US 7/4.5 mm crochet hook

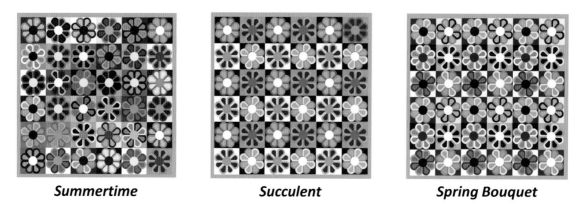

Summertime   Succulent   Spring Bouquet

Figure 1: Three Color Stories for Blanket

GAUGE

18 sts x 36 rows = 4"/10 cm in garter st

NOTES

- Three Color Stories (CS) are shown in Figure 1:

    Summertime: 14 colors with no repeating flower color combinations,

    Succulent: 8 colors with 4 repeating flower color combinations, and

    Spring Bouquet: 9 colors with 6 repeating flower combinations.

- Figure 2 is an overview of the construction. This blanket is composed of 36 Blocks worked individually then sewn together. A Block has an 8–petaled flower with a center and a background. Flower petals are worked flat and shaped using: decreases, wrap & turn, and a 3-needle bind-off; and are worked with stitches picked up and knit from the edges of previously completed petals. The center is worked flat from stitches picked up and knit on the inner edges of Petals, then closed with a short seam. The Block Background is picked up and knit around the edges of the flower, and Blocks are finished with a crochet edge and sewn together. After assembly, the blanket border is picked up and knit on the edges of the blanket.

- The larger needle is used only for 3-needle bind-off. Use smaller needle for all other parts.

- Charts for pattern stitches begin on page 48.

BLANKET INSTRUCTIONS

There are instructional videos for making the Petal and Edge and Corner shapes. See "Supplemental Material" on page 206.

BLOCK

See Figure 4 for Block shapes and color key.

Make 36 Blocks in chosen Color Story (CS) shown in Figures 10–12, where colors [C1][C2][C3][C4][C5] are shown for each Block.

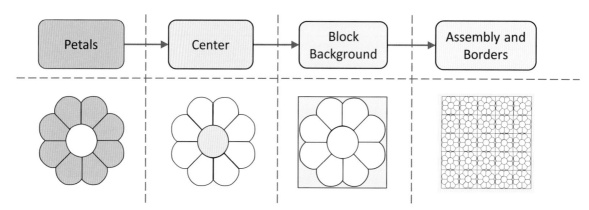

Figure 2: Construction Overview

Petals 1–8

See Figure 3 for construction.

Notes:

- Do not cut C1, C2, and C3 yarns until all 8 Petals are complete. Yarns are carried over to the following Petals by draping with a little slack from one use to the next.

- There are two types of markers used on Petals. Figure 5 shows the Petal construction details and the placement of markers for even- and odd-numbered Petals.

  - The Background Marker (BGM) is placed in the Cast On st for Petals. It is left in place until it is used later while working the Block background.

  - The marker (m) referred to in the Petal instructions, is a removable marker placed on the needle during Cast On.

- Refer to Figures 10–12, for colors (C1–C3) for Petals.

Petal 1 (P1) With C1, CO 8, leaving 12"/30 cm tail, pm (m), CO 6, pm in last st added (Background Marker, "BGM"), CO 18 – 32 sts. Work [Petal].

Petal 2 (P2) With C2, and starting at red triangle on edge of prev Petal, pu&k 7 sts (one per CO st), turn and CO 1, pm (m), CO 11, pm in last st added (BGM), CO 13 – 32 sts. Work [Petal].

Petal 3 (P3) With C1 and starting at red triangle on edge of prev Petal, pu&k 7 sts (one per CO st), turn and CO 1, pm (m), CO 6, pm in last st added (BGM), CO 18 – 32 sts. Work [Petal].

Petal 4 (P4) Rep Petal 2.

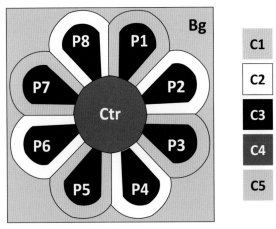

Figure 4: Shapes and Colors

Petal – 32 sts dec'ing to 1 st

See also Petal chart on page 48.

Row 1 (WS): Knit.
Row 2 (RS): Knit to m, k2tog, k2, k2tog, k4, k2tog, k2, k2tog, knit to end – 4 sts dec'd; 28 sts.
Row 3: Knit.
Change to C3 for Block. Do not cut C1.
Rows 4 & 5: Knit.
Row 6: Knit to m, k2tog, k1, k2tog, k2, k2tog, k1, k2tog, knit to 3 sts bef end, w&t – 4 sts dec'd; 24 sts.
Row 7: Knit to 3 sts from end, w&t.
Row 8: Knit to m, rm, k2tog 4 times, k2, w&t – 4 sts dec'd; 20 sts.
Row 9: K8, w&t.
Row 10: K1, cdd twice, knit to end – 4 sts dec'd; 16 sts.
Row 11: K8. Turn RS tog and use larger needle to 3-needle BO rem sts.
Enlarge the last loop on the needle, insert yarn skein through it and pull to tighten. Do not cut C3.

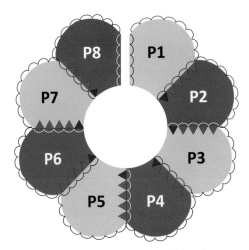

Figure 3: Construction of Petals

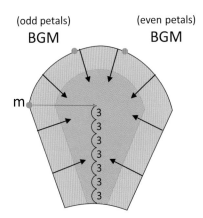

Figure 5: Petal Construction and Marker Placement

Petals 5–8 (P5–P8) Rep [Petal 3 and Petal 4] twice more. Cut C1, C2, and C3, and fasten off.

Center (Ctr)

See Figure 6 and Figure 7.

With C4, starting at the yellow triangle in Figure 6 and working clockwise, pu&k 7 sts on the inner curved edge of each Petal – 56 sts.

> *Note*: Draped C1, C2, and C3 yarns can be tacked to the WS during the Center pu&k by alternately inserting the needle above and below the draped yarns at the back of the work. Or, tack yarns to the pick-up row by leaving a 30"/75 cm tail of C4 when attaching yarn for the Center, threading the tail onto a tapestry needle and, on the WS, tacking the draped yarns to the pick-up row.

Work [Ctr]. Cut C4 leaving 12"/30 cm tail.

Center (Ctr) – 56 sts dec'ing to 8 sts

See also Center chart on page 48.
Row 1 and all odd (WS) rows to 11: Knit.
Row 2 (RS): (K5, k2tog) 8 times – 8 sts dec'd; 48 sts.
Row 4: (K2, k2tog, k2) 8 times – 8 sts dec'd; 40 sts.
Row 6: (K2tog, k3) 8 times – 8 sts dec'd; 32 sts.
Row 8: (K2, k2tog) 8 times – 8 sts dec'd; 24 sts.
Row 10: (K2tog, k1) 8 times – 8 sts dec'd; 16 sts.
Row 12: (K2tog) 8 times – 8 sts dec'd; 8 sts.
Cut yarn, leaving 15"/40 cm tail. Thread tail onto tapestry needle. Insert needle through rem sts, pull to tighten and fasten off securely.

With long tail from Center and mattress stitch, sew red dotted seam in Figure 7 to close Center. With long tail from P1's cast-on and mattress st, sew blue dotted seam in Figure 7 bet P1 and P8 utilizing only the lower 7 CO sts on each Petal edge.

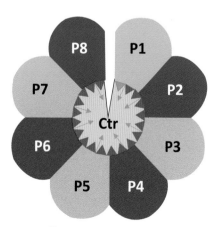

Figure 6: Center (Ctr)

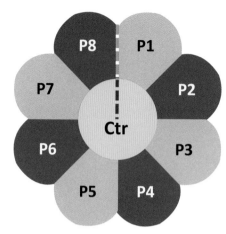

Figure 7: Flower Seaming

BLOCK BACKGROUND (BG)

See Figure 8 and Figure 9. Block's background shapes, Corners and Edges, are worked counter-clockwise around the Flower to turn it into a square.

Corner 1 (Crn1) and Edge 1 (Ed1)

On RS, attach C5 for Block at BGM at the red-outlined triangle in Figure 8 labeled "Start" (on rounded P8 edge) by pulling one loop from back and placing on R needle (1 st).

*Pu&k 10 sts to end of Petal, 1 st in join bet Petals, pm, and pu&k 11 sts to next BGM (red-outlined triangle) – 23 sts. Work [Crn].

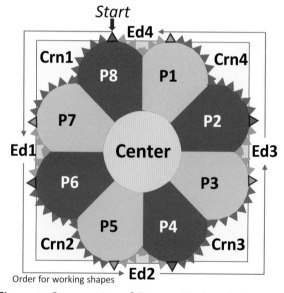

Figure 8: Construction of Corners (Crn) and Edges (Ed)

With crochet hook, work 13 sl sts loosely along left edge of Crn1 to BGM of next Petal. Transfer loop from last sl st to needle, pu&k 5 sts to end of Petal, 1 st in join bet Petals, pm, and pu&k 6 sts to BGM on next petal – 13 sts.

Work [Ed]. With crochet hook, work 6 slip sts loosely along left edge of Ed1 to BGM on next Petal, and transfer loop to needle.*

Corner (Crn) – 23 sts dec'ing to 1 st

See also Corner chart on page 48.
Row 1 and all odd (WS) rows to 19: Knit.
Row 2 (RS): K2tog, knit to 2 sts bef m, rm, cdd, pm, knit to last 2 sts, ssk – 4 sts dec'd; 19 sts.
Row 4: K2tog, k3, bli, knit to 2 sts bef m, rm, cdd, pm, knit to 5 sts bef end, bli, k3, ssk – 2 sts dec'd; 17 sts.
Rows 6 & 8: Rep [Row 4] – 4 sts dec'd; 13 sts.
Row 10: Knit to 2 sts bef m, rm, cdd, pm, knit to end – 2 sts dec'd; 11 sts.
Rows 12, 14, 16, & 18: Rep [Row 10] 4 times – 8 sts dec'd; 3 sts.
Row 20: Rm, cdd – 2 sts dec'd; 1 st.

Edge (Ed) – 13 sts dec'ing to 1 st

See also Edge chart on page 48.
Row 1 (WS): Knit.
Row 2 (RS): K2tog, knit to 2 sts bef m, rm, cdd, pm, knit to last 2 sts, ssk – 4 sts dec'd; 9 sts.
Rows 3 & 4: Rep [Rows 1 & 2] – 4 sts dec'd; 5 sts.
Row 5: Knit.
Row 6: Rm, cdd2 – 4 sts dec'd; 1 st.

Key

 Sl st from fasten off point for Crn to pu&k point for next Ed

Sl st from fasten off point for Ed to pu&k point for next Crn

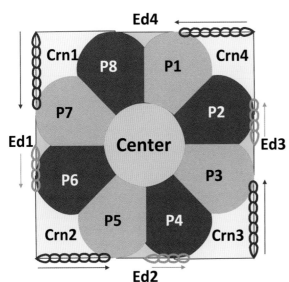

Figure 9: Locations for Working Slip Stitch

Crn2, Ed2, Crn3, Ed3, Crn4, and Ed4

Cont in a counterclockwise direction around the Flower, rep bet * and * 3 times.

After completing Ed4, work single crochet (sc) loosely around edge of the Block, making 2 sc to turn each corner, and 38 sc per edge (13 along each Crn edge and 12 along each Ed edge). When reaching the end of the round, slip st in first sc. Cut yarn and fasten off, leaving a 40"/100 cm tail.

ASSEMBLY

Arrange Blocks as shown in Figure 10, Figure 11, or Figure 12 selected for Color Story. Using whip st, and inserting needle only into the back loops of the sc border, sew Blocks tog into horizontal Strip, then sew Strip tog, matching Block corners, using long tails from Crn's and Ed's when available. Otherwise, cut 40"/100 cm of C5 of one of the two Blocks being sewn.

BORDERS

RIGHT BORDER

On RS, starting at the lower-right corner of blanket, with L, pu&k 264 sts along right edge of blanket (44 sts per Block). Knit 11 rows. BO loosely, do not cut yarn and leave last st on needle.

TOP BORDER

Pu&k 5 sts on top edge of Border, 1 st in the join bet Border and blanket, 264 sts across top of blanket – 271 sts. Knit 11 rows. BO loosely, do not cut yarn and leave last st on needle.

LEFT BORDER

Rep as for Top Border, starting the pu&k at top-left corner of Top Border.

BOTTOM BORDER

Pu&k 5 sts on left edge of Left Border, 1 st in the join bet Border and blanket, 264 sts across bottom of blanket, 1 st in join bet Border and blanket, 6 sts on edge of Right Border – 278 sts. Knit 11 rows. BO loosely. Cut yarn and fasten off.

FINISHING

Weave in ends.

Figure 10: Block Color Scheme for Summertime Color Story

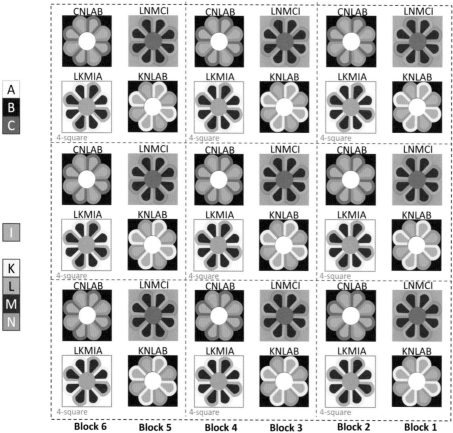

Figure 11: Block Color Scheme for Succulent Color Story

Dotted lines show repeats of 4–flower color scheme

Figure 12: Block Color Scheme for Spring Color Story

Dotted lines show repeat of 6–flower color scheme

CHARTS

CHART SYMBOLS

◥ RS: slip, slip, knit (ssk)   ⋀ RS: central double decrease (cdd)   ℓ RS: backwards loop increase (bli)

⊂ RS: wrap & turn (w&t)   ⊃ WS: wrap & turn (w&t)   ⌒ 3-needle bind-off

☐ marker (m)   ▨ sts not worked in this row   ▨ no stitch

▨ worked in 3-needle BO
with sts 25-32 of row

PETAL

CENTER (CTR)

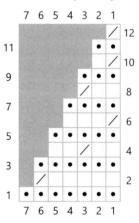

Note: Make color change from C1/C2 to C3 at beg of Row 4 of Petal chart

EDGE (ED)

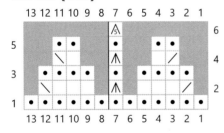

CORNER (CRN)

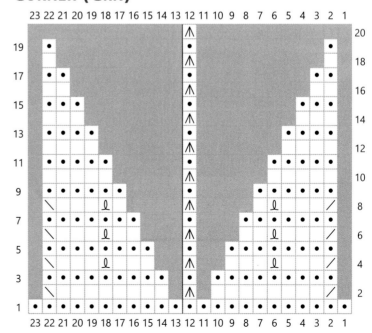

Make a Flower Show pillow to try out the pattern!

This pillow is worked by making one Block of the Blanket, and then picking up and knitting a striped border around the edges of the Block.

See the blanket pattern for yarn colors, needle size, equipment, gauge, notes, and Block instructions.

SIZE

18"/45 cm square Pillow Cover

SUPPLIES

18"/45 cm square pillow form
18"/45 cm zipper
Sewing thread matching yarn color
Sewing needle and safety pins

PILLOW FRONT

Yarn Requirements

The yarn requirements for working the front side only are:

C1: Edge of Petals 1, 3, 5, and 7: 14 yds/14 m of D
C2: Edge of Petals 2, 4, 6, and 8: 14 yds/14 m of G
C3: Inner part of Petals 1–8: 31 yds/29 m of A
C4: Center (Ctr): 12 yds/11 m of J
C5: Background (BG) around flower: 45 yds/42 m of L

The border is composed of three color stripes. Yarn requirements for these are:

Inner Border: 66 yds/60 m of H
Middle Border: 83 yds/76 m of A
Outer Border: 100 yds/92 m of J

Instructions

Using yarns C1–C5, make a Block (see instructions for "Block" on page 42).

BORDERS

Right Border

Inner Border With H, and starting at bottom right corner of Block, pu&k 44 sts evenly to next corner. Knit 1 row. Work [Border] 5 times (6 ridges completed), ending after WS row – 54 sts. Cut yarn and fasten off, leaving 10"/25 cm tail.

Border
Row 1 (RS): Kf&b, knit to last st, kf&b – 2 sts inc'd. **Row 2 (WS):** Knit.

Illustration of Flower Show Pillow

Middle Border With A, work [Border] 6 times (6 ridges completed), ending after a WS row – 66 sts. Cut yarn and fasten off, leaving a 10"/25 cm tail.

Outer Border With J, work [Border] 7 times (7 ridges completed), ending after a WS row – 80 sts. BO loosely. Cut yarn and fasten off, leaving 10"/25 cm tail.

Top, Left, and Bottom Borders

Rep as for Right Border, attaching yarn at the top-right, top-left, and bottom-left corners, respectively.

Using matching long tails and mattress st, sew open corners tog, aligning color transitions.

PILLOW BACK

Either repeat the Pillow Front (yarn amounts for the Pillow Front should be doubled) or work a plain garter stitch back (instructions below).

Yarn Requirements

360 yds/325 m of J (the Outer Border color for the Front of the pillow)

Instructions

CO 80 sts. Knit 159 rows (80 ridges). BO loosely.

PILLOW FRONT/BACK ASSEMBLY

See "Assembling Pillows with a Zipper Closure" on page 192.

LOVE BUG

Make a funky blanket featuring a pop culture icon from the 1970s.

TECHNIQUES

Intarsia, wrap & turn, 3-needle BO

SIZE

48.5 x 65"/123 x 165 cm

YARN

Malabrigo Rios, worsted (100% superwash merino wool; 210 yds/192 m; 3.5 oz/100 g):

Pattern color ID	Color swatch	Color ID	Color name	Color description	# Hanks
A		RIO704	Ivory	off-white	5
B		RIO655	Chaja	yellow	1
C		RIO695	Peachy	peach	2
D		RIO896	Living Coral	red-orange	2
E		RIO886	Diana	mixed med	2
F		RIO277	Siri	mixed light	1
G		RIO093	Fucsia	fuchsia	1
H		RIO869	Cumparsita	burgundy	1
I		RIO057	English Rose	dusty pink	2
J		RIO708	Cucumber	mint green	2
K		RIO011	Apple Green	avocado green	1
L		RIO687	Aquamarine	light blue	2
M		RIO210	Blue Jeans	royal blue	2
N		RIO809	Solis	green-blue	1
O		RIO215	Cowboy	dark navy blue	1

NEEDLES

US Size 7/4.5 mm circular needles of minimum length 60"/150 cm and 1 US 10/6 mm needle for 3-needle BO

NOTIONS

Removable stitch markers, tapestry needle, stitch holder, US 7/4.5 mm crochet hook

GAUGE

19 sts x 38 rows = 4"/10 cm in garter st

Notes

- This blanket is composed of Blocks. The Blocks are joined with Strips of knitting and a 3-needle BO. Borders are picked up and knit from the blanket edges.

- A Block is constructed in 7 steps (see Figure 1):

  1. **Car Top:** Roof and Window of the car, worked with shaping.

  2. **Body:** worked from stitches left from Car Top and pu&k'ed on lower edge of Car Top. The Hood and the Wheel Covers are worked with shaping and intarsia.

  3. **Arch Right:** Stitches are generated via pu&k, and shaping is used.

  4. **Arch Left:** Stitches are generated via pu&k, and shaping is used.

  5. **Inner Frame:** continued from stitches of Arches and from pu&k on the upper curve of each Wheel Cover. Shaped knitting and w&t are used.

  6. **Outer Frame:** continued from stitches of Inner Frame, and from pu&k on the lower, outer edges of Wheel Covers. Shaping is used.

  7. **Bottom:** worked from stitches on holder from Body, and from stitches pu&k on the bottom edge of the Outer Frame. Intarsia is used.

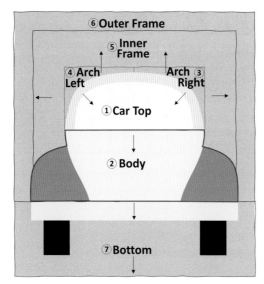

Figure 1: Steps for Making Block

- When working intarsia from written instructions, yarn color changes are abbreviated as follows: <current yarn color> » <next yarn color>. For instance, the abbreviation: "SC»NC" means: "drop SC and continue with NC."

- Figure 2 shows the color identification and abbreviations for the Block. Colors for Blocks are:

  RC: Roof Color
  WC: Window Color
  MC: Middle Color
  SC: Side Color
  BC: Background Color
  FC: Fender Color
  TC: Tire Color
  LC: Light Color
  (**HC:** Heart Color) *if used in Block*

- To avoid tangling of yarn ends and intarsia yarns, weave in yarn ends as soon as the current step is complete or wind ends up and pin to WS.

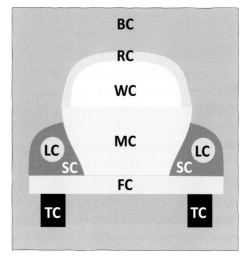

Figure 2: Color Abbreviations

BLANKET INSTRUCTIONS

Make 20 Blocks in color schemes shown in Figure 7 on page 55, where color schemes are specified as:

[RC][WC][MC][SC][BC][FC][TC][LC][(HC)]

Block

Car Top see Figure 3
In RC, CO 19 sts, pm, CO 19 sts – 38 sts.

Row 2 and all WS rows to 22: Knit.
Row 3 (RS): K9, k2tog, k16, k2tog, k9 – 2 sts dec'd; 36 sts.
Cut RC after Row 4.
Row 5: With WC, k4, k2tog, k5, k2tog, k10, k2tog, k5, k2tog, k4 – 4 sts dec'd; 32 sts.
Row 7: K6, k2tog, k16, k2tog, k6 – 2 sts dec'd; 30 sts.
Row 9: (K4, k2tog) twice, k6, (k2tog, k4) twice – 4 sts dec'd; 26 sts.

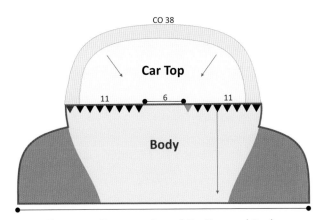

CO 38

Car Top

11   6   11

Body

Figure 3: Construction of Car Top and Body

Row 11: K4, k2tog, k2, k2tog, k6, k2tog, k2, k2tog, k4 – 4 sts dec'd; 22 sts.
Row 13: K7, k2tog, k4, k2tog, k7 – 2 sts dec'd; 20 sts.
Row 15: K3, (k2tog, k2) 3 times, k2tog, k3 – 4 sts dec'd; 16 sts.
Row 17: K3, k2tog, k6, k2tog, k3 – 2 sts dec'd; 14 sts.
Row 19: K1, k2tog twice, k4, k2tog twice, k1 – 4 sts dec'd; 10 sts.
Row 21: K2tog twice, k2, k2tog twice – 4 sts dec'd; 6 sts. Place rem 6 sts on holder for Body.
Weave in ends.

Body see Figure 3

See also Body chart on page 60. Before working this section, see "Intarsia" on page 196.

Row 1: With MC, and starting at red triangle in Figure 3, pu&k 11 sts to the beg of sts on holder, knit 6 sts off holder, pu&k 11 sts from green triangle to corner of Car Top – 28 sts.
Rows 2–6: Knit.
Row 7 (RS): With SC, make slip knot on Right needle, and k1. With separate strand of MC, knit to last st; with separate strand of SC, k1 (the last st). Turn and with SC, CO 1 st – 2 sts inc'd; 30 sts.
Row 8 (WS): With SC, k2, SC»MC, knit to last 2 sts, MC»SC, k2. Turn and CO 2 sts – 2 st inc'd; 32 sts.
Row 9: With SC, k4, SC»MC, knit to last 2 sts, MC»SC, k2. Turn and CO 2 sts – 2 sts inc'd; 34 sts.
Row 10: With SC, k4, SC»MC, knit to last 4 sts, MC»SC, k4. Turn and CO 2 sts – 2 sts inc'd; 36 sts.
Row 11: With SC, k6, SC»MC, knit to last 4 sts, k4. Turn and CO 2 sts – 2 sts inc'd; 38 sts.
Row 12: With SC, k6, SC»MC, knit to last 6 sts, MC»SC, k6.
Row 13: With SC, k7, SC»MC, knit to last 7 sts, MC»SC, k7.
Row 14: With SC, k7, SC»MC, knit to last 7 sts, MC»SC, k7. Turn and CO 1 st – 1 st inc'd; 39 sts.

Row 15: With SC, k8, SC»MC, knit to last 7 sts, MC»SC, k7. Turn and CO 1 st – 1 st inc'd; 40 sts.
Row 16: With SC, k8, SC»MC and knit to 8 sts from end, MC»SC, knit to end.
Rows 17–20: With SC, k9, SC»MC and knit to 9 sts from end, MC»SC, knit to end.
Rows 21–24: With SC, k10, SC»MC and knit to 10 sts from end, MC»SC, knit to end.
Rows 25 & 26: With SC, k11, SC»MC and knit to 11 sts from end, MC»SC, knit to end.
Cut yarns and fasten off. Place 40 sts on holder.
Note: For ease of working on the Frame pieces, it is more convenient to place stitches on a string or waste yarn rather than a rigid stitch holder.

Arches see Figure 4

Arches may be worked on straight needles, but a circular needle will flex to accommodate the shape and be more comfortable. See also Arch Right and Left charts on page 60.

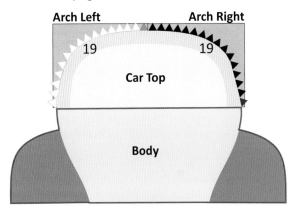

Arch Left   Arch Right

19   19

Car Top

Body

Figure 4: Arches

Arch Right

With BC, and starting at red triangle on right-bottom corner of Top, pu&k 19 sts (1 st per CO st) to center of curved edge of Top ending at the green triangle.

Row 2 (WS): Sl1, knit to last 2 sts, w&t.
Row 3: K6, bli, k1, bli, k6, w&t – 2 sts inc'd; 21 sts.
Row 4: Knit to 2 sts bef prev wrap, w&t.
Row 5: K5, bli, k1, bli, k5, w&t – 2 sts inc'd; 23 sts.
Row 6: Rep Row 4.
Row 7: K4, bli, k5, w&t – 1 st inc'd; 24 sts.
Rows 8–11: Rep Row 4.
Row 12: K1, w&t.
Row 13: Knit to end.
Pm. Do not cut yarn.

Arch Left

See Figure 4 on page 53. With yarn from Arch Right, and starting at green triangle, pu&k 19 sts to bottom-left corner of Car Top.

Note: Stitch counts are from m to end of row.

Row 2: Sl1, knit to last 4 sts bef m, w&t.

Row 3: K6, bli, k1, bli, k5, w&t – 2 sts inc'd; 21 sts.

Row 4: Knit to 2 sts bef prev wrap, w&t.

Row 5: K5, bli, k1, bli, k4, w&t – 2 sts inc'd; 23 sts.

Row 6: Rep Row 4.

Row 7: K5, bli, k3, w&t – 1 st inc'd; 24 sts.

Rows 8–10: Rep Row 4.

Row 11: K1, w&t.

Row 12: Knit to end.

Do not cut yarn.

Counting on RS, there are 24 sts before the m, and 24 sts after the m – 48 sts.

Rm.

Inner Frame see Figure 5

On RS of work, pm (m1), on lower right edge, bet 4th and 5th ridges from bottom edge as shown in Figure 5. Pm (m4) on lower left edge, bet 4th and 5th ridges from bottom edge. Pm on 12th st from beg of row (m2), and on 12th st from end of row (m3). *Note:* Markers m2 and m3 are placed through the stitch and may be advanced to the last row worked after each WS row. Bli's are worked on either side of sts marked m2 and m3.

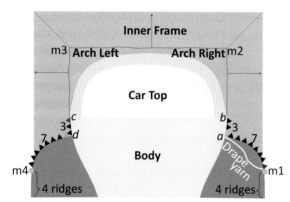

Figure 5: Inner Frame

Row 1 (RS): With BC still attached, drape yarn from *a* to m1, leaving a little slack, then starting at red triangle pu&k 7 sts from m1 to *a*, simultaneously weaving draped yarn. See "Tacking Draped Yarn" on page 202. Cont at the yellow triangle, pu&k 3 sts (1 st per garter st ridge) bet *a* and *b*.

K11 (to 1 st bef m2), bli, k1, bli; knit to 1 st bef m3, bli, k1, bli, knit to end.

Starting at the blue triangle (at *c*) pu&k 3 sts (1 st per ridge) bet *c* and *d*, then 7 sts bet *d* (at green triangle) and m4 – 24 sts inc'd; 72 sts.

Row 2 (WS): Knit to 7 sts bef end, w&t.

Row 3: Knit to 1 st bef m2, bli, k1, bli, knit to 1 st bef m3, bli, k1, bli, knit to 7 sts bef end, w&t – 4 sts inc'd 76 sts.

Row 4: Knit to and including prev wrapped st, w&t.

Row 5: Knit to 1 st bef m2, bli, k1, bli, knit to 1 st bef m3, bli, k1, bli, knit to and including prev wrapped st, w&t – 4 sts inc'd; 80 sts.

Row 6: Rep Row 4.

Rows 7–16: Rep [Rows 5 & 6] 5 times – 20 sts inc'd; 100 sts.

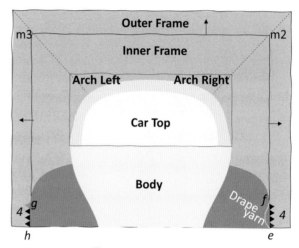

Figure 6: Outer Frame

Outer Frame see Figure 6

Row 17 (RS): With BC still attached, drape yarn from *f* to *e* in, leaving a little slack. Starting at red triangle at *e*, pu&k 4 sts (1 st per garter st ridge) from *e* to *f*, simultaneously weaving draped yarn.

Knit to 1 st bef m2, bli, k1, bli, knit to 1 st bef m3, bli, k1, bli, knit to end. Starting at green triangle at *g*, pu&k 4 sts (1 st per garter st ridge) to *h* – 12 sts inc'd; 112 sts. Rm m1 and m4.

Row 18 (WS): Knit.

Row 19: Knit to 1 st bef m2, bli, k1, bli, knit to 1 st bef m3, bli, k1, bli, knit to end – 4 sts inc'd; 116 sts.

Row 20: Knit.

Rows 21 & 22: Rep [Rows 19 & 20] once – 4 sts inc'd; 120 sts.

BO loosely, leaving last st on needle. Do not cut yarn. Weave in ends.

Bottom see Figure 8

See also Bottom chart on page 61.

Row 1 (RS): Working on RS, with BC still attached, and 1 loop rem on needle from Outer Frame, starting at red triangle in Figure 8, pu&k 3 sts to *h* (1 st per garter st ridge), then with FC, knit 40 sts off holder from Body, then cont at the green triangle at

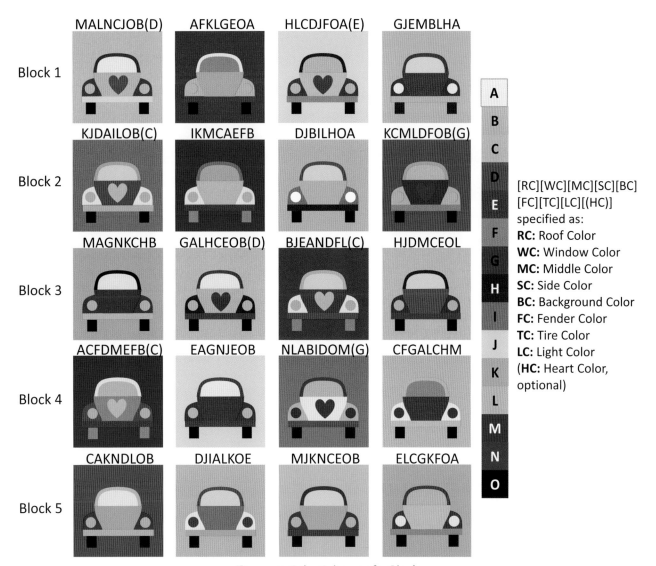

	MALNCJOB(D)	AFKLGEOA	HLCDJFOA(E)	GJEMBLHA
Block 1				
	KJDAILOB(C)	IKMCAEFB	DJBILHOA	KCMLDFOB(G)
Block 2				
	MAGNKCHB	GALHCEOB(D)	BJEANDFL(C)	HJDMCEOL
Block 3				
	ACFDMEFB(C)	EAGNJEOB	NLABIDOM(G)	CFGALCHM
Block 4				
	CAKNDLOB	DJIALKOE	MJKNCEOB	ELCGKFOA
Block 5				

A
B
C
D
E
F
G
H
I
J
K
L
M
N
O

[RC][WC][MC][SC][BC]
[FC][TC][LC][(HC)]
specified as:
RC: Roof Color
WC: Window Color
MC: Middle Color
SC: Side Color
BC: Background Color
FC: Fender Color
TC: Tire Color
LC: Light Color
(**HC:** Heart Color,
optional)

Figure 7: Color Schemes for Blocks

e, with a separate strand of BC, pu&k 3 sts (1 st per garter st ridge) to corner – 46 sts.

Row 2 (WS): With BC, k3, BC»FC, knit to last 3 sts, FC»BC, knit to end.

Rows 3–6: Rep [Row 2] 4 times. Cut FC.

Row 7 (RS): With BC still attached, k5, with TC, k5, with separate strand of BC, k26, with separate strand of TC, k5, with separate strand of BC, k5.

Row 8: With BC, k5, BC»TC, k5, TC»BC, k26, BC»TC, k5, TC»BC, k5.

Rows 9–18: Rep [Row 8] 10 times. Do not cut BC used on left edge. Cut all other yarns.

Rows 19–30: With BC still attached, knit 12 rows. BO loosely.

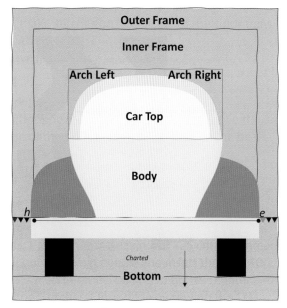

Figure 8: Bottom

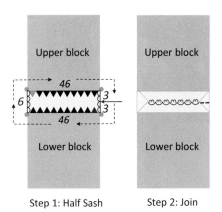

Step 1: Half Sash   Step 2: Join

Figure 9: Joining of Blocks to Make Strips

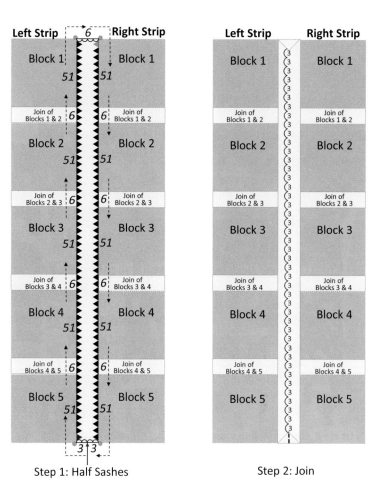

Step 1: Half Sashes

Figure 10: Joining of Strips

ASSEMBLY

Lay out Blocks as shown in Figure 7.

Figure 9 and Figure 10 show the detailed assembly. The blue dots indicate the locations of markers, black dashed lines indicate direction of stitch generation, red dashed lines indicate locations of seams, and numbers in italics are the number of stitches to generate on the edges of a shape.

JOINING OF BLOCKS TO MAKE STRIPS

Make 4 vertical Strips of Blocks as follows:

Join Blocks 1 and 2 of Strip

1) Half Sashes see Step 1 of Figure 9

With A, and shorter circular needles, leaving a 10"/25 cm tail, CO 3 sts, pm (m1). Turn needle and starting at red triangle at the top-right corner of Lower Block, pu&k 46 sts (1 per BO st), to top-left corner of Lower Block. Pm (m2), turn and CO 6 sts, pm (m3), turn and starting at green triangle on the bottom-left corner of Upper Block, pu&k 46 sts (1 per BO st) to bottom-right corner of Upper Block. Pm (m4). Turn needle and CO 3 sts – 104 sts.

Work [Sash]. Do not cut yarn.

2) Join see Step 2 of Figure 9

Work [Join].

Join Remaining Pairs of Blocks

For rem pairs of Blocks: 2 and 3, 3 and 4, 4 and 5, work as for Join of Blocks 1 and 2 of Strip. The Lower Block of the prev Join becomes the Upper Block of the current Join.

Sash

Row 2 (WS): Knit.
Row 3 (RS): (Knit to 2 sts bef m, ssk, k2tog) 4 times, knit to end – 8 sts dec'd; 96 sts.
Row 4: Knit.
Row 5: Rep Row 3 – 8 sts dec'd; 88 sts.
Row 6: Rm m1 and m4 (1st and last m's). Cdd, knit to 2 sts bef m, rm (m2 and m3), cdd, pm, cdd, knit to 3 sts bef end of row, cdd – 8 sts dec'd; 80 sts.

Join

Bring needle tips together with RS of work tog.

Split stitches at the marker bet the cdd's and push stitches on each side of split toward needle tips.

With larger needle, perform 3-needle BO of all stitches. Cut yarn and insert end through rem loop on needle, and tighten.

Using long CO tail and tapestry needle, with mattress stitch, sew tog open seam along red dashed line.

JOINING OF STRIPS

Join Strips 1 and 2

1) Half Sashes see Step 1 of Figure 10

With A, and longer circular needles, leaving a 10"/25 cm tail, CO 3 sts, pm (m1). Turn needle and starting at red triangle at the bottom-right corner of Block 5 of Left Strip, pu&k 279 sts (51 sts per Block and 6 sts per Join) to top-left corner of Block 1 of Left Strip. Pm (m2), turn and CO 6 sts, pm (m3), turn and starting at green triangle on top-left corner of Block 1 of Right Strip, pu&k 279 sts (51 sts per Block and 6 sts per Join) to bottom-left corner of Block 5 of Right Strip. Pm (m4). Turn needle and CO 3 sts – 570 sts.

Work [Sash]. Do not cut yarn.

2) Join see Step 2 of Figure 10

Work [Join].

Join Remaining Pairs of Strips

For rem pairs of Strips: 2 and 3, 3 and 4; rep as for Join Strips 1 and 2. The Right Strip of the prev Join becomes the Left Strip of the current Join.

BORDERS

RIGHT BORDER

With A, and starting at bottom right corner of blanket, pu&k 279 sts (51 sts per Block and 6 sts per Join). Knit 11 rows. BO loosely, leaving last st on needle. Do not cut yarn.

TOP BORDER

Pu&k 6 sts on top edge of Right Border, 202 sts (46 sts per Block and 6 sts per Join) on top edge of blanket– 209 sts. Knit 11 rows. BO loosely, leaving last st on needle. Do not cut yarn.

LEFT BORDER

Pu&k 6 sts on left edge of Top Border, and 279 sts (51 sts per Block and 6 sts per Join) on left edge of blanket – 286 sts. Knit 11 rows. BO loosely, leaving last st on needle. Do not cut yarn.

BOTTOM BORDER

Pu&k 6 sts on the bottom edge of Left Border, and 202 sts (46 sts per Block and 6 sts per Join) on bottom edge of blanket, and 7 sts on right edge of Right Border – 216 sts. Knit 11 rows. BO loosely.

FLOWERS

Make 20 Flowers in color schemes [Petal Color (PC)] [Center Color (CC)] then sew to front of blanket at locations indicated in Figure 11. For sewing, see "Tacking Embellishments" on page 189.

FLOWER

Petals see also Petal chart on page 59
With PC, CO 3 sts.

Petal 1

Row 2 (RS): Knit.
Row 3 (WS): K3, turn and CO 2 sts – 2 sts inc'd; 5 sts.
Row 4: K4, w&t.
Row 5: K4, turn and CO 1 st – 1 st inc'd; 6 sts.
Row 6: K4, w&t.
Rows 7 & 8: Rep [Rows 5 & 6] once – 1 st inc'd; 7 sts.
Row 9: Knit.
Row 10: K3, w&t.
Rows 11 & 12: Rep [Rows 9 & 10] once.
Row 13: Knit.
Row 14: K4, w&t.
Row 15: Knit.
Row 16: K2tog, k3, w&t – 1 st dec'd; 6 sts.
Row 17: Knit.
Row 18: Rep Row 16 – 1 st dec'd; 5 sts.
Row 19: Knit.
Row 20: K2tog, BO 3 – 4 sts dec'd; 1 st.
Row 21: CO 2 – 2 sts inc'd; 3 sts.

Petals 2–5

Rep Petal 1 (4) more times, ending Petal 5 after Row 20. Cut yarn leaving 10"/25 cm tail and fasten off.

Center see Figure 12, Step 1

On RS of Petals, starting at red triangle on the inner curved edge and working clockwise, with CC, pu&k 12 sts evenly to end of inner curved edge at **a**.

Row 2 (WS): Knit.
Row 3 (RS): K2tog 6 times – 6 sts dec'd; 6 sts.
Row 4: Knit.

Cut yarn leaving 10"/20 cm tail. Thread tail onto tapestry needle. Insert needle through 6 loops on needle. Pull yarn taut and fasten off securely.

Seaming of Flower

See Figure 12, Step 2. With tail of Ctr still on needle, working on RS, and using mattress stitch, sew open edges of Ctr together, then fasten off yarn. With long tail from P5, sew opening between P1 and P5, seaming tog only the 3 CO and BO sts.

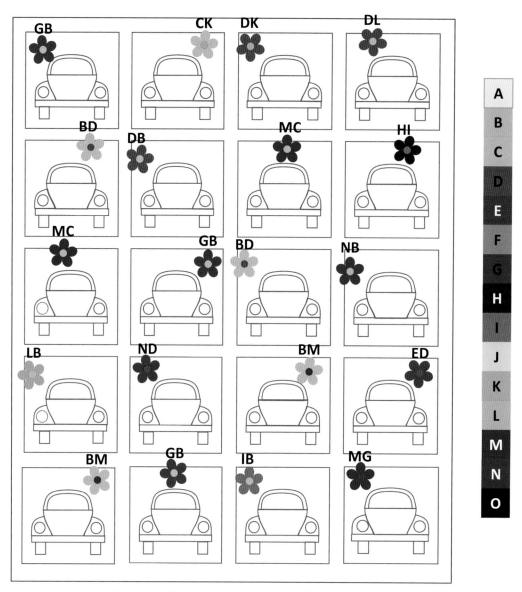

Figure 11: Flower Color Schemes [PC][CC] and Locations

HEARTS

Make 8 hearts in color schemes shown in Figure 7.

With HC, CO 7 sts. See also Heart Chart on page 59.

Row 2 (WS): Knit to end, turn and CO 3 sts – 3 sts inc'd; 10 sts.

Row 3: K9, w&t.

Row 4: K9, turn and CO 1 – 1 st inc'd; 11 sts.

Row 5: K8, w&t.

Row 6: K8.

Row 7: K7, w&t.

Row 8: K7.

Row 9: K6, w&t.

Row 10: K6.

Row 11: K2tog, k3, w&t – 1 st dec'd; 10 sts.

Row 12: K4.

Row 13: BO 3, w&t (6th from end) – 3 sts dec'd; 7 sts.

Row 14: K1, turn and CO 3 – 3 sts inc'd; 10 sts.

Row 15: K4, w&t.

Row 16: K4, turn and CO 1 – 11 sts.

Row 17: K5, w&t.

Row 18: K5.

Row 19: Rep Row 9.

Row 20: K6.

Row 21: Rep Row 7.

Row 22: K7.

Row 23: K2tog, k6, w&t – 1 st dec'd; 10 sts.

Row 24: K7.

Row 25: K2tog, BO the k2tog st, k6, w&t – 2 sts dec'd; 8 sts.

Row 26: K7.

Row 27: K2tog, BO the k2tog st, BO rem sts – 1 st.

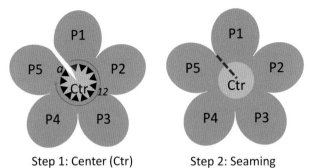

Step 1: Center (Ctr)	Step 2: Seaming

Figure 12: Flower Center and Seaming

Cut yarn, leaving 12"/30 cm tail. Insert tail through remaining stitch on needle and tighten.

Using long tail, sew hearts in locations indicated in Figure 7.

HEADLIGHTS

For colors and locations to attach headlights, see Figure 7 on page 55.

There are two options for working the headlights: single crochet or knitted with a small seam.

Option 1: Single Crochet

Wrap LC for Block twice around L index finger. Slide wraps off finger and pinch circle between thumb and index finger of L hand.

Foundation round: With crochet hook, draw working yarn through center of circle, chain 1 (ch1), make 8 single crochet (sc) through center of circle, then slip st in first sc.

Next round: Ch1, work 2 sc in each foundation row sc, slip st in 1st st of round. Cut yarn leaving 12"/30 cm tail. Pull short yarn to close hole. Fasten off securely. With long tail, sew headlight to car.

Option 2: Knitted with a Small Seam

With LC for Block, CO 18 sts.

Row 2: Knit.
Row 3: K2tog 9 times – 9 sts dec'd; 9 sts.
Row 4: Knit.

Cut yarn leaving 12"/30 cm tail. Thread tail onto tapestry needle and insert tail through 9 sts on needle. Pull taut and fasten off securely.

With long tail, sew headlights to cars

FINISHING

Weave in ends.

HEART

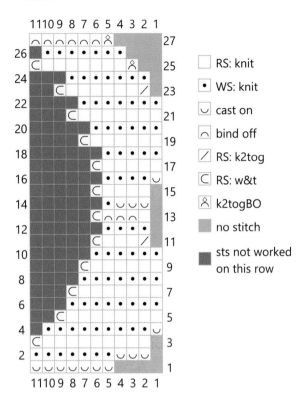

- ☐ RS: knit
- • WS: knit
- ⌣ cast on
- ⌢ bind off
- ╱ RS: k2tog
- ⊂ RS: w&t
- ⅄ k2togBO
- (gray) no stitch
- (dark) sts not worked on this row

PETAL

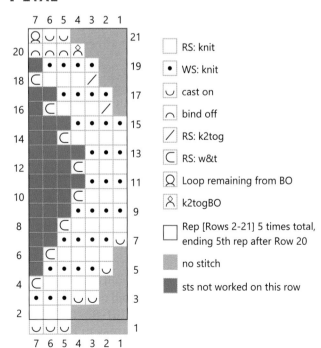

- ☐ RS: knit
- • WS: knit
- ⌣ cast on
- ⌢ bind off
- ╱ RS: k2tog
- ⊂ RS: w&t
- ℺ Loop remaining from BO
- ⅄ k2togBO
- ☐ Rep [Rows 2-21] 5 times total, ending 5th rep after Row 20
- (gray) no stitch
- (dark) sts not worked on this row

BODY

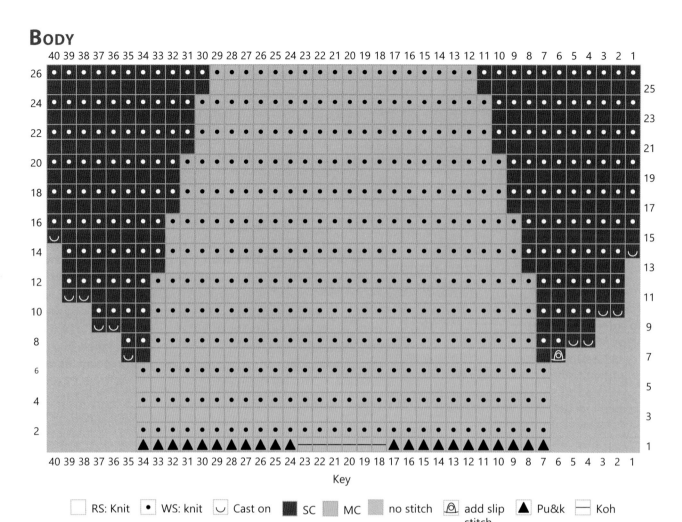

Key

| | RS: Knit | • WS: knit | ⌣ Cast on | ■ SC | ▨ MC | ▨ no stitch | ⓐ add slip stitch | ▲ Pu&k | — Koh |

ARCH RIGHT

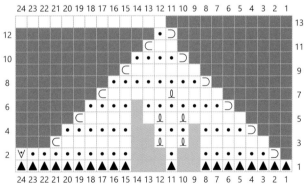

ARCH LEFT

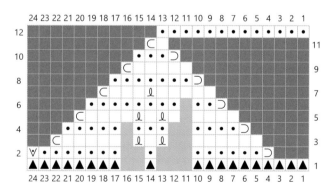

| | RS: knit | • WS: knit | ℓ RS: bli | C RS: w&t | ⊃ WS: w&t | ▨ no stitch | ▲ RS: pu&k | ■ sts not worked on this row | ⱴ WS: slip |

Bottom

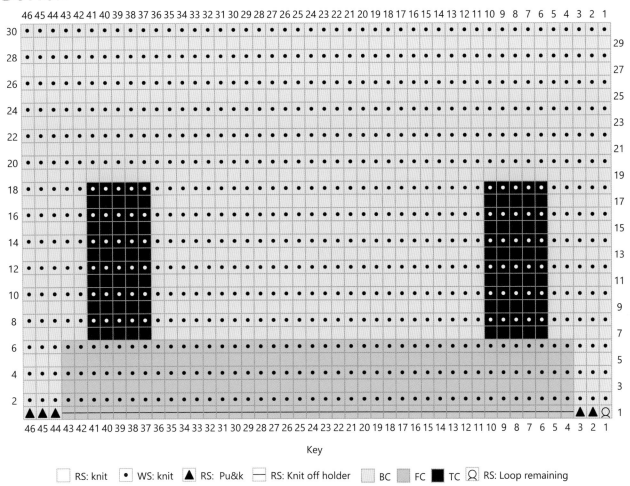

Key

☐ RS: knit   ● WS: knit   ▲ RS: Pu&k   ⊢ RS: Knit off holder   ☐ BC   ☐ FC   ■ TC   ꩜ RS: Loop remaining

Make a Love Bug pillow to try out the pattern!

This pillow is worked by making one Block of the Blanket, and then picking up and knitting a border around the edges of the Block.

See the blanket pattern for yarn colors, needle size, equipment, gauge, notes, and Block instructions.

SIZE

18"/45 cm square Pillow Cover

SUPPLIES

18"/45 cm square pillow form
18"/45 cm zipper
Sewing thread matching yarn color O
Sewing needle and safety pins

PILLOW FRONT

Yarn Requirements

The yarn requirements for working the front side only are:

	yds	meters		yds	meters		yds	meters
A	11	10	C	90	82	G	20	18
J	2	2	K	20	18	L	10	9
M	10	9	N	270	250	O	5	5

where color scheme for Block is: NAKMCLOB(G). See explanation in Figure 7 on page 55.

Instructions

Make a Block (see instructions for "Block" on page 52).

With G for petals and J for center, make Flower (see instructions for "Flower" on page 57). Using long tail of G, sew Flower at location indicated in Figure 13.

With G, make a Heart (see instructions for "Heart" on page 59).

With B, make two headlights (see instructions for "Headlights" on page 59).

Borders

Right Border

With N, on RS of Block, and starting at bottom-right corner, pu&k 51 sts to corner. Knit 37 rows (19 ridges). BO loosely leaving last st on needle.

Illustration of Love Bug Pillow

Top Border

With yarn still attached, pu&k 19 sts on top edge of Right Border and 46 sts on top edge of Block – 66 sts. Knit 31 rows (16 ridges). BO loosely leaving last st on needle.

Left Border

With yarn still attached, pu&k 16 sts on bottom edge of Top Border, and 51 sts on left edge of Block – 68 sts. Knit 37 rows (19 ridges). Bind off loosely leaving last st on needle.

Bottom Border

With yarn still attached, pu&k 19 sts on bottom edge of Left Border, 46 sts on bottom edge of Block, and 20 sts on bottom edge of Right Border – 86 sts. Knit 31 rows. BO loosely.

PILLOW BACK

Either repeat the Pillow Front (yarn amounts for the Pillow Front should be doubled), or work a plain garter stitch back (instructions below).

Yarn Requirements

395 yds/360 m of O

Instructions

CO 84 sts. Knit 167 rows (84 ridges). BO loosely.

PILLOW FRONT/ BACK ASSEMBLY

See "Assembling Pillows with a Zipper Closure" on page 192.

OACLNMPB(H)

Figure 13: Pillow Color Scheme

MORE THAN A FELINE

Express your colorful side with this purr-fectly pleasing blanket of kitties.

TECHNIQUES

Intarsia, sewing, crochet (slip stitch), simple crochet (for eyes)

SIZE

74.5 x 61.5"/189 x 156 cm

YARN

Sugarbush Bold, worsted (100% extra fine superwash merino; 190 yds/174 m; 3.5 oz/100 g):

Pattern color ID	Color swatch	Color name	Color description	# Balls
A		Clover	yellow-green	1
B		Fir	pine green	1
C		Pine Pass	lightest green	1
D		Truro Teal	teal	1
E		Yukon Gold	yellow	1
F		Prairie Gold	gold	1
G		Mango Mob	red-orange	1
H		Rusty Road	rust	1
I		Powell Pink	light pink	1
J		Fleur de Rose	hot pink	1
K		Plumtastic	burgundy	1
L		Lac Lavender	medium purple	1
M		Cabot Blue	light blue	1
N		Trinity Bay Blue	royal blue	1
O		Avalon Aqua	light aqua	1
P		Georgian Gray	slate gray	6
Q		Fresh Snow	white	4
R		Rockies	black	2

NEEDLES

US Size 7/4.5 mm 40"/100 cm circular needles

NOTIONS

US Size 7/4.5 mm crochet hook, tapestry needle, stitch markers, stitch holders

GAUGE

17 sts x 34 rows = 4"/10 cm in garter st

NOTES

- The blanket is worked entirely from charts, which are on page 71. Vertical Strips of Cats are worked and then sewn together. A Cat consists of a Neck (Nk) and a Head (H1, H2, or H3 depicted in Figure 1). In Figure 2, there are white lines to mark the beginning and end of each Cat.

Ear Section is Rows 43-56
of charts H1, H2, and H3

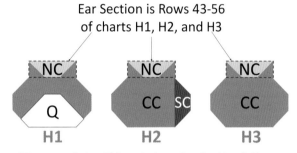

Figure 1: Color Abbreviations for Cat Head Charts

- All Cat Head charts, H1–H3, end with an Ear section worked in intarsia using the color of the current cat (CC) for the ears and the color of the next cat (NC) for the bottom area of the Neck, as shown in the red dashed sections in Figure 1. Head 1 is worked in intarsia with CC and Q (for nose area). Heads 2 and 3 are used at the edges to create parts of the Border. Head 2 (H2) is worked in intarsia with CC and Side Color (SC). Head 3 is worked in one color, CC, until the Ear section.

- Strips are numbered 1–12 from left to right in the blanket. Strips 1, 2, 3, 10, 11, and 12 require working a portion of a chart.

- Strips can be worked in any order. To become familiar with the knitted shapes gradually, work Strips in order (6, 9), (5, 8), (4, 7), 3, 2, 1, 10, 11, 12. The Strips in rounded braces in the ordering are worked the same.

- In some of the Ear sections of Strips 1, 2, 10, 11, and 12, CC and NC are the same color. When this is the case, no color change (intarsia) is required.

- When cutting CC yarns after completing Ear Section, leave a 30"/75 cm tail at left ear for sewing seams.

BLANKET INSTRUCTIONS

See Figure 2 for yarn colors.

STRIP 1

With P, CO 21 sts, with F CO 7 sts – 28 sts.

Cat 1: Work [H1 chart, Rows 15–56, sts 1–28], replacing k2tog at end of Row 41 with a knit st – 7 sts dec'd; 21 sts.

Cat 2: Work [Neck chart, sts 1–21] replacing the kf&b at end of Row 3 with a knit st – 7 sts dec'd; 14 sts. Work [H1 chart, sts 1–21].

Cat 3: Work [Neck chart, sts 1–14] – 7 sts dec'd; 7 sts. Work [H1 chart, sts 1–14] – 7 sts.

Cat 4: Work [Neck chart, Rows 1–14, sts 1–7] – 6 sts dec'd; 1 st. Cut yarn and fasten off.

Main Cat – 21 sts inc'ing to 35 sts, dec'ing to 21 sts

> *Note:* Main Cat is the predominant Cat used in the blanket. It starts with the Neck and ends with Head 1 (H1), which is the cat head with the white inset for the face.
>
> In CC for Cat, work [Neck chart].
>
> With CC, Q, and NC, work [H1 chart]. Cut CC. Do not cut NC. It becomes CC for the next cat.

STRIP 2

Cat 1: In CC for Cat 1, CO 21 sts. Knit 14 rows.

Cats 2–4: Work [Main Cat] 3 times.

Cat 5: Work [H2, sts 1–28], replacing k2tog at end of Row 41 with a knit st.

Cats 6–8: Work as for Strip 1, Cats 2–4.

STRIP 3

Cat 1: In CC for Cat 1, CO 21. Knit 14 rows. Work [H1 chart]. Cut CC. Do not cut NC. It becomes CC for the next cat.

Cats 2–7: Work [Main Cat] 6 times.

Cat 8: In P, work [Neck chart], then work [H3 chart, rows 1–28, sts 1–28] replacing kf&b at end of Row 1 with a knit st – 7 sts inc'd; 28 sts. Place rem 28 sts on holder for Border.

STRIP 4

Cat 1: In CC for Cat 1, CO 28 sts, in SC for Cat 1, CO 7 sts – 35 sts. Work [H2 chart, Rows 13–56], replacing kf&b at beg and end of row 13 with knit st. Cut SC, and do not cut CC – 14 sts dec'd; 21 sts.

Cats 2–8: Work [Main Cat] 7 times. Place rem 21 sts on holder for Border.

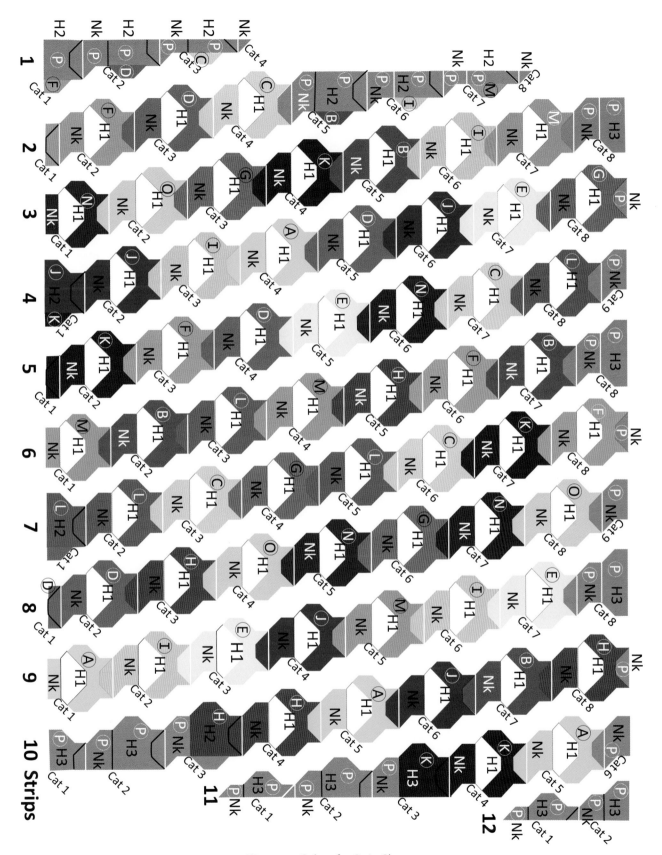

Figure 2: Colors for Strip Shapes

STRIP 5

Cat 1: CO 21 in CC for Cat 1, knit 14 rows.

Cats 2–8: Work [Main Cat] 7 times.

Cat 9: Cont with P, work [Neck chart]. Place rem 21 sts on holder for Border.

STRIP 6

Cat 1: In CC for Cat 1, CO 21. Knit 14 rows. Work [H1 chart] in CC, Q, and NC for cat. Cut CC. Do not cut NC. It becomes CC for the next cat.

Cats 2–7: Work [Main Cat] 6 times.

Cat 8: Cont with P, work [Neck chart], then work [H3 chart, rows 1–28]. Place rem 35 sts on holder for Border.

STRIP 7

Work as for Strip 4.

STRIP 8

Work as for Strip 5.

STRIP 9

Work as for Strip 6.

STRIP 10

Cat 1: With P, CO 21 sts. Work [H3 chart, Rows 13–56, sts 15–35], replacing kf&b at end of Row 13 with knit sts – 7 sts dec'd; 14 sts.

Cat 2: With P, work [Neck chart, sts 8–28] replacing the ssk at beg of row 15 with a knit st – 7 sts inc'd; 21 sts. With P, work [H3 chart, sts 8–35], replacing kf&b on beg of Row 1 with a knit st, and k2tog at beg of Row 41 with a knit st.

Cat 3: With P, work [Neck chart]. With CC and SC, work [H2 chart].

Cats 4–8: Work [Main Cat] 5 times. Place rem 21 sts on stitch holder for Border.

STRIP 11

Cat 1: With P, CO 1 st. Work [Neck chart, Rows 1–28, sts 21–28], omitting the kf&b at the end of Row 15 – 6 sts inc'd; 7 sts. With P, work [H3, sts 22–35].

Cat 2: With P, work [Neck chart, sts 15–28] – 7 sts inc'd; 14 sts. With P, work [H3 chart, sts 15–35].

Cat 3: With P, work [Neck chart, sts 8–28], replacing k2tog at beg of Row 15 with knit st – 7 sts inc'd; 21 sts. With CC, work [H3 chart, sts 8–35], replacing kf&b

at beg of Row 1 with knit st, and replacing k2tog at beg of Row 41 with knit st.

Cats 4 and 5: Work [Main Cat] twice.

Cat 6: In P, work [Neck chart]. Place rem 21 sts on holder for Border.

STRIP 12

Cat 1–2: Work as for Strip 11, Cat 1–2, ending Cat 2 after Row 28 of H3 chart.

Place rem 21 sts on holder for Border.

EDGE PIECES – MAKE 4

With P, CO 1 st, work [H3 chart, rows 1–42, sts 1–7], omitting kf&b on Row 1 and k2tog on Row 41. Cut yarn and fasten off.

EMBELLISHMENTS

There are instructional videos for the embellishments. See "Supplemental Material" on page 206.

These embellishments are added to the 59 cats worked from H1 chart, and for ease of work, should be added before sewing Strips together.

EYES

Make 24 in color F for use on Cats of colors K, L, and N. Make 94 in color R for the remaining Cats. *Tip:* Using Figure 5 as a reference for eye colors, circle the 24 cats that use color F in Figure 2.

Wrap yarn twice around L index finger. With crochet hook draw long end through center of circle, pinching circle with thumb and index finger of R

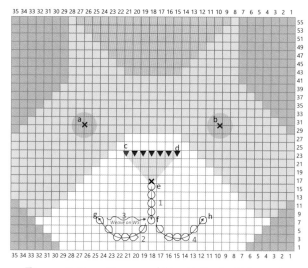

Figure 3: Eyes, Nose, and Mouth Embellishments

hand, ch1, make 8 sc through center of circle, sl st in 1st sc. Cut yarn and fasten off, leaving 8"/20 cm tail. Pull starting tail (of the circle) to close hole.

With long tail, sew Eye to Cat face at **a** and **b** in Figure 3.

NOSE

See Figure 3. On RS, turn work upside down. With R, pu&k 7 sts in the garter stitch "bumps" from the red triangle at **c** to **d**.

Row 1 (WS): Knit.
Row 2: (RS): K2tog, knit to last 2 sts, ssk – 2 sts dec'd; 5 sts.
Rows 3 & 4: Rep [Rows 1 & 2] 1 time – 2 sts dec'd; 3 sts.
Row 5: Knit.
Row 6: Cdd – 2 sts dec'd; 1 st. Cut yarn and fasten off, leaving 6"/15 cm tail. Using long tail, sew bottom of nose to location **e** in Figure 3. *Note:* Diagonal edges of Cat Nose are not sewn down.

MOUTH

Note: The instructions use a crochet hook, but a tapestry needle may be used instead.

1) Insert crochet hook through the attachment point at bottom of nose at **e** and pull a loop of yarn color R from the WS of work. Sl st 5 to **f**, inserting crochet hook front-to-back between garter stitch ridges as shown in Figure 3.

2) Cont, making additional sts at locations indicated along arrow 2 to **g**. After last sl st at **g**, draw yarn around end of loop to back, securing loop of last st, and fasten off on WS. Cut yarn, leaving 18"/40 cm tail.

3) Thread tail onto tapestry needle and on WS, weave yarn through garter st bumps on WS to **f**. Unthread tapestry needle.

4) With crochet hook pull loop of yarn to RS, then sl st at locations indicated in Figure 3, along arrow 4 to **h**. After last sl st, draw yarn around end of loop to back, securing loop of last st and tying off on WS.

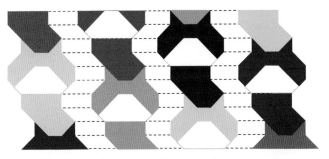

Figure 4: Alignment of Corners for Sewing Strips

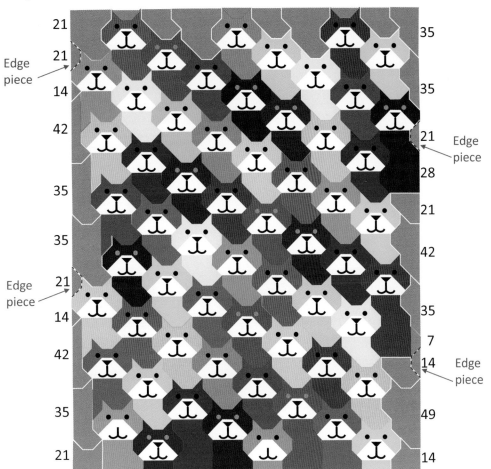

Figure 5: Edge Pieces and Stitch Counts for Borders

ASSEMBLY

Lay out completed Strips as shown in Figure 2. Using long tails from ears sections where available and mattress st, sew Strips tog matching corners of adjacent Strips as shown in Figure 4. Sew Edge pieces to blanket edge on right and left side at locations indicated in Figure 5.

Tip: After each new Strip is attached, transfer live sts to circular needle.

BORDERS

See Figure 5 for the number of sts to generate, per shape, for Right and Left Borders.

RIGHT BORDER

With P and starting at lower right corner of blanket, pu&k 301 sts to end of edge. Knit 15 rows. BO loosely, and do not cut yarn, leaving last st on needle.

TOP BORDER

With P, pu&k 8 sts on edge of Right Border, knit 245 sts from holders to needle – 254 sts. Knit 15 rows. BO loosely, and do not cut yarn, leaving last st on needle.

LEFT BORDER

With P, pu&k 8 sts on edge of Top Border, 301 sts on left edge of blanket – 310 sts. Knit 15 rows. BO loosely, and do not cut yarn, leaving last st on needle.

BOTTOM BORDER

With P, pu&k 8 sts on edge of Left Border, 245 sts on bottom edge of blanket (1 st per CO st), and 9 sts on edge of Right Border – 263 sts. Knit 15 rows. BO loosely. Cut yarn and fasten off.

FINISHING

Weave in ends.

CHARTS

CHART SYMBOLS

☐	RS: knit
⊡	WS: knit
⊽	RS: kf&b
◺	RS: ssk
◹	RS: k2tog
☐	Current Color (CC)
☐	New Color (NC)
☐	Q (white)
☐	Side Color (SC)
☐	no stitch
☐	Worked as knit st(s) on strips where sts to the right of this column are omitted
☐	Worked as knit st(s) on strips where sts to the left of this column are omitted
✚	Add new yarn color here

HEAD 1 (H1)

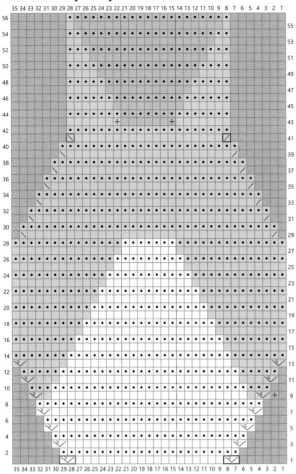

HEAD 2 (H2)

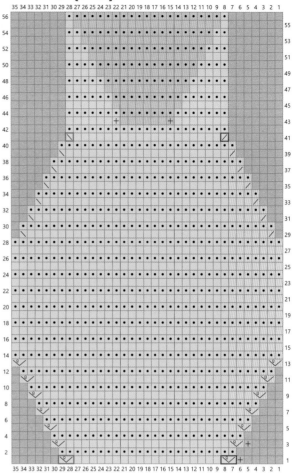

HEAD 3 (H3)

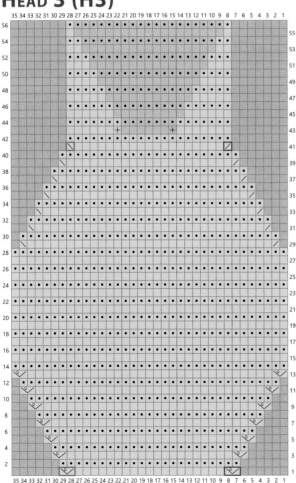

NECK (NK)

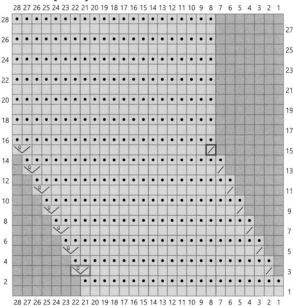

Make a More Than a Feline pillow to try out the pattern!

This pillow is worked by making five Strips of Cats, then sewing the Strips together.

See the blanket pattern for needle size, notions, Main Cat pattern stitch, charts, embellishments, and notes. Refer to Figure 1 for shape identification, and Figure 3 for embellishments.

SIZE

21.5"/55 cm square Pillow Cover

SUPPLIES

22"/55 cm square pillow form
22"/55 cm zipper
Sewing thread matching yarn color A
Sewing needle and safety pins

PILLOW FRONT

Yarn Requirements

The yarn requirements for working the front side only are:

A (background color; dark gray): 150 yds/138 m
B (left cat; teal): 80 yds/74 m
C (bottom-center cat; yellow): 60 yds/55 m
D (bottom-right cat; chartreuse): 40 yds/37 m
E (top-center cat; orange): 50 yds/46 m
F (top-right cat; purple): 50 yds/46 m
G (snouts; cream): 80 yds/74 m
H (eyes, noses, mouths): 30 yds/28 m

Instructions

See Figure 6 for yarn colors and construction of Strips. The order of the Instructions for Strips is 1 through 5, however, to work the simpler Strips first, work in this order: Strip 3, 4, 2, 1, then 5.

Strip 1

Cat 1: With A, CO 7 sts. Knit 14 rows.

Work [H2 chart, Rows 1–56, sts 1–14].

Cat 2: Cont with A, work [Neck chart, sts 1–7] – 6 sts dec'd; 1 st. Cut yarn and fasten off.

Illustration of More Than a Feline Pillow

Strip 2

Cat 1: With CC for Cat (color B), CO 28 sts, and with SC for Cat (color C), CO 7 sts. Work [H2 chart, Rows 13–56, sts 1–35], replacing kf&b's at beg and end of Row 13 with knit stitches – 14 sts dec'd; 21 sts.

Cat 2: Work [Main Cat] once. Do not cut NC (A). It becomes CC for the next cat.

Cat 3: Cont with A, work [Neck chart], then work [H3 chart, rows 1–28, sts 1–28], replacing ssk at the end of Row 1 with a knit st. BO loosely.

Strip 3

Cat 1: With C, CO 21 sts. Knit 14 rows.

Cats 2 & 3: Work [Main Cat] twice. BO loosely.

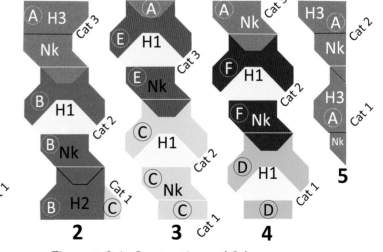

Figure 6: Strip Construction and Colors

Strip 4

With D, CO 21 sts.

Cat 1: Knit 14 rows. Work [H1 chart]. Do not cut NC. It becomes CC for next cat.

Cat 2: Work [Main Cat].

Cat 3: Cont with NC (A), work [Neck chart]. BO loosely.

Strip 5

Cat 1: With A, CO 1 st. Work [Neck chart, Rows 1–28, sts 21–28], omitting the kf&b at the end of Row 15 – 6 sts inc'd; 7 sts.

With A, work [H3 chart, sts 22–35].

Cat 2: With A, work [Neck chart, sts 15–28] – 7 sts inc'd; 14 sts. With A, work [H3 chart, rows 1–28, sts 15–35] – 7 sts inc'd; 21 sts. BO loosely.

Edge Pieces

Ed1: With A, CO 1 st, work [H3 chart, rows 1–42, sts 1–7], omitting kf&b on Row 1 and k2tog on Row 41. Cut yarn and fasten off.

Ed2: With A, CO 7 sts, work [H3, rows 13–40 sts 29–35], replacing kf&b at end of Row 13 with a knit st – 6 sts dec'd; 1 st. Cut yarn and fasten off.

Front Assembly

See Figure 7.

Lay out completed Strips as shown. Using matching long tails from Ears sections where available and mattress st, sew Strips tog matching corners of adjacent Strips as shown by dashed lines. Sew Edge pieces, Ed1 and Ed2, at locations indicated.

Pillow Back

Either repeat the Pillow Front (yarn amounts for the Pillow Front should be doubled), or work a plain garter stitch back (instructions below).

Yarn Requirements

460 yds/420 m of A for a solid color back. If short on yarn for the back, work it in stripes from multiple colors. For clean color changes, change colors at the beg of RS rows. For interlaced color changes, change colors at the beg of WS rows.

Instructions

CO 91sts. Knit 181 rows (91 ridges). BO loosely.

Pillow Front/Back Assembly

See "Assembling Pillows with a Zipper Closure" on page 192.

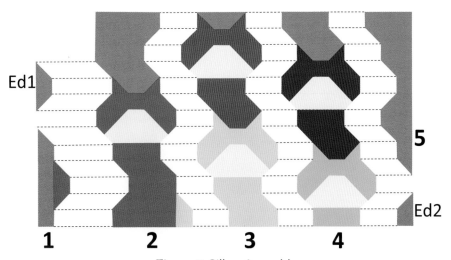

Figure 7: Pillow Assembly

OCEANFRONT

Fresh breezes, warm days, cool nights, sand, sailing, surf, and sky—
this blanket reminds us of all the things we love about the ocean.

TECHNIQUES

Sewing, intarsia

SIZE

61 x 69"/155 x 175 cm

YARN

Berroco Vintage, worsted (52% acrylic/40% wool/8% nylon; 218 yds/199 m; 3.5 oz/100 g):

Pattern color ID	Color swatch	Color ID	Color name	Color description	# Hanks
A		5162	Envy	avocado green	1
B		5124	Kiwi	pale green	2
C		5185	Tide Pool	dark teal	2
D		5163	Caribbean Sea	medium teal	2
E		51133	Electric	light, bright teal	2
F		5120	Gingham	dusty light teal	6
G		5122	Banane	light yellow	2
H		5121	Sunny	bright yellow	2
I		51130	Tangerine	orange	2
J		5173	Red Pepper	burnt orange	5
K		5102	Buttercream	off-white	2
L		51109	Beet Root	dark burgundy	2

NEEDLES

US Size 7/4.5 mm 40"/100 cm circular needles

NOTIONS

Tapestry needle, 3 medium bobbins, 2 stitch markers, stitch holders

GAUGE

18 sts x 36 rows = 4"/10 cm in garter st

NOTES

This blanket is composed of diagonal Strips of Houses that are sewn together. After the Houses are complete, the beach is picked up from the edges of the House section. The Sea is worked separately and sewn to the beach. The Border is pu&k from blanket edges. Charts are on page 82 and Figures are at the end of pattern. All BOs are performed loosely.

BLANKET INSTRUCTIONS

HOUSE STRIPS

House Strips can be worked in any order. See Figure 1 on page 78 for an overview of shapes.

To become familiar with the knitted shapes gradually, work Strips 8 and 9, then Strips 1–7, then Strips 10–15.

House colors and construction are shown in Figure 2, page 79 (Strips 1–7) and Figure 3, page 80 (Strips 8–16). Strips are worked from right to left. Shape names are in italics.

In the instructions and House charts, "MC" refers to the main color for the House and CO; "WC" refers to the color for the windows and door.

As shown on Hf and Hp charts (Row 32; a WS row), the lower 16 sts of Hp are bound off, and 16 sts rem on needle to start the next House. CO additional sts as instructed for next House. In Strip 7, sts for Hf1–Hf5 and Hbf are not BO but are placed on holder for mitered Triangle (Tm).

Roofs are attached below Hp and Hbp houses. Roofs may be added as each Strip is worked or after all are complete.

Strip 1

Hp: In MC for Hp, CO 32 sts. Work [Hp] – 16 sts.

Hbp: In MC for Hbp, work [Hbp]. BO loosely.

Strips 2 (3, 4, 5, 6)

Hp1: In MC for Hp1, CO 32 sts. Work [Hp] – 16 sts.

Hp2–Hp3 (Hp5, Hp7, Hp9, Hp11): Turn, and in MC for Hp, CO 16 sts – 32 sts. Work [Hp] – 16 sts.

Hbp: In MC for Hbp, work [Hbp]. BO loosely.

Strip 7

Hp1–Hp7: Work as for Strip 2, rep Hp2 6 times (7 Hp's total).

Hp8: In MC for Hp8, turn and CO 16 sts – 32 sts. Work [Hp, Rows $1 31], then Row 32 as follows:

Houses are worked from charts that begin on page 82. See notes for tips about working intarsia. Cut MC after completing each House, leaving a 25"/65 cm tail for sewing seams.

House flat (Hf) – 32 sts

Work [House flat (Hf) chart, Rows 1–32, sts 1–32].

House peaked (Hp) – 32 sts dec'ing to 24 sts, inc'ing to 32 sts

Work [House peaked (Hp) chart, Rows 1–32, sts 1–32].

House top (Ht)

Work [House flat (Hf) chart, Rows 1–32, sts 1–16].

House bottom flat (Hbf) – 16 sts

Work [House flat (Hf) chart, Rows 1–32, sts 17–32].

House bottom peaked (Hbp) – 16 sts dec'ing to 8 sts, inc'ing to 16 sts

Work [House peaked (Hp) chart, Rows 1–32, sts 17–32].

Row 32: K16 and place on holder, knit to end.

Hf1–Hf5: In MC for Hf, turn and CO 16 sts – 32 sts. Work [Hf, Rows 1–31], then Row 32 as follows:

Row 32: K16 and place on holder, knit to end – 16 sts.

Hbf: In MC for Hbp, turn and work [Hbf, rows 1–31], then Row 32 as follows:

Row 32: Knit, then place 16 sts on holder.

Tm1: With G and starting at the lower-left corner of Hf1 at red triangle, pu&k 16 sts to next corner, pm, knit 16 sts from holder to needle – 32 sts. Work [Tm].

Tm2–Tm6: Work as for Tm1, beg at the lower-left corners of Hf2–Hf5 and Hbf.

Tm7: With G, CO 16 sts, pm, knit 16 sts of Hbf from needle to holder. Work [Tm].

Strips 8 and 9

Hp1: In MC for Hp1, CO 32 sts. Work [Hp] – 16 sts.

Hp2–Hp7: In MC for Hp, turn and CO 16 sts – 32 sts. Work [Hp] – 16 sts.

Hbp8: In MC for Hp, turn and CO 16 sts, work [Hbp, rows 1–31], then Row 32 as follows:

Row 32: Knit.

BO loosely.

Triangles

Triangle mitered (Tm) – 32 sts dec'ing to 1 st
Row 1 (WS): Knit.
Row 2 (RS): K2tog, knit to 2 sts bef m, ssk, sm, k2tog, knit to last 2 sts, ssk – 4 sts dec'd; 28 sts.
Rows 3–14: Rep [Rows 1 & 2] 6 times – 24 sts dec'd; 4 sts.
Row 15: Ssk, k2tog – 2 sts dec'd; 2 sts.
Row 16: K2tog – 1 st dec'd; 1 st.
Cut yarn and fasten off.

Triangle small (Ts) – 16 sts dec'ing to 1 st
Row 1 (WS): Knit.
Row 2 (RS): K2tog, knit to last 2 sts, ssk – 2 sts dec'd; 14 sts.
Rows 3–14: Rep [Rows 1 & 2] 6 times – 12 sts dec'd; 2 sts.
Row 15: K2tog – 1 st dec'd; 1 st.
Cut yarn and fasten off, leaving 10"/25 cm tail.

Triangle (Tr) – 16 sts dec'ing to 1 st
Row 1 (RS): K2tog, knit to end – 1 st dec'd; 15 sts.
Row 2 (WS): Knit.
Rows 3–30: Rep [Rows 1 & 2] 14 times – 14 sts dec'd; 1 st.
Cut yarn and fasten off.

Strip 10

Ht: In MC for Ht, CO 16 sts. Work [Ht].

Hp1–Hp6: Work as for Strip 9, Hp1 to Hp6.

Ts1: With G; knit 1 row, then work [Ts].

Strips 11 (12, 13, 14)

Ht: In MC for Ht, CO 16 sts. Work [Ht].

Hp1–Hp5 (Hp4, Hp3, Hp2): In MC for Hp, turn and CO 16 sts – 32 sts. Work [Hp] – 16 sts.

Ts1: In MC for Ts, knit 1 row, then work [Ts].

Ts2: With color for Ts2, pu&k 16 sts from the red triangle on right-top corner of final Hp of Strip to next corner. Work [Ts].

Strip 15

Work as for Strip 11, working Ht, Hp1, and Ts2.

Strip 16

Ht: In MC for Ht, CO 16 sts. Work [Ht].

Tr: In color for Tr, work [Tr].

Ts2: With color for Ts2, pu&k 16 sts from red triangle on right-top corner of Ht to next corner. Work [Ts].

ROOFS UNDER HOUSES

See Figure 2 (page 79) and Figure 3 (page 80) for construction and Roof colors.

On the bottom of each Hp, in space labeled "Rf," with color for Roof, pu&k 11 sts from red triangle to next corner, 1 st in corner of peak, pm, and 11 sts to next corner – 23 sts. Work [Rf].

Roof

Roof (Rf) – 23 sts dec'ing to 1 st
Row 1 (WS): Knit.
Row 2 (RS): K2tog, knit to 2 sts bef m, rm, cdd, pm, knit to last 2 sts, ssk – 4 sts dec'd; 19 sts.
Rows 3–10: Rep [Rows 1 & 2] 4 times – 16 sts dec'd; 3 sts.
Row 11: Cdd – 2 sts dec'd; 1 st.
Cut yarn and fasten off.

ASSEMBLY OF STRIPS

With long BO tails from Houses and Ts's and mattress stitch, sew tog Strip along red dotted lines as shown in Figure 4 (page 81), matching corners.

BEACH

See Figure 4. With G and starting at the top-left of assembled Houses at red triangle, (pu&k 22 sts along edge of Tm, then 23 sts along next Tm) 3 times, then 22 sts along edge of 7th Tm, pm (m1), knit 32 sts of Strip 8 off holder, knit 32 sts of Strip 9 off holder, pm (m2), (pu&k 22 sts bet first two red dots, 23 sts between next pair of red dots) 3 times, then 22 sts bet last 2 red dots – 378 sts.

Note: In the instructions below, the numbers in parenthesis after each line of instructions represent these stitch counts:

(beg to m1 – m1 to m2 – m2 to end)

Row 1 (WS): Knit. (157–64–157)
Row 2 (RS): Kf&b, knit to last st, kf&b – 2 sts inc'd; 380 sts. (158–64–158)
Row 3: Knit.
Row 4: Kf&b, knit to 2 sts bef m1, ssk, k2tog, knit to 2 sts bef m2, ssk, k2tog, knit to last st, kf&b – 2 sts dec'd; 378 sts. (158–62–158)
Row 5: Knit.
Rows 6–13: Rep [Rows 2–5] twice. (160–58–160).
Rows 14–15: Rep [Rows 2 & 3] once – 2 sts inc'd; 380 sts. (161–58–161)
BO loosely. Cut yarn and fasten off, leaving 120"/300 cm for sewing beach to sea.

SEA

See Figure 5 on page 82 for construction concept and colors for boats. On Rows where charts are first introduced (37, 97, and 159), the black numbers are stitch counts for charts and red numbers are stitch counts between charts. Red stitch counts before first and after last boat include the increases made when working the Row.

With F, CO 58 sts.

Row 1 (RS): Kf&b, knit to last st, kf&b – 2 sts inc'd; 60 sts.

Row 2 (WS): Knit.

Rows 3–36: Rep [Rows 1 & 2] 17 times – 34 sts inc'd; 94 sts.

Row 37: Kf&b, k2, and with colors shown in Figure 5, work [Sailboat chart Row], k14, work [Wave chart Row], k15, work [Sailboat chart Row], k2, kf&b – 2 sts inc'd; 96 sts.

Row 38: Knit all sts, in same color as prev RS row.

Rows 39–96: Rep [Rows 37 & 38] working next row of established charts. *Note:* Last row of charts is Row 96 (48 ridges completed) – 58 sts inc'd; 154 sts.

Row 97: Kf&b, k1, *work [Sailboat chart Row], k14, work [Wave chart Row], k15; rep from * once, work [Sailboat chart Row], k1, kf&b – 2 sts inc'd; 156 sts.

Row 98: Rep [Row 38].

Rows 99–156: Rep [Rows 97 & 98], working next row of established charts. *Note:* last row of charts is 156 (78 ridges complete) – 58 sts inc'd; 214 sts.

Row 157: Kf&b, *work [Sailboat chart Row], k14, work [Wave chart Row], k15; rep from * twice more, work [Sailboat chart Row], kf&b – 2 sts inc'd; 216 sts.

Row 158: Rep [Row 38].

Row 159–216: Rep [Rows 157 & 158], working next row of established charts. *Note:* Last row of charts is 216 (108 ridges completed) – 58 sts inc'd; 274 sts.

Rows 217–230: Rep [Rows 1 & 2] 7 times – 14 sts inc'd; 288 sts.

Place sts on holder for Left Border.

Using mattress st and long tail from Beach, sew Sea edge to Beach edge along dotted red line in Figure 4.

BORDERS

See Figure 4 for stitch counts per edge shape.

RIGHT BORDER

On RS, starting at the lower right corner of blanket, with L, pu&k 288 sts along right edge of blanket (32 per Hf). Knit 19 rows. BO loosely, leaving last st on needle. Do not cut yarn.

TOP BORDER

Pu&k 9 sts along top edge of Right Border, 1 st in Join bet Border and blanket, and 252 sts along Top Border of blanket (16 sts per House/Tm, 12 sts along the edge of the beach) – 263 sts. Knit 19 rows. BO loosely, leaving last st on needle. Do not cut yarn.

LEFT BORDER

Pu&k 9 sts along left edge of Top Border, 1 st in Join between Border and blanket, then knit 288 sts from holder – 299 sts. Knit 19 rows. BO loosely, leaving last st on needle. Do not cut yarn.

BOTTOM BORDER

Pu&k 9 sts along bottom edge of Left Border, 1 st in Join between Border and blanket, 252 sts along Bottom Border of blanket (12 sts along the edge of the beach, 16 per House/Tr), and 11 sts along bottom edge of Right Border – 274 sts. Knit 19 rows. BO loosely. Cut yarn and fasten off.

FINISHING

Weave in ends.

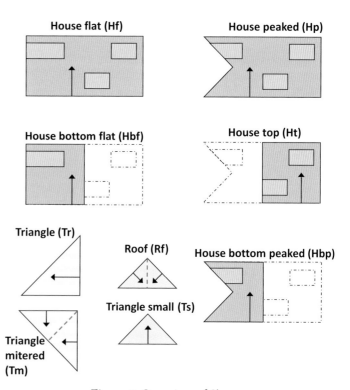

Figure 1: Overview of Shapes

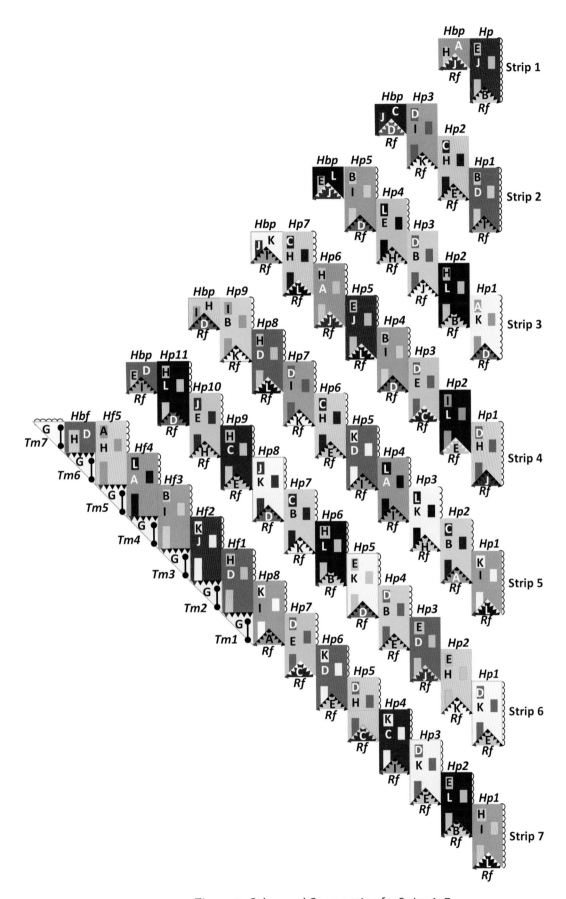

Figure 2: Colors and Construction for Strips 1–7

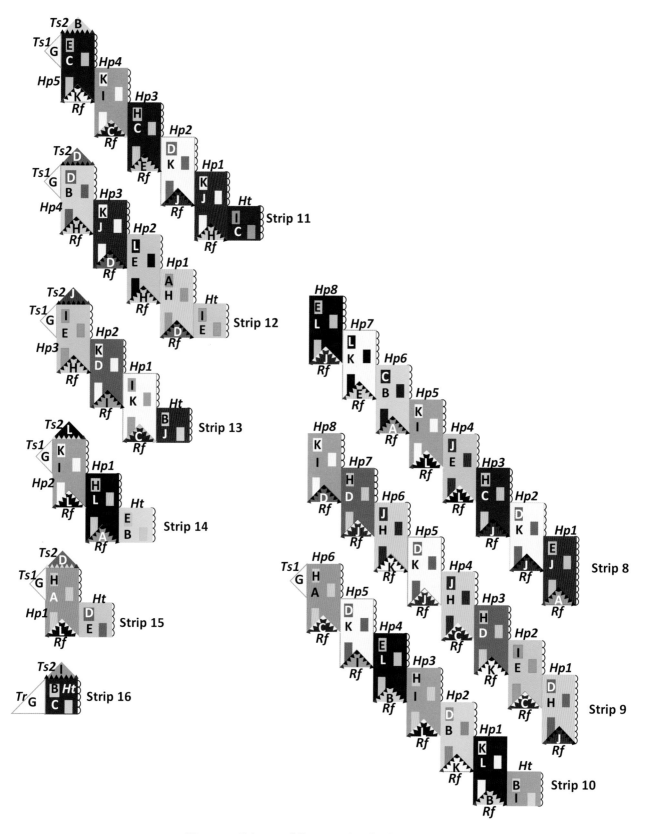

Figure 3: Colors and Construction for Strips 8–16

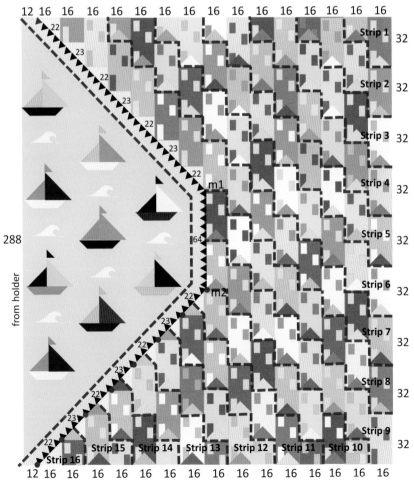

Figure 4: Assembly of House Strips, Beach Construction, and Seaming of Sea to Beach

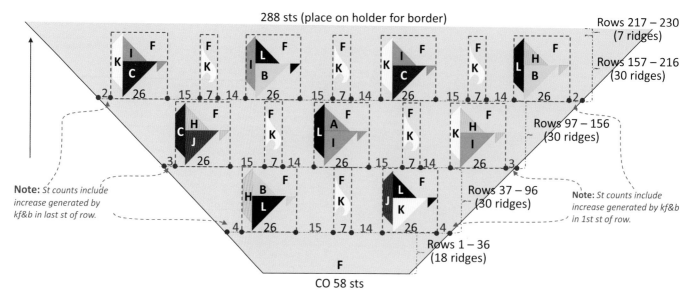

Figure 5: Construction Concept for Sea and Colors for Boats

CHARTS

Each area worked with a separate strand for intarsia contains a yardage estimate. Use this estimate to work the first intarsia area then adjust as needed for subsequent areas.

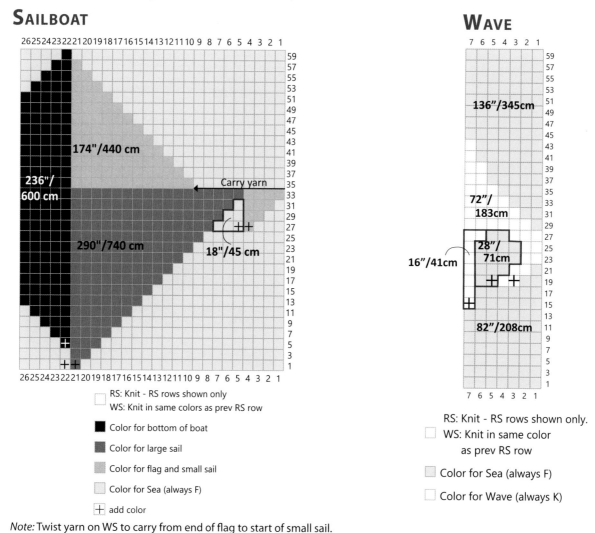

SAILBOAT

174"/440 cm

236"/600 cm

Carry yarn

290"/740 cm

18"/45 cm

RS: Knit - RS rows shown only
WS: Knit in same colors as prev RS row

■ Color for bottom of boat

■ Color for large sail

■ Color for flag and small sail

□ Color for Sea (always F)

+ add color

Note: Twist yarn on WS to carry from end of flag to start of small sail.

WAVE

136"/345cm

72"/183cm

16"/41cm

28"/71cm

82"/208cm

RS: Knit - RS rows shown only.
WS: Knit in same color as prev RS row

■ Color for Sea (always F)

□ Color for Wave (always K)

House Flat (Hf)

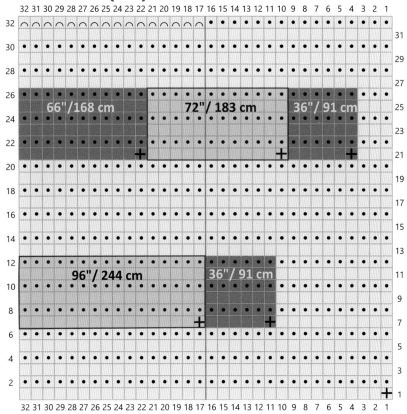

House Peaked (Hp)

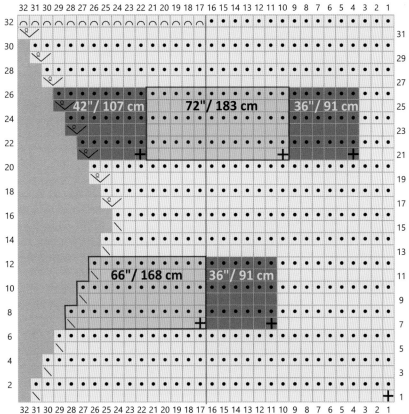

Notes about Charts

- Yarn amounts for small areas of color are specified. Use these amounts as estimates when working the first pieces, adjust to match actual yarn usage.

- Areas with no yarn amount specified should be worked directly from the skein.

- See "Intarsia" on page 196.

- ▮ WC- Window Color
- ▨ MC - Main Color
- ☐ RS: knit
- • WS: knit
- ◥ RS: ssk
- ◺ RS: kf&b
- ∩ bind off
- ＋ Add color
- ▮ no stitch

Make an Oceanfront pillow to try out the pattern!

See the blanket pattern for yarn color identification, needle size, gauge, notions, notes, House Strip notes, pattern stitches, and charts.

SIZE

20.5"/52 cm square Pillow Cover

SUPPLIES

20"/50 cm square pillow form
20"/50 cm zipper
Sewing thread matching yarn color G
Sewing needle and safety pins

PILLOW FRONT

Yarn Requirements

See blanket pattern for yarn brand and color identification. The yarn requirements for working the front side only are:

	yds	meters		yds	meters		yds	meters
A	30	28	B	10	10	C	30	28
D	10	10	E	30	28	F	200	183
G	110	101	H	20	19	I	40	37
J	10	10	K	20	19	L	30	28

Instructions

See Figure 6 for Strip construction and colors.

Strip 1

Hp: With E, CO 32 sts. Work [Hp] – 16 sts.

Ts1: With G. Knit 1 row, work [Ts].

Ts2: With D, and starting at red triangle on right-top corner of Hp, pu&k 16 sts to next corner. Work [Ts].

Strip 2

Hp1: With MC, CO 32 sts. Work [Hp] – 16 sts.

Hp2: Turn and with MC, CO 16 sts – 32 sts. Work [Hp].

Ts1: With G. Knit 1 row, work [Ts].

Ts2: With color for Ts2, and starting at red triangle on right-top corner of Hp, pu&k 16 sts to corner. Work [Ts].

Strip 3

Ht: With MC, CO 16 sts. Work [Ht].

Hp: Turn, and with MC, CO 16 sts – 32 sts. Work [Hp].

Ts1: With G. Knit 1 row, work [Ts1].

Illustration of Oceanfront Pillow

Ts2: With color for Ts2, and starting at the red triangle on right-top corner of Hp, pu&k 16 sts to next corner. Work [Ts].

Strip 4

Ht: With MC, CO 16 sts. Work [Ht].

Tr: With MC, work [Tr].

Ts2: With color for Ts2, and starting at red triangle on right-top corner of Hp, pu&k 16 sts to next corner. Work [Ts].

Top Triangle (Tt)

With G, CO 16 sts. Work [Ts].

Roofs under Houses

On the bottom of each of the 4 Hp's, in space labeled "Rf," with color for Roof, pu&k 11 sts from red triangle to next corner, 1 st in corner of peak, pm, and 11 sts to next corner – 23 sts. Work [Rf].

Assembly of Strips see Figure 7

With BO tails and mattress stitch, sew tog Strip and Tt along red dotted lines, matching corners.

Beach see Figure 7

With G, pu&k 22 sts bet red triangle at corner of Tt and 1st two purple dots, (23 sts bet next pair of dots; 22 sts bet next pair of dots) twice – 112 sts.

Row 1 (WS): Knit.
Row 2: Kf&b, knit to last st, kf&b – 2 sts inc'd; 114 sts.
Row 3: Knit.
Rows 4–15: Rep [Rows 2 & 3] 8 times – 16 sts inc'd; 130 sts. BO loosely. Cut yarn and fasten off, leaving 120"/300 cm tail.

Sea see Figure 8

On Rows where charts are first introduced (58 and 118), the black numbers are stitch counts for charts and red numbers are stitch counts between charts. Stitch counts after last boat include the increase made at the end of the Row.

With F, CO 1 st.

Row 1 (WS): Knit.
Row 2 (RS): Knit to last st, kf&b – 1 st inc'd; 2 sts.
Row 3 (WS): Knit.
Rows 4–57: Rep [Rows 1 & 2] 27 times – 27 sts inc'd; 29 sts.
Row 58: K2, and with color from Figure 8, work [Sailboat chart Row] over next 26 sts, knit to last st, kf&b – 1 st inc'd; 30 sts.
Row 59: Knit, working sts in same colors as prev RS row.
Row 60–117: Rep [Rows 58 & 59] 29 times – 29 sts inc'd; 59 sts.
Row 118: With F, k11, work [Wave chart Row], with F, k14, work [Sailboat chart Row], knit to last st, kf&b – 1 st inc'd; 60 sts.
Row 119: Rep Row 59.
Rows 120–177: Rep [Rows 118 & 119] 29 times – 29 sts inc'd; 89 sts.
Row 178: With F, knit to last st, kf&b – 1 st inc'd; 90 sts.
Row 179: Knit.
Rows 180–183: Rep [Rows 178 & 179] twice – 2 sts inc'd; 92 sts. BO loosely.

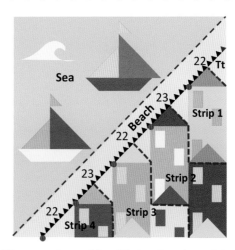

Figure 7: Assembly of Strips, Beach, and Sea

Assembly of Houses/Beach and Sea

Using mattress st and long tail of G, sew Sea edge to Beach edge along dotted red line in Figure 7, using long tail from Beach and matching corners.

PILLOW BACK

Either repeat the Pillow Front (yarn amounts for the Pillow Front should be doubled) or work a plain garter stitch back (instructions below).

Yarn Requirements

460 yds/420 m of F are needed for a solid back.

Instructions

CO 92 sts. Knit 183 rows (92 ridges). BO loosely.

PILLOW FRONT/BACK ASSEMBLY

See "Assembling Pillows with a Zipper Closure" on page 192.

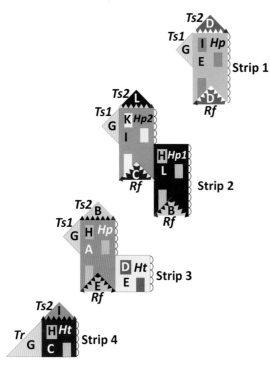

Figure 6: Pillow Strip Construction

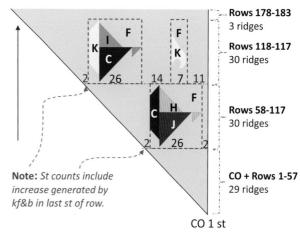

Note: *St counts include increase generated by kf&b in last st of row.*

Figure 8: Concept and Colors for Sea

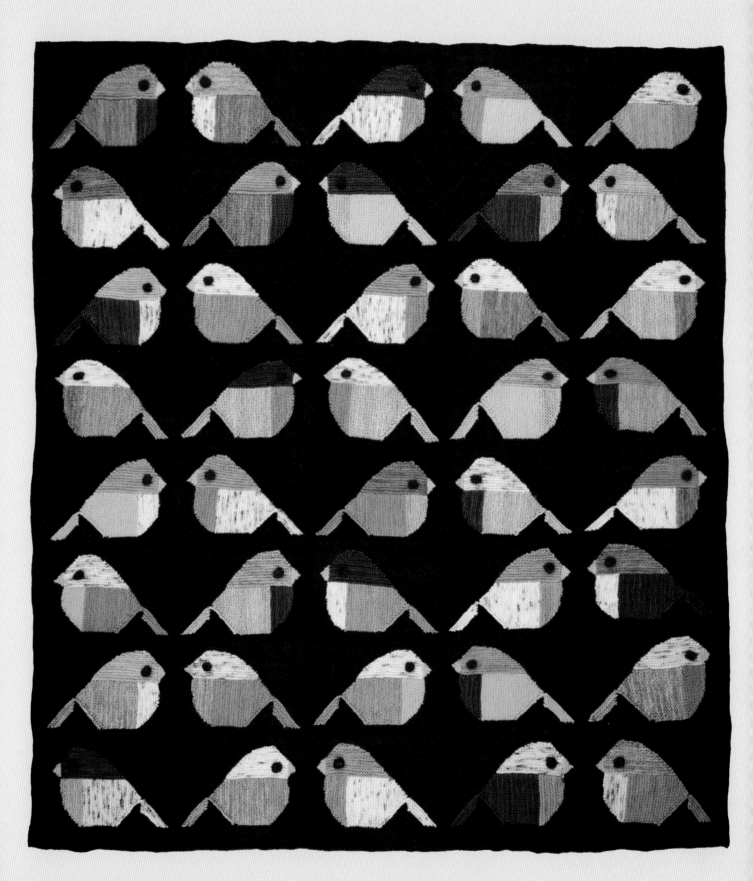

ROW ROBIN

These colorful birds are a reminder of the joys to be found in a lifelong commitment.

TECHNIQUES

Sewing, 3-needle BO

SIZES

Small (Large): 48.5 x 60.5"/123 x 154 cm (54.5 x 72"/138 x 183 cm)

YARN

SweetGeorgia, Superwash Worsted (100% superwash merino wool; 200 yds/182 m; 4 oz/115 g):

Pattern color ID	Color swatch	Color name	Color description	# Hanks for Size	
				Small	Large
A		Ultraviolet	dark purple	10	16
B		Bubble Wand	off white with green, pink and purple		1
C		Rosé Day	off white with pink and peach	1	1
D		Starlight	light blue	1	1
E		Silver	light gray		1
F		Mermaid	dark aqua with blue	1	1
G		Buttercup	yellow	1	1
H		Papaya	yellow-orange		1
I		Chili Pepper	red-orange	1	1
J		Grapefruit	dark peach		1
K		Rose Gold	peach with pink and ivory	1	1

NEEDLES

US Size 7/4.5 mm 40"/100 cm circular needles, (1) US Size 7/4.5 mm dpn, and a larger needle for 3-needle BO

NOTIONS

Tapestry needle, 2 stitch markers, stitch holders, crochet hook (optional)

GAUGE

17 sts x 34 rows = 4"/10 cm in garter st.

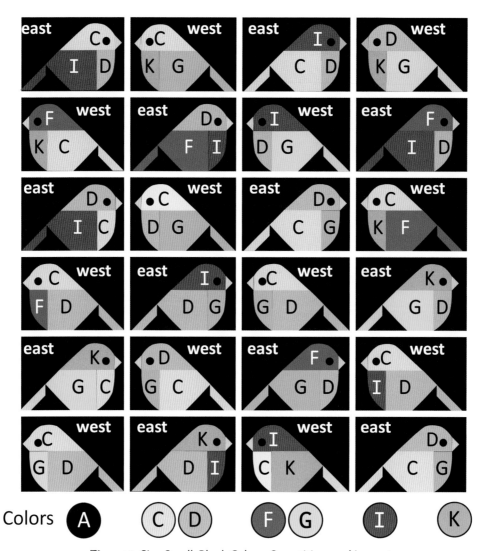

Colors (A) (C) (D) (F) (G) (I) (K)

Figure 1: Size Small: Block Colors, Quantities, and Layout

NOTES

- Instructions are for Size Small, with changes for Large in parenthesis.

- The blanket is worked in Blocks that are joined later. There are two Blocks: west Block and east Block, named for the orientation of the Bird. Construction of a Block begins with the Bird. The dark purple background pieces are pu&k around the completed Bird to convert the shape into a rectangle. Completed Blocks are joined into horizontal Strips with pu&k and a 3-needle BO, and then the Strips are joined in the same manner. A border is pu&k on the edges of the completed blanket. Eye and Leaf embellishments are knitted separately and tacked onto the blanket after assembly.

- Figure 1 (Figure 3) shows the colors for each of the 24 (40) Blocks, and Figure 2 identifies the color abbreviations used in the instructions.

- For all Blocks, Color A is used for the Frame pieces and Eyes embellishments, and I is used for Beak pieces.

- Stitch generation, which is either a knitted CO or pu&k, counts as Row 1 in all pattern stitches.

- Complete written instructions are included, and most pattern stitches have a corresponding chart at the end of the pattern.

East Block   ## West Block

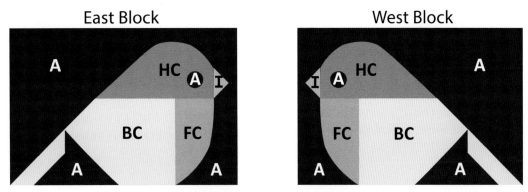

Figure 2: Color Identification and Abbreviations

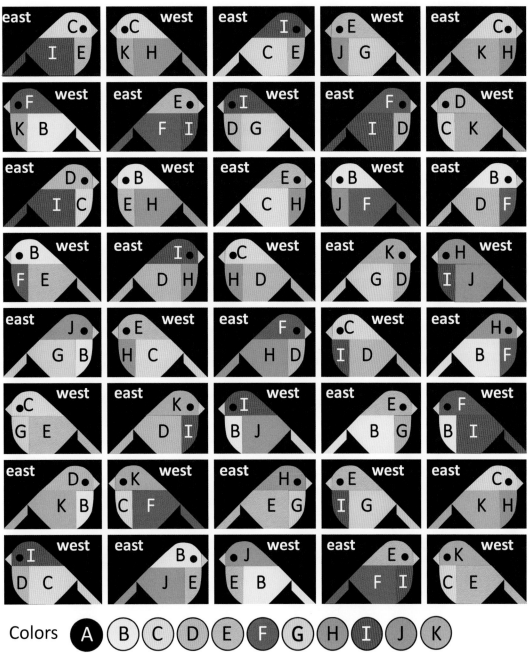

Colors Ⓐ Ⓑ Ⓒ Ⓓ Ⓔ Ⓕ Ⓖ Ⓗ Ⓘ Ⓙ Ⓚ

Figure 3: Size Large: Block Colors, Quantities, and Layout

INSTRUCTIONS

West Block

Make 12 (20) in colors specified in Figure 1 (Figure 3) on page 88 (89). The four parts of the Bird are: Front, Back, Head, and Beak. The names of these parts are prefixed with "west" to distinguish from those of the east Block.

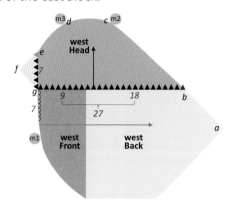

Figure 4: West Bird Parts

West Front see Figure 4

With Front Color (FC) for Block, CO 6 stitches.

Row 2 (WS): K6, turn and CO 4 –10 sts.

Row 3 and all odd (RS) rows to 17: Knit.

Row 4: Knit to end, turn and CO 2 – 12 sts. Pm (m1) through edge of CO chain bet 10th and 11th sts.

Row 6: Knit to end, turn and CO 2 – 14 sts.

Row 8: Knit to end, turn and CO 1 – 15 sts.

Rows 10, 12, 14, 16: Rep Row 8 – 4 sts inc'd; 19 sts.

Row 18: Knit. Cut FC.

West Back see Figure 4

Note: Row numbering is continued from **west Front**.

Rows 19–44: With BC, knit. (26 rows/13 ridges).

Row 45 (RS): K2tog, knit to end – 1 st dec'd; 18 sts.

Row 46 (WS): Knit.

Rows 47–54: Rep [Rows 45 & 46] 4 times – 4 sts dec'd; 14 sts.

Rows 55–65: Work [Tr] until 2 sts rem after RS row.

Row 66 (WS): K2tog – 1 st dec'd; 1 st. Cut BC and fasten off.

Triangle (Tr)
Row 1 (RS): K2tog, knit to last 2 sts, ssk – 2 sts dec'd. **Row 2 (WS):** Knit.

West Head see Figure 4

With HC and starting at the red triangle, pu&k 27 sts (1 per ridge, with 18 on top edge of Bird Back, and 9 sts on top edge of Bird Front).

Row 2 and all even (WS) rows through 24: Knit.

Row 3: K2tog, knit to end – 1 st dec'd; 26 sts.

Rows 5, 7, 9, 11, 13: Rep [Row 3] – 5 sts dec'd; 21 sts.

Row 15: K2tog, knit to last 2 sts, ssk – 2 sts dec'd; 19 sts.

Row 17: Rep Row 15 – 2 sts dec'd; 17 sts.

Row 19: K2tog, BO 1, knit to last 2 sts, ssk – 3 sts dec'd; 14 sts.

Rows: 21, 23, 25: Rep [Row 19] – 9 sts dec'd; 5 sts. BO loosely. Pm through sts on both ends of Row 23. Markers are at **c** (m2) and **d** (m3).

West Beak see Figure 4

With I, pu&k 7 sts from green triangle **e** to **g**. Work [Tr] until 3 sts rem, ending after WS row.

Next row (RS): Cdd – 2 sts dec'd; 1 st. Cut yarn and fasten off.

Frame 1 see Figure 5

With A, CO 17 sts, then starting at green triangle at **a**, pu&k 9 sts to **b**, and 16 sts from the hot pink triangle at **b** to the marked stitch m2 at **c**, rm2 and place on needle, pu&k 8 sts from **c** to m3 at **d**, rm m3 and place on needle, and pu&k 12 sts from **d** to end of the beak at **f** – 62 sts (42–8–12).

Note: Numbers after the row stitch count are the numbers bet markers when RS is facing, as follows:

<beg to m2> - <m2 to m3> - <m3 to end of row>.

Row 2 and all even (WS) rows to 10: Knit.

Row 3: K2tog, knit to 1 st bef m2, kf&b, sm, kf&b, knit to 1 st bef m3, kf&b, sm, kf&b, knit to end – 3 sts inc'd; 65 sts (42–10–13).

Row 5 (RS): K2tog, knit to end – 1 st dec'd; 64 sts (41–10–13).

Row 7: Rep [Row 3] – 3 sts inc'd; 67 sts (41–12–14).

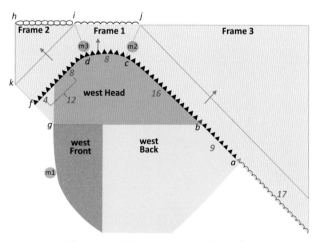

Figure 5: West - Frames 1, 2, and 3

Rows 9 & 11: Rep [Row 5] – 2 sts dec'd; 65 sts (39–12–14).
Row 12 (WS): Knit first 14 sts to m3. Turn to RS leaving rem sts on row unworked. Do not cut yarn.

Frame 2 see Figure 5
Work [Tr] until 2 sts rem, ending after a RS row.
Next row (WS): K2tog – 1 st dec'd; 1 st.
Either:
1) Cut yarn and fasten off, then reattach at *i*, or
2) With crochet hook, work 10 slip sts bet corner of Frame 2 at *h* and m3 at *i*. BO 12 sts bet *i* and *j* (until 39 sts rem on needle), then cont on WS, knit to end.

Frame 3 see Figure 5
Work [Tr] until 3 sts rem, ending after WS (plain knit) row.
Next row (RS): Cdd – 2 sts dec'd; 1 st. Cut yarn and fasten off.

Frame 4 see Figure 6
Note: Numbers after the row stitch count are the numbers bet markers when RS is facing, as follows:
<beg to m4> - <m4 to m1> - <m1 to end of row>.

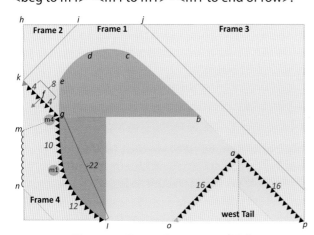

Figure 6: West - Frame 4 and Tail

Starting at the green triangle at *k*, pu&k 8 sts to *g*, pm (m4), pu&k 10 sts to m1, rm m1 and place on needle, then pu&k 12 sts to *l* – 30 sts (8–10–12).

Row 2 (WS): K2tog, knit to end – 1 st dec'd; 29 sts (8–10–11).
Row 3 (RS): K2tog, knit to 2 sts bef m, ssk, sm, k2tog, knit to 1 st bef next m, kf&b, sm, kf&b, knit to last 2 sts, ssk – 2 sts dec'd; 27 sts (6–10–11).
Row 4 and even-numbered (WS) rows to 16: Knit.
Row 5: K2tog, knit to last 2 sts, ssk – 2 sts dec'd; 25 sts (5–10–10).
Row 7: Rep [Row 3] – 2 sts dec'd; 23 sts (3–10–10).
Row 9: Rep [Row 5] – 2 sts dec'd; 21 sts (2–10–9).

Row 11 (RS): Rm's. K2tog, BO 11 sts starting with the k2tog st to *n*, until 9 sts rem on needle, knit to last 2 sts, ssk – 13 sts dec'd; 8 sts.
Rows 13 -17: Work [Tr] until 2 sts rem after RS row.
Row 18 (WS): K2tog – 1 st dec'd; 1 st. Cut yarn, fasten off.

West Tail see Figure 6
With BC, and starting at yellow triangle at *o*, pu&k 16 sts to *a*, and 16 sts to *p* – 32 sts. See "Single Crochet for Edging" on page 189.

See "Intarsia" on page 196.
Row 2: Cont with BC, knit.
Row 3: With A, k2tog, k12, ssk, while alternately inserting needle over and under BC to tack BC to WS. Cont with BC, k2tog, knit to last 2 sts, ssk – 4 sts dec'd; 28 sts (14 of A and 14 of BC).
Row 4 (WS) and all WS rows to 8: Knit to color transition, drop BC, cross, and with A, knit to end.
Row 5: With A, k2tog, knit to 2 sts bef color transition, ssk, drop A, cross, and with BC, k2tog, knit to last 2 sts of row, ssk – 4 sts dec'd; 24 sts.
Row 7: Rep [Row 5] – 4 sts dec'd; 20 sts (10 of A, 10 of BC). Cut BC after WS Row 8 and pm after 10th st.
Row 9: Cont with A, k2tog, knit to 2 sts bef m, ssk, sm, k2tog, knit to last 2 sts, ssk – 4 sts dec'd; 16 sts.
Row 10 (WS): Knit.
Rows 11–14: Rep [Rows 9 & 10] twice – 8 sts dec'd; 8 sts.
Row 15: (K2tog, ssk) twice – 4 sts dec'd; 4 sts.
Row 16 (WS): Sl2 kwise, k2tog, psso – 3 sts dec'd; 1 st. Enlarge rem loop and insert ball through, tighten. Cut yarn. *Note:* If color transition area is loose, leave a 12"/30 cm tail, and with tapestry needle, on WS, make stitches on either side of the color transition to close gaps.
Weave in all ends.

Eye
Work [Eye].
Position the eye with lower edge just above the 3rd ridge of the bird head and 3 sts in from the beak. Pin in place. Sew eye to Block.
See "Tacking Embellishments" on page 189.

Eye

With A, and long-tail cast-on method, CO 10 sts. Knit 1 row. Cut yarn leaving 10"/25 cm tail. Thread tail onto tapestry needle and insert through 10 sts on needle twice, pulling to tighten center and gather stitches. Close circle by sewing the CO edges tog.

East Block

Make 12 (20) in colors specified in Figure 1 (Figure 3) on page 88 (89). The four parts of the Bird are: Front, Back, Head, and Beak. The names of these parts are prefixed with "east" to distinguish from those of the west Block.

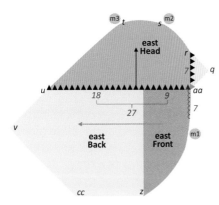

Figure 7: East Bird parts

East Front see Figure 7

With Front Color (FC) for Block, CO 6 stitches.

Row 2 and all even-numbered (WS) rows to 18: Knit.

Row 3: Knit, turn and CO 4 – 4 sts inc'd; 10 sts.

Row 5: Knit, turn and CO 2 – 2 sts inc'd; 12 sts. Pm (m1) through edge of CO chain bet 10th and 11th sts.

Row 7: Knit, turn and CO 2 – 2 sts inc'd; 14 sts.

Row 9: Knit, turn and CO 1 – 1 st inc'd; 15 sts.

Rows 11, 13, 15, and 17: Rep Row 9 – 4 sts inc'd; 19 sts.

Cut FC after WS Row 18.

East Back see Figure 7

Note: Row numbering is continued from **east Front**.

Rows 19–44: With BC, knit. (26 rows/13 ridges).

Row 45 (RS): Knit to 2 sts from end, ssk – 1 st dec'd; 18 sts.

Row 46 (WS): Knit.

Rows 47–54: Rep [Rows 45 & 46] 4 times – 4 sts dec'd; 14 sts.

Rows 55–65: Work [Tr] until 2 sts rem, ending after RS row.

Row 66 (WS): K2tog – 1 st dec'd; 1 st. Cut BC and fasten off.

East Head see Figure 7

With HC and starting at the red triangle, pu&k 27 sts (1 per ridge, with 9 on top edge of east Front, and 18 sts on top edge of east Back).

Row 2 and all odd (WS) rows through 18: Knit.

Row 3: Knit to last 2 sts, ssk – 1 st dec'd; 26 sts.

Rows 5, 7, 9, 11, and 13: Rep [Row 3] – 5 sts dec'd; 21 sts.

Row 15: K2tog, knit to last 2 sts, ssk –2 sts dec'd; 19 sts.

Rows 17 & 19: Rep Row 15 – 4 sts dec'd; 15 sts.

Row 20 (WS): K2tog, BO 1, knit to end – 2 sts dec'd; 13 sts.

Row 21: K2tog, knit to end – 1 st dec'd; 12 sts.

Rows 22–25: Rep [Rows 20 & 21] twice – 6 sts dec'd; 6 sts.

Pm through sts on both ends of Row 23. Markers are at locations **s** (m2) and **t** (m3) in Figures.

Row 26: Rep Row 20 – 2 sts dec'd; 4 sts. BO rem 4 sts. Cut yarn and fasten off.

East Beak see Figure 7

With I, pu&k 7 sts from red triangle at **aa** to **r**. Work [Tr] until 3 sts rem, ending after WS row.

Next row (RS): Cdd – 2 sts dec'd; 1 st. Cut yarn and fasten off.

Frame 5 see Figure 8

With A, starting at green triangle at **q**, pu&k 4 sts to **r**, 8 sts to **s**, rm m2 and place on needle, pu&k 8 sts from **s** to **t**, 16 sts to **u**, and 9 sts to **v**. Turn and CO 17 sts – 62 sts (12–8–42).

Note: Numbers after the row stitch count are the numbers bet markers when RS is facing, as follows:

<beg to m2> - <m2 to m3> - <m3 to end of row>.

Row 2 and all even (WS) rows to 10: Knit.

Row 3: Knit to 1 st bef m2, kf&b, sm, kf&b, knit to 1 st bef m3, kf&b, sm, kf&b, knit to last 2 sts, ssk – 3 sts inc'd; 65 sts (13–10–42).

Row 5: Knit to last 2 sts, ssk – 1 st dec'd; 64 sts (13–10–41).

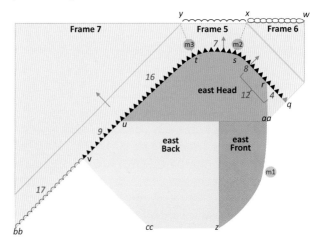

Figure 8: East - Frames 5, 6, and 7

Row 7: Rep [Row 3] – 3 sts inc'd; 67 sts (14–12–41).
Row 9: Rep [Row 5] – 1 st dec'd; 66 sts (14–12–40).
Frame 6 see Figure 8
Rm2. Work [Tr] over first 14 sts of row until 2 sts rem after a RS (dec) row.

Next row (WS): K2tog – 1 st dec'd; 1 st. Either:
1) Cut yarn and fasten off, then reattach at **x**, or,
2) With crochet hook, work 10 slip sts bet corner of Frame 6 at **w** and m2 at **x**.

BO 12 sts bet **x** and **y** (until 40 sts rem on needle), then, cont on RS, knit to last 2 sts, ssk – 39 sts.

Frame 7 See Figure 8

Work [Tr], until 3 sts rem, ending after a WS (plain knit) row.

Next row (RS): Cdd – 2 st dec'd; 1 st. Cut yarn and fasten off.

Frame 8 see Figure 9

Note: Numbers after the row stitch count are the numbers bet markers when RS is facing, as follows:

<beg to m1> - <m1 to m4> - <m4 to end of row>.

Starting at the green triangle at **z**, pu&k 12 sts to m1, rm m1 and place on needle, pu&k 10 sts to **aa**, pm (m4), then 8 sts to **w** – 30 sts (12–10–8).

Row 2 (WS): Knit to last 2 sts, ssk – 1 st dec'd; 29 (11–10–8) sts.

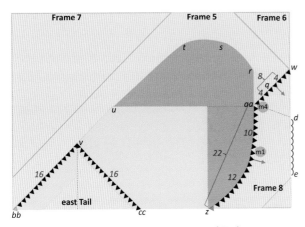

Figure 9: East - Frame 8 and Tail

Row 3 (RS): K2tog, knit to 1 st bef m, kf&b, sm, kf&b, knit to 2 sts bef next m, ssk, sm, k2tog, knit to last 2 sts, ssk – 2 sts dec'd; 27 sts (11–10–6).
Row 4 and even-numbered (WS) rows to 10: Knit.
Row 5: K2tog, knit to last 2 sts, ssk – 2 sts dec'd; 25 sts (10–10–5).
Row 7: Rep [Row 3] – 2 sts dec'd; 23 sts (10–10–3).
Row 9: Rep [Row 5] – 2 sts dec'd; 21 sts (9–10–2).

Row 11: Rep [Row 5] – 2 sts dec'd; 19 sts (8–10–1).
Row 12 (WS): Rm's. K2tog, BO 10 sts starting with the k2tog st to **e**, until 8 sts rem then knit to end – 11 sts dec'd; 8 sts.
Rows 13–17: Work [Tr] until 2 sts rem after RS row.
Row 18 (WS): K2tog – 1 st dec'd; 1 st. Cut yarn and fasten off.

East Tail see Figure 9

With BC, and starting at yellow triangle at **bb**, pu&k 16 sts to **v**, pm, and 16 sts from **v** to **cc** – 32 sts. See "Single Crochet for Edging" on page 189.
Row 2: Cont with BC, knit.

See "Intarsia" on page 196
Row 3: Cont with BC, k2tog, knit to 2 sts bef m, ssk, rm, and with A, k2tog, knit to last 2 sts, ssk – 4 sts dec'd; 28 sts (14 of BC and 14 of A).
Row 4 (WS) and all WS rows to 8: With A, knit to color transition, drop A, cross, and with BC, knit to end of row.
Row 5: With BC, k2tog, knit to 2 sts bef color transition, ssk, drop BC, cross, and with A, k2tog, knit to last 2 sts of row, ssk – 4 sts dec'd; 24 sts (12 of BC and 12 of A).
Row 7: Rep Row 5 – 4 sts dec'd; 20 sts (10 of BC, 10 of A).
Row 8: Rep [Row 4].
Cut BC after completing WS Row 8 and pm after 10th st.
Drape A to start of next row, loosely.
Row 9: With A, k2tog, knit to 2 sts bef m while alternately inserting needle above and below draped A, ssk, sm, k2tog, knit to last 2 sts, ssk – 4 sts dec'd; 16 sts.
Row 10: Knit.
Rows 11–14: Rep [Rows 9 & 10] twice – 8 sts dec'd; 8 sts.
Row 15: (K2tog, ssk) twice – 4 sts dec'd; 4 sts.
Row 16 (WS): Sl2 kwise, k2tog, psso – 3 sts dec'd; 1 st. Enlarge rem loop and insert ball through, tighten. Cut yarn. *Note:* If color transition area is loose, leave a 12"/30 cm tail, and with tapestry needle, on WS, take stitches on either side of the color transition to close gaps. Weave in all ends.

Eye

Work [Eye, page 91]. Position the Eye with lower edge just above the 3rd ridge of the Bird Head and 3 sts in from the Beak. Pin in place. Sew Eye to Block. See "Tacking Embellishments" on page 189.

ASSEMBLY

Lay out completed Blocks as in Figure 1 (Figure 3) on page 88 (89). Blocks are joined into horizontal Strips then the Strips are joined.

BLOCK JOIN see Figure 10

Bet each pair of neighbor Blocks, with a circular needle and A, starting at red triangle, pu&k 34 sts on left edge of Right Block, turn and CO 2 sts, pm, and starting at green triangle, pu&k 34 sts on the right edge of the Left Block – 70 sts.

Work [Join].

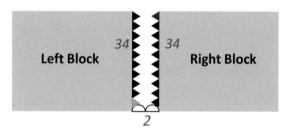

Figure 10: Pu&k for Block Join

Join

Note: Pu&k counts as Row 1.
Row 2 (WS): Knit to 2 sts bef m, rm, cdd, pm, cdd, knit to end – 4 sts dec'd.
Split stitches at marker pushing sts to tips of both needles. Orient work with RS together and WS facing outward. With 3rd, larger needle, 3-needle BO all sts. Cut yarn, insert end through rem st on needle, and fasten off.

STRIP JOIN see Figure 11

Bet each pair of neighbor Strips, with a circular needle, starting at blue triangle, pu&k 198 (248) sts (48 per Block, 2 per Join) on top edge of Lower Strip, turn and CO 2 sts, pm, starting at green (orange) triangle, pu&k 198 (248) sts on bottom edge of Upper Strip.

Work [Join].

BORDERS

RIGHT BORDER

With A, and starting at bottom-right corner of blanket, pu&k 214 (286) sts (34 per Block, 2 per Join) to corner. Knit 11 rows, BO loosely leaving last st on needle.

TOP BORDER

Cont with A, at top-right corner of blanket, pu&k 7 sts on Right Border, 198 (248) sts on top Border (48 per Block, 2 sts per Join) – 206 (256) sts. Knit 11 rows, BO loosely leaving last st on needle.

LEFT BORDER

Cont with A, at top-left corner of Top Border, pu&k 7 sts on Top Border, 214 (286) sts (34 per Block, 2 per join) to bottom-left corner of blanket – 222 (294) sts. Knit 11 rows. BO loosely, leaving last st on needle.

BOTTOM BORDER

Cont with A, at bottom-left corner of Left Border, pu&k 7 sts on Left Border, 198 (248) sts (48 per Block, 2 per Join) on bottom edge of blanket, and 8 sts on right edge of Right Border – 214 (264) sts. Knit 11 rows. BO loosely. Cut yarn and fasten off.

FINISHING

Weave in ends.

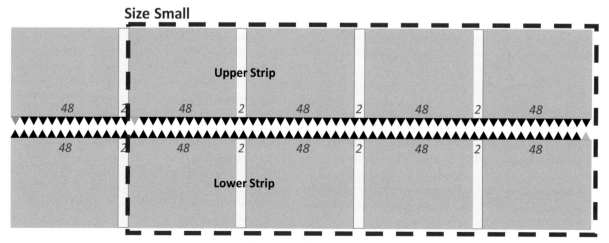

Figure 11: Strip Join

CHART SYMBOLS

☐	RS: knit	●	WS: knit	/	RS: k2tog
\	RS: ssk	＼•	WS: k2tog	☒	RS: kf&b
⋀	RS: central double decrease	⋀₄	RS: slip 2 sts, k2tog, psso	▲	pu&k
⌒	bind off	⋊	K2togBO	▧	no stitch
☐	marker 1 (m1)	☐	marker 2 (m2)	☐	marker 3 (m3)
☐	marker 4 (m4)				

WEST FRONT

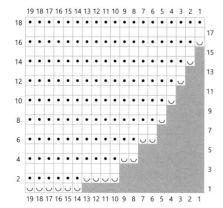

WEST HEAD

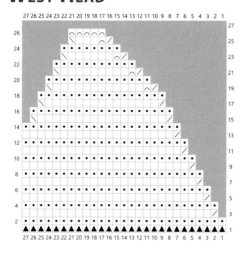

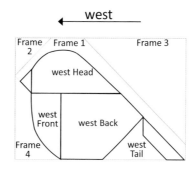

WEST BACK

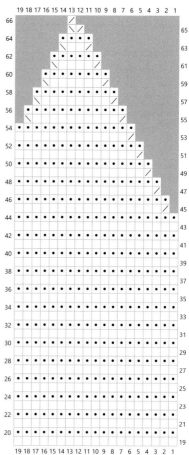

FRAME 1

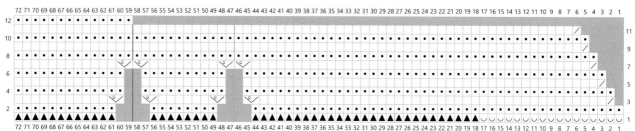

FRAME 4

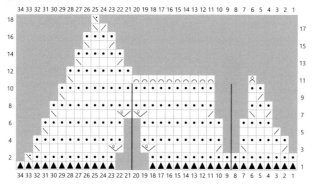

WEST TAIL

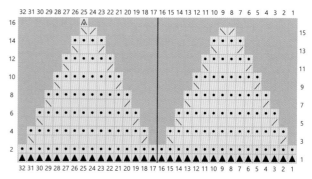

EAST FRONT

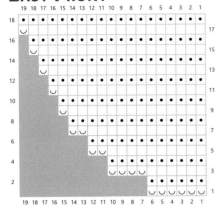

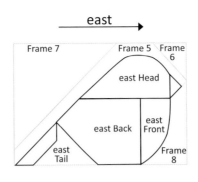

EAST BACK

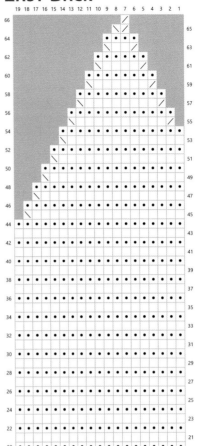

EAST HEAD

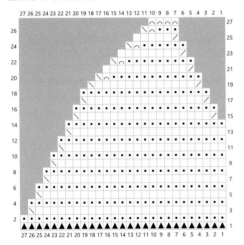

FRAME 5

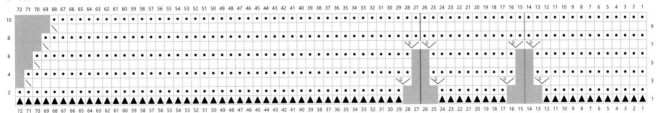

FRAME 8

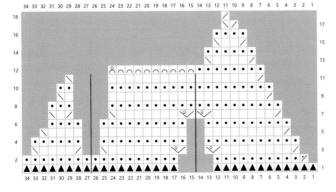

EAST TAIL

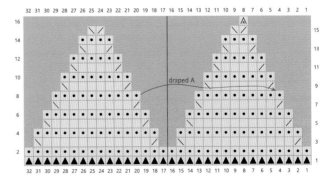

Make a Row Robin pillow to try out the pattern!

See the blanket pattern for yarn color identification, notions, notes, pattern stitches, and charts.

SIZE

19.5"/50 cm square Pillow Cover

SUPPLIES

20"/50 cm square pillow form
20"/50 cm zipper
Sewing thread matching yarn color A
Sewing needle and safety pins
Stitch markers
Tapestry needle

Illustration of Row Robin Pillow

PILLOW FRONT

Yarn Requirements

Pillow is worked in DK weight so the pillow will not be too large. The color names and abbreviations are the same as those specified in the yarn requirements for the blanket on page 87:

SweetGeorgia, Superwash DK (100% superwash merino wool; 256 yds/234 m; 4 oz/115 g):

	yds	meters		yds	meters		yds	meters
A	350	320	C	62	60	F	62	60
G	62	60	J	62	60	K	62	60
M	62	60						

Needles

(2) US 5/3.75 mm circular needles of minimum length 24"/60 cm

Gauge

21 sts x 42 rows = 4"/10 cm in garter st

Instructions

West Block Make 2 in colors specified in Figure 12, using instructions on page 90. *Note:* for pillow, beaks are worked in color J, rather than I.

East Block Make 2 in colors specified in Figure 12, using instructions on page 92.

Assembly of Blocks

Lay out completed Blocks, RS up, as shown in Figure 12. Join top pair of Blocks as specified in Figure 10 on page 94.

Rep Join for bottom pair of Blocks, forming horizontal Strips.

Assembly of Strips

See Figure 11 on page 94.

Bet each pair of neighbor Strips, with a circular needle, starting at red triangle, pu&k 102 sts (50 per Block, 2 per Join) on top edge of Lower Block, turn and CO 2 sts, pm, starting at green triangle, pu&k 102 sts on bottom edge of Upper Block. Work [Join, page 94].

BORDERS

Top Border

On RS, beg at the top-right corner of the top Strip, pu&k 102 sts (50 per Block, 2 per Join) to end of edge. Knit 22 rows (11 ridges). On RS, BO loosely. Cut yarn leaving long tail for sewing.

Bottom Border

Work as for Top Border, beg pu&k at bottom-left corner of bottom Strip, and knitting 38 rows (19 ridges).

PILLOW BACK

Either repeat the Pillow Front (yarn amounts for the Pillow Front should be doubled), or work a plain garter stitch back (instructions below).

Yarn Requirements

475 yds/435 m of A are needed for a solid color back worked in DK weight.

Instructions

CO 102 sts. Knit 203 rows (102 ridges). BO loosely.

PILLOW FRONT/BACK ASSEMBLY

See "Assembling Pillows with a Zipper Closure" on page 192.

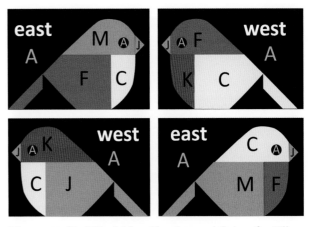

Figure 12: Bird Block Identification and Colors for Pillow

SAFE AT HOME

A colorful blanket reminding us that home and family is our safe place.

TECHNIQUES

Sewing, intarsia

SIZE

55"/140 cm square

YARN

Malabrigo, Worsted Merino (100% kettle dyed pure merino wool; 210 yds/192 m; 3.5 oz/100 g):

Pattern color ID	Color swatch	Color ID	Color name	Color description	# Hanks
A		150	Azul Profundo	dark blue	2
B		051	Vaa*	dark green-blue	3
C		032	Jewel Blue	sky blue	2
D		037	Lettuce	avocado green	2
E		083	Water Green	mint green	2
F		007	Cadmium	bright yellow	2
G		035	Frank Ochre	dull gold	2
H		096	Sunset	orange-yellow	2
I		019	Pollen	light yellow or cream	2
J		123	Rhodesian	rust	2
K		184	Shocking Pink	bright pink	2
L		610	Red Mahogany	dark red-brown	2

Note: If working Method D of Assembly (pu&k with 3-needle BO, requiring no sewing), an extra 300 yds/275 m of the color B are needed in addition to what is required in the yarn table.

NEEDLES

US Size 7/4.5 mm 40"/100 cm circular needle

A second US Size 7/4.5 mm 40"/100 cm circular needle for Method D (optional)

US 10/6 mm straight or circular needle of any length for Method D (optional)

Notions

Tapestry needle for weaving ends, stitch holders or scrap yarn

Gauge

17 sts and 34 rows = 4"/10 cm in garter st

Notes

- This blanket is worked in 9 horizontal Strips, worked right to left.

- Color Scheme (CS) names [C1][C2][C3][C4][C5] are used in Figure 5 on page 105 and refer to the 5 parts of Blocks. They are described as follows with the approximate yardage per part in parentheses.

  C1: Background of Ground Floor *(12 yds/11 m)*
  C2: Windows *(1 yd/1 m per Window)*
  C3: Door, 1st and all odd stripes of the Roof *(7.5 yds/7 m)*
  C4: 2nd and all even stripes of the Roof *(4.5 yds/4.5 m)*
  C5: Sky *(4.5 yds/4.5 m per Sky)*

- The Ground Floor of each House uses Intarsia. Before beginning, see "Intarsia" on page 196.

- Work the GF directly from skeins or cut yarns for House parts and wind onto bobbins. Yardage provided above is an estimate. Knit one Block using these estimates and adjust as needed.

- Strip instructions are for working each Block (Ground Floor, Roof, then Skies) in its entirety then working subsequent Blocks of the Strip. However, the Ground Floors (GFs) of the Strip may all be worked continuously, and Roofs and Skies added afterwards. If this is done, the stitches of a completed GF do not need to be placed on a holder.

- An overview of construction options is provided in Figure 1.

  - There are two methods (A and B) for working the Sky parts. In Method A, a triangle shape is worked on each roof edge, then the adjacent edges of the triangles are seamed. In Method B, no sewing is required. The adjacent Sky parts between Houses are worked in one piece using intarsia for the color change.

  - There are two methods (C and D) for assembling the completed Strips. In Method C, the Strips are sewn together using long tails from Skies. In Method D there is no sewing required. Stitches are pu&k on the edges of adjacent Strips and a 3-needle BO is used to join the Strips. The narrow separator between each Strip adds 3"/7.5 cm to the vertical length of the blanket and requires an extra 300 yds/254 m of yarn color B.

- Figure 2 shows the Construction and Color Scheme abbreviations for the GF and Roof.

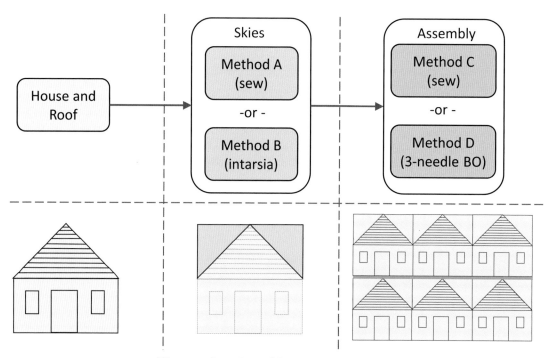

Figure 1: Overview of Construction Options

BLANKET INSTRUCTIONS

STRIPS 1–9

Block 1

Ground Floor

CO 12 sts.

Work [GF chart, Rows 1–47] using Color Scheme (CS) for the Block (see Figure 5). Cut yarn and fasten off. Place 12 sts on holder.

Note: on the GF chart, only RS rows are shown. On the WS rows, work sts in same color as prev RS row. Change colors on RS (odd) rows as shown.

Roof

With C3 and starting at red triangle in Figure 2, pu&k 24 sts (one st per garter st ridge) across the right edge of the GF.

Work [Rf], attaching C4 at the beg of Row 2, then alternating C3 and C4 every 2 rows, and carrying non-working yarn along edge. Cut yarns and fasten off.

Roof (Rf) – 24 sts dec'ing to 1 st

Row 1 (WS): Knit.
Change to alternate color.
Row 2 (RS): K2tog, knit to last 2 sts, ssk – 2 sts dec'd; 22 sts.
Row 3: Knit. Change to alternate color.
Rows 4–23: Rep [Rows 2 & 3] 10 times – 20 sts dec'd; 2 sts.
Row 24: With C5, k2tog – 1 sts dec'd; 1 st.

Blocks 2 – 9

Transfer 12 sts from prev Block from holder to needle. Work as for Block 1 (omitting CO for GF and beg on Row 1), using CS for Block specified in Figure 5 on page 105. At the end of Block 9 [GF Row 48], BO sts instead of placing on holder.

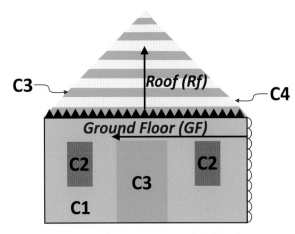

Figure 2: Construction and Colors for Ground Floor and Roof

GROUND FLOOR (GF) CHART

Chart shows RS rows only. WS rows are knitted using same color as prev RS row.

Key

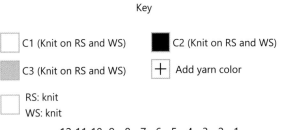

- C1 (Knit on RS and WS)
- C2 (Knit on RS and WS)
- C3 (Knit on RS and WS)
- $+$ Add yarn color
- RS: knit
- WS: knit

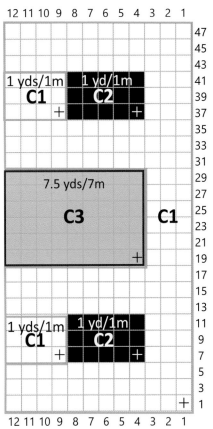

Skies

Work using either Method A or Method B.

Sky - Method A see Figure 3

A Sky piece is worked on each roof edge, then skies of adjacent Houses are seamed. Skies may be worked as soon as the Roof they attach to is complete.

Left Sky Starting at peak of Roof at green triangle, leave a 10"/25 cm tail of C5 and pu&k 17 sts evenly along edge. Work [Tr]. Cut yarn and fasten off, leaving 12"/30 cm tail for sewing skies.

Right Sky Starting at the lower right corner of Roof at red triangle, with C5, pu&k 17 sts evenly along edge. Work [Tr]. Cut yarn and fasten off, leaving 20"/55 cm tail if using Assembly Method C.

Thread long CO tail of Left Sky onto tapestry needle. Insert needle in right corner of Left Sky and then into left corner of Right Sky, to tie these two pieces together. Pull to tighten, then fasten off securely.

Using long tail from Right Sky and mattress st, sew tog Right Sky edge of current Block to Left Sky edge of prev Block along red dashed lines. Before tying off, take a few discrete sts to fully close the corner where the roof corners meet.

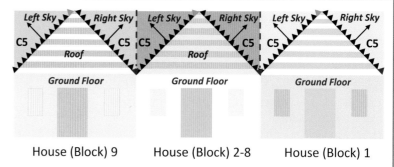

House (Block) 9 House (Block) 2-8 House (Block) 1

Figure 3: Method A for Skies

Triangle (Tr) – 17 sts dec'ing to 1 st

Row 1 (WS): Knit.
Row 2 (RS): K2tog, knit to last 2 sts, ssk – 2 sts dec'd; 15 sts.
Row 3: Knit.
Rows 4–15: Rep [Rows 2 & 3] 6 times – 12 sts dec'd; 3 sts.
Row 16: Cdd – 2 sts dec'd; 1 st.

Sky - Method B see Figure 4

Work Right Sky of Block 1 and Left Sky of Block 9 as in Method A. Between each pair of Houses, with C5 for House on the right (C5–R), and starting at the green triangle, pu&k 17 sts to next corner. Drop C5–R but do not cut. With C5 for the House on the Left (C5–L), pu&k 17 sts from the orange triangle to the Roof peak of House on the Left. Work [DS].

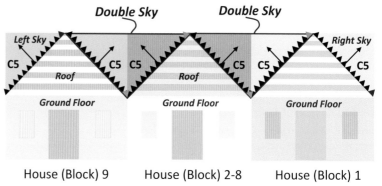

House (Block) 9 House (Block) 2-8 House (Block) 1

Figure 4: Method B for Skies

Double Sky (DS) – 34 sts dec'ing to 2 sts

Row 1 (WS): Knit.
Row 2 (RS): K2tog, knit to last 2 sts of C5–R, ssk, twist C5–R and C5–L on WS of work, and cont with C5–L, k2tog, knit to last 2 sts, ssk – 4 sts dec'd; 30 sts.
Row 3: Knit C5–L sts, bring both C5–L and C5–R to WS (toward you), twist yarns, then move C5–R to RS (away from you), and with C5–R knit to end.
Rep [Rows 2 & 3] until 6 sts rem, ending after WS row.
Next row: Cdd, twist C5–R and C5–L at back of work, Cdd – 4 sts dec'd; 2 sts.
Cut yarn, and if working Method C for Assembly, leave a 20"/55 cm tail. Thread tail onto tapestry needle and insert through both sts rem on needle. Fasten securely.

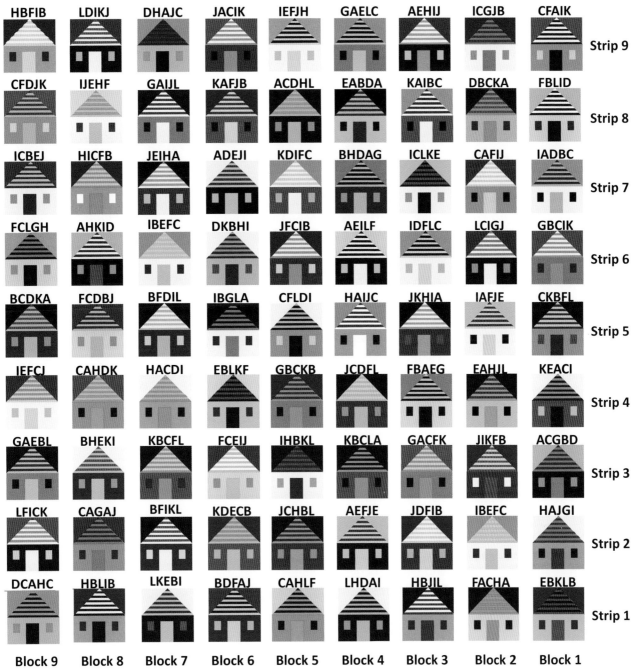

HBFIB	LDIKJ	DHAJC	JACIK	IEFJH	GAELC	AEHIJ	ICGJB	CFAIK	Strip 9
CFDJK	IJEHF	GAIJL	KAFJB	ACDHL	EABDA	KAIBC	DBCKA	FBLID	Strip 8
ICBEJ	HICFB	JEIHA	ADEJI	KDIFC	BHDAG	ICLKE	CAFIJ	IADBC	Strip 7
FCLGH	AHKID	IBEFC	DKBHI	JFCIB	AEILF	IDFLC	LCIGJ	GBCIK	Strip 6
BCDKA	FCDBJ	BFDIL	IBGLA	CFLDI	HAIJC	JKHIA	IAFJE	CKBFL	Strip 5
IEFCJ	CAHDK	HACDI	EBLKF	GBCKB	JCDFL	FBAEG	EAHJL	KEACI	Strip 4
GAEBL	BHEKI	KBCFL	FCEIJ	IHBKL	KBCLA	GACFK	JIKFB	ACGBD	Strip 3
LFICK	CAGAJ	BFIKL	KDECB	JCHBL	AEFJE	JDFIB	IBEFC	HAJGI	Strip 2
DCAHC	HBLIB	LKEBI	BDFAJ	CAHLF	LHDAI	HBJIL	FACHA	EBKLB	Strip 1
Block 9	Block 8	Block 7	Block 6	Block 5	Block 4	Block 3	Block 2	Block 1	

Figure 5: Color Schemes for Blocks

ASSEMBLY

Work using either Method C or Method D. Arrange Strips 1–9 as shown in Figure 5.

ASSEMBLY - METHOD C (SEWING)

Using long tails of Sky pieces and mattress st, sew Strips tog.

ASSEMBLY - METHOD D (PU&K AND 3-NEEDLE BO)

Note 1: Requires 300 yds/275 m of additional yarn in color B.

Note 2: This assembly method creates a ⅜"/1 cm) high horizontal Strip between each pair of House Strips.

Join Strip 1 and Strip 2

With B and a circular needle, starting at the right-top corner of Block 1 of the lower Strip and working on the RS, *pu&k 24 sts evenly to end of House, pm; rep from * to end of Strip – 216 sts. Knit 1 row (on WS). Cut yarn and fasten off, leaving sts on needle.

With a separate strand of B and a second circular needle, starting at the bottom-left corner of Block 9 of the upper Strip and working on the RS, *pu&k 24 sts evenly to end of the House; rep from * to end of Strip – 216 sts. Knit 1 row (on WS). Do not cut yarn.

Turn lower and upper Strips RS tog, with the upper Strip at back and needle tips parallel. With 3rd, larger needle, use 3-needle BO to BO all sts (see "3-needle Bind-Off" on page 190"3-needle Bind-Off" on page 190). The purpose of markers is to assist in aligning the Block corners. Markers may be removed when encountered.

Join Remaining Strips

Rep as for Join Strip 1 and 2 for the seven remaining pairs of Strips.

BORDERS

All pu&k is performed on the RS of work.

RIGHT BORDER

(If Assembly Method C used) On RS, starting at right-bottom corner of blanket, with B, pu&k 24 sts per Block on right edge of blanket – 216 sts. Knit 15 rows. BO loosely. Leave rem st on needle and do not cut yarn.

(If Assembly Method D used) On RS, starting at right-bottom corner of blanket, with B, pu&k 24 sts per

Block, and 2 sts on each Join – 232 sts. Knit 15 rows. BO loosely. Leave rem st on needle, and do not cut yarn.

TOP BORDER

Pu&k 8 sts on edge of Right Border, 24 sts per Block on top edge of blanket – 225 sts. Knit 15 rows. BO loosely. Leave rem st on needle and do not cut yarn.

LEFT BORDER

(If Assembly Method C used) Rep as for Top Border, picking up sts on left edge of Top Border and left side of blanket.

(If Assembly Method D used) Pu&k 8 sts on left edge of Top Border, 24 sts per Block, and 2 sts on each Join – 241 sts. Knit 15 rows. BO loosely. Leave rem st on needle and do not cut yarn.

BOTTOM BORDER

Pu&k 8 sts on bottom-left corner of Left Border, 24 sts per Block on bottom edge of blanket, and 9 sts on bottom edge of Right Border – 234 sts. Knit 15 rows. BO loosely. Cut yarn and fasten off.

FINISHING

For yarn ends of Windows and Door, on WS, with crochet hook or tapestry needle, pull each tail through the loop next to where the yarn is emerging. Pull to tighten, then weave in tail. This will eliminate the small holes in the fabric.

Weave in remaining ends.

Make a Safe at Home pillow to try out the pattern!

This pillow is worked by making 9 House Blocks, then sewing them together.

See the blanket pattern for needle size, notions, pattern stitches, chart, notes, and Block instructions.

SIZE

17"/43 cm square Pillow Cover

SUPPLIES

- 18"/45 cm square pillow form
- 18"/45 cm zipper
- Sewing thread matching yarn color A
- Sewing needle and safety pins

PILLOW FRONT

Yarn Requirements

The yarn requirements for working the front side only are:

	yds	meters		yds	meters		yds	meters
A	21	20	B	24	20	C	26	24
D	35	33	E	15	14	F	34	32
G	8	8	H	28	26	I	14	13
J	38	35	K	28	26	L	34	32

Instructions

See Figure 2 (page 103) for Block construction diagram and color scheme arrangement and Figure 6 for Color Schemes (CS).

Strips 1–3

Work Block 1 (page 103) and Blocks 2 and 3 (page 103). After Block 3, BO sts loosely. *Note:* There are 2 methods (A and B) for working Skies.

Front Assembly

Arrange Strips 1–3 as shown in Figure 6. Using long tails of Sky pieces and mattress st, sew Strips tog.

PILLOW BACK

Either repeat the Pillow Front (yarn amounts for the Pillow Front should be doubled) or work a plain garter stitch back (instructions below).

Illustration of Safe at Home Pillow

Yarn Requirements

290 yds/270 m of A for a solid color back. If short on yarn for the back, work it in stripes from multiple colors. For clean color changes, change colors at the beg of RS rows. For interlaced color changes, change colors at the beg of WS rows.

Instructions

CO 72 sts. Knit 143 rows (72 ridges). BO loosely.

PILLOW FRONT/BACK ASSEMBLY

See Pillow Assembly instructions on page 192.

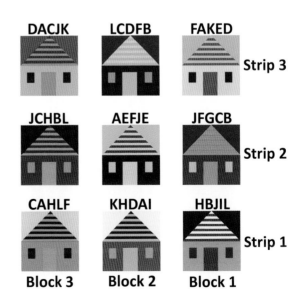

Figure 6: Pillow Color Schemes and Layout

Leftover yarn? Make a table runner!

This table runner is worked in two Strips that are joined with a 3-needle BO.

See the blanket pattern for notions, pattern stitches, chart, notes, and Block instructions.

NEEDLES

(2) US size 7 (4.5 mm) circular needles of minimum length 50"/120 cm.

(1) US Size 10 straight or circular needle for 3-needle BO

SIZE

14 x 104.5"/36 x 265 cm

The table runner has Strips of 18 House Blocks and will fit a table of length 84 to 96" (215 to 245 cm), with a drop (overhang) of 4 to 10" (10 to 25 cm) on each end of the table. To make the runner shorter or longer add or remove Blocks from the Strips. Each Block is 5.5"/14.5 cm square.

YARN REQUIREMENTS

The yarn requirements for working the House Strips only are:

	yds	meters		yds	meters		yds	meters
A	95	87	B	85	78	C	131	120
D	62	57	E	73	67	F	132	121
G	50	46	H	106	97	I	162	149
J	97	89	K	89	82	L	109	100

An additional 380 yds/350 m of the color that will be used for Borders and Separators between Strips is required. The runner is illustrated with color G for Borders and Separators.

INSTRUCTIONS

See Figure 2 (page 103) for Block construction diagram and color scheme arrangement and Figure 7 (page 108) for Color Schemes (CS) for Blocks.

STRIPS 1 & 2

Work Blocks 1–2 (page 103). Rep Block 2 sixteen times for a total of 18 Blocks.

After Block 18, BO sts loosely.

SEPARATOR

See Figure 8 at right. With G and circular needle, pu&k 432 sts from red triangle on the top-right corner of Strip 1 to end of Strip (24 sts per Block). Knit 3 rows.

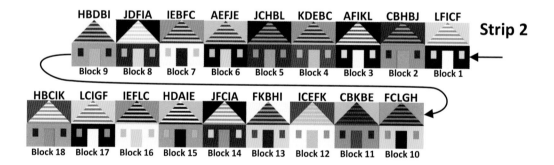

Strip 2

Strip 1

Figure 7: Colors and Strip Arrangement for Table Runner

Leave stitches on needle.

Cut yarn and fasten off.

With G and 2nd circular needle, pu&k 432 sts from yellow triangle at the top-right corner of Strip 2 to end of Strip.

Knit 3 rows. Do not cut yarn.

Orient Strips 1 and 2 with RS tog and needle tips parallel. Turn so that Strip 2 is behind Strip 1. With G still attached to Strip 2, and 3rd (larger) needle, 3-needle BO all sts on both needles.

Cut yarn and fasten off.

BORDERS

RIGHT BORDER

With G, and starting at bottom-right corner of assembled runner, pu&k 52 sts to next corner (24 sts on edge of each Block and 4 sts on edge of Separator).

Knit 3 rows. BO loosely.

LEFT BORDER

Rep as for Right Border, attaching yarn at top-left corner of runner.

TOP BORDER

With G, and starting at top-right corner of Right Border, pu&k 5 sts on top edge of Right Border, 432 sts along House Blocks (24 sts per Block), and 5 sts on top edge of Left border – 442 sts.

Knit 3 rows. BO loosely.

Illustration of Safe at Home Table Runner

BOTTOM BORDER

Rep as for Top Border, attaching yarn at bottom-left corner of Left Border.

FINISHING

Weave in ends and block to measurements.

Figure 8: Separator Construction

SAFE IN THE CITY

A stash-busting blanket with a colorful city scene.

TECHNIQUES

Sewing, intarsia

SIZE

58 x 78"/148 x 199 cm

YARN

Plymouth Encore, Worsted (75% acrylic, 25% wool; 200 yds/183 m; 3.5 oz/100 g):

Pattern color ID	Color swatch	Color ID	Color name	Color description	# Skeins
A		146	Natural	off-white	2
B		133	Royal	royal blue	2
C		848	Navy	navy blue	3
D		1383	Orange	orange	2
E		478	Neon Pink	bright pink	2
F		686	Wine Heather	burgundy	2
G		703	Amber Blush	tan	1
H		154	Blue Haze	light aqua-gray	2
I		459	Lagoon	aqua	2
J		9852	Teal-A-Delphia	teal	1
K		0233	Lilac	light mauve	2
L		158	Purple Amethyst	purple	2
M		215	Light Yellow	yellow	1
N		1382	Daffodil	orange-yellow	1
O		450	Honeydew Melon	light green	2
P		6004	Shamrock Heather	avocado green	2
Q		217	Black	black	2

NEEDLES

US Size 7/4.5 mm 40"/100 cm circular needles

NOTIONS

Tapestry needle, stitch markers, 4 bobbins, 10 stitch holders or scrap yarn

GAUGE

18 sts and 36 rows = 4"/10 cm in garter st

NOTES

- The blanket is worked in diagonal Strips. There are 1 Sky Strip and 11 House Strips. Roofs are added to the lower edge of each Strip. Instructions are for working Roofs last, after the Sky and all House Strips are complete; however, a Roof can be added as soon as the House it is attached to is completed.

- Before beginning, see "Intarsia" on page 196.

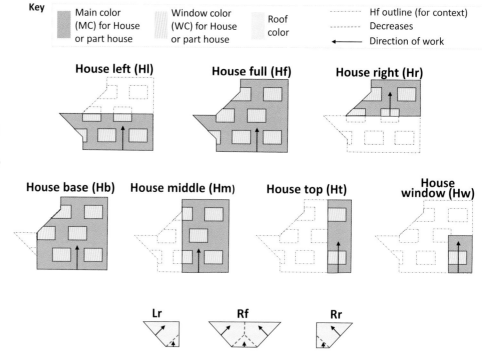

Figure 1: Shape Catalog

BLANKET INSTRUCTIONS

HOUSE STRIPS

Figure 1 is a catalog of House and Roof pattern stitch shapes used in Strips. House shapes in Figure 1 are rotated 90 degrees from their orientation in the blanket.

Houses are worked from a chart (page 117). The predominant shape for Houses is House full (Hf), that includes all rows and sts of House chart. The other house shapes (partial Houses) omit some rows and/ or stitches of House chart. The row and stitch range to work for a partial House is specified in the green pattern stitch box for Houses on the top-left of page 113. In Figure 1, the omitted parts are outlined with dashed lines, for context.

See Figure 2 for construction and Figure 3 for color schemes. All full (Hf) and partial Houses (Hr, Hl, Hb, Hm, Ht, and Hw) are worked in two colors: main (MC) and window (WC), stated in Figure 3 as [MC][WC].

Do not BO sts between Houses within a Strip. Leave a 25"/65 cm tail of MC when cutting yarn after finishing the last House of a Strip, for sewing seams.

Yarns for small areas of intarsia may be cut and wound onto bobbins, using estimated amounts shown on House chart. Yarns for windows and spaces between windows can be trimmed after they are complete.

Although instruction order for House Strips is to work 1–11, to get familiar with the House chart and shaping, Strip 2 of the Houses may be worked first.

Strips 1, 3, 5, and 7

House right (Hr) With WC for Hr, CO 7, with MC, CO 5, with separate strand of WC, CO 7, with separate yarn of MC, CO 8 – 27 sts. Work [Hr] – 18 sts.

House full 1–8 (Hf1) With MC, turn and CO 9 sts – 27 sts. Work [Hf] – 18 sts.

House left (Hl) With MC, turn and CO 9 sts – 27 sts. Work [Hl] – 36 sts. Place rem 36 sts on holder. Cut yarn and fasten off.

Strips 2, 4, and 6

Hf1 With MC for right-most House on Strip, CO 27 sts and work [Hf] – 18 sts.

Hf2 – Hf9 With MC, turn and CO 9 sts – 27 sts. Work [Hf] – 18 sts. After Hf9, place rem 18 sts on holder.

Strip 8

Hb With MC, CO 27 sts, work [Hb] – 18 sts.

Hf1 – Hf8 With MC, turn and CO 9 sts – 27 sts. Work [Hf] – 18 sts. After Hf8, place rem 18 sts on holder.

Houses (Hf, Hl, Hr, Hb, Hm, Ht, and Hw)

Work [House chart] working the row and stitch range specified for the House shape as follows:

House full (Hf)
Work [House chart, Rows 1–54, sts 1–36].

House base (Hb)
Work [House chart, Rows 1–54, sts 1–27]. On Rows 7 through 16, work st 27 in MC, not WC. On Row 9, work st 27 as knit instead of kf&b.

House middle (Hm)
Work [House chart, Rows 1–54, sts 1–18]. On Row 45, work st 18 as knit instead of ssk.

House top (Ht)
Work [House chart, Rows 1–54, sts 1–9]. On Rows 23–32, work st in MC, not WC.

House window (Hw)
Work [House chart, Rows 1–28, sts 1–9]. On Rows 23–28, work st 9 in MC, not WC.

House right (Hr)
Work [House chart, Rows 29–54, sts 1–27].

House left (Hl)
Work [House chart, Rows 1–28, sts 1–36]. On Row 28, knit sts 28–36 instead of BO.

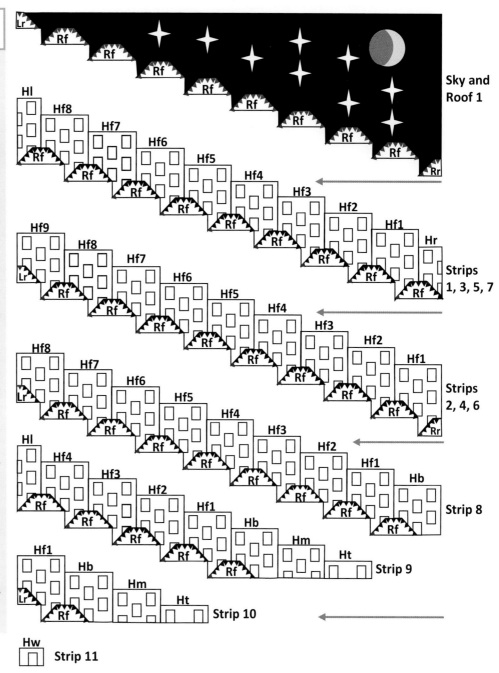

Figure 2: Strip and Roof Construction

Strip 9
Ht With MC for Ht, CO 9 sts, work [Ht].

Hm With MC for Hm, turn and CO 9 sts – 18 sts. Work [Hm].

Hb With MC for Hb, turn and CO 9 sts – 27 sts, work [Hb] – 18 sts.

Hf1 – Hf4 With MC Hf, turn and CO 9 sts – 27 sts. Work [Hf] – 18 sts.

Hl With MC for Hl, turn and CO 9 sts – 27 sts. Work [Hl] – 36 sts. Place rem 36 sts on holder.

Strip 10
Work as for Strip 9 [Ht – Hf1]. Place rem 18 sts on holder.

Strip 11
With MC for Hw, CO 9 sts, work [Hw]. Place rem 9 sts on holder.

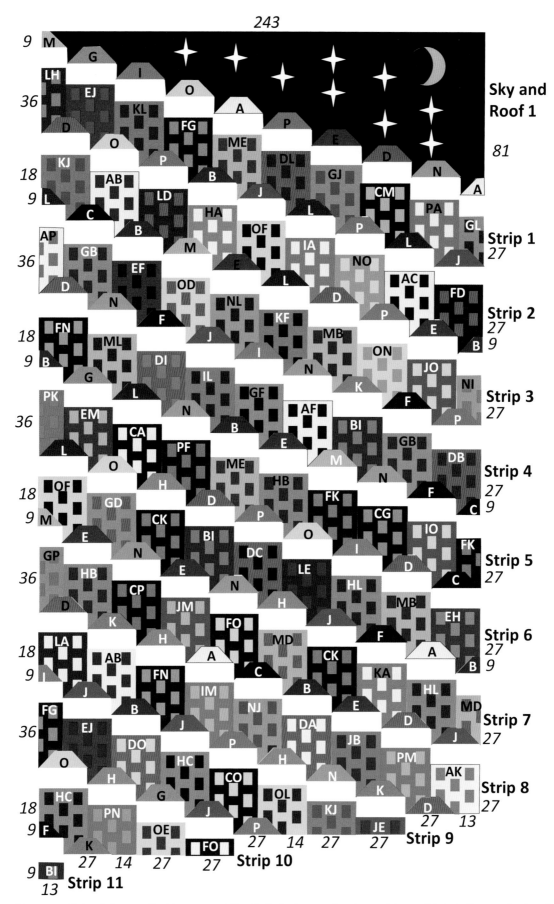

Figure 3: Color Schemes for Houses and Roofs, Strip Layout for Assembly, and Stitch Counts for Borders

Sky

See Figure 4 for construction. Shapes are rotated 90 degrees from their orientation in the blanket.

Charts for Moon and Star are on page 118 with yarn amounts per color section. Cut Moon and Star yarns after completing each intarsia shape.

The Sky is constructed by working Repeats of the Sky pattern stitch. When Moon or Stars are used in a Repeat, they start on Row 1. Once it is started, continue working the chart until it ends. The Star chart ends on Row 26 of the Repeat, and the Moon chart on Row 44 of the Repeat.

With Q, CO 81 sts.

1st Rep (81 sts inc'ing to 90, dec'ing to 72 sts)
  Rows 1–10: Knit.
  Rows 11–46: Work [Sky, Rows 17–52].

2nd Rep (72 sts inc'ing to 81 sts dec'ing to 63 sts)
  Row 47: K9, work [Moon chart row], k5, (work [Star chart row], k3) twice.
  Rows 48–100: Cont with established charts, work [Sky].

Sky

Setup row (WS): Knit.
Row 1 (RS)–16 (WS): Knit.
Row 17 (RS): Knit to last st, kf&b – 1 st inc'd.
Row 18 (WS): Knit.
Rows 19–32: Rep [Rows 17 & 18] 7 times – 7 sts inc'd.
Row 33: Rep Row 17 – 1 st inc'd.
Row 34: BO 9 sts, knit to end – 9 sts dec'd.
Row 35: Knit to last 2 sts, ssk – 1 st dec'd.
Row 36: Knit.
Rows 37–52: Rep [Rows 35 & 36] 8 times – 8 sts dec'd.

3rd Rep (63 sts inc'ing to 72 sts dec'ing to 54 sts)
  Row 101: K2, work [Star chart row], k12, work [Star chart Row], k12.
  Rows 102–154: Cont with established charts, work [Sky].

4th Rep (54 sts inc'ing to 63 sts dec'ing to 45 sts)
  Row 155: K18, work [Star chart row], k3, work [Star chart row], k3.
  Rows 156–208: Cont with established charts, work [Sky].

5th Rep (45 sts inc'ing to 54 sts dec'ing to 36 sts)
  Row 209: K18, work [Star chart row], k12.
  Rows 210–262: Cont with established charts, work [Sky].

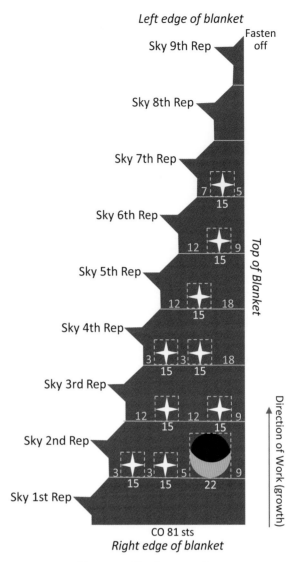

Figure 4: Sky Construction

6th Rep (36 sts inc'ing to 45 sts dec'ing to 27 sts)
  Row 263: K9, work [Star chart row], k12.
  Rows 264–316: Cont with established charts, work [Sky].

7th Rep (27 sts inc'ing to 36 sts dec'ing to 18 sts)
  Row 317: K5, work [Star chart row], k7.
  Rows 318–370: Cont with established charts, work [Sky].

8th Rep (18 sts inc'ing to 27 sts dec'ing to 9 sts)
  Row 371: Knit.
  Rows 372–424: Work [Sky].

9th Rep (9 sts inc'ing to 18 sts dec'ing to 0 st)
  Row 425: Knit.
  Rows 426–476: Work [Sky, Setup row - Row 50].
Cut yarn and fasten off.

Right roof (Rr) – 18 sts dec'ing to 1 st

Row 1 (WS): Knit.
Row 2 (RS): K2tog, knit to m, k2tog, knit to end – 2 sts dec'd; 16 sts.
Rows 3–8: Rep [Rows 1 & 2] 3 times – 6 sts dec'd; 10 sts.
Row 9: Knit.
Row 10: Rm. K2tog, knit to last 2 sts, ssk – 2 sts dec'd; 8 sts.
Row 11: Knit.
Rows 12–15: Rep [Rows 10 and 11] twice – 4 sts dec'd; 4 sts.
Row 16: K2tog, ssk – 2 sts dec'd; 2 sts.
Row 17: K2tog – 1 st dec'd; 1 st.

Roof (Rf) – 35 sts dec'ing to 1 st

Row 1 (WS): Knit.
Row 2 (RS): K2tog, knit to m, k2tog, knit to 2 sts bef next m, ssk, knit to last 2 sts, ssk – 4 sts dec'd; 31 sts.
Rows 3–6: Rep [Rows 1 & 2] twice – 8 sts dec'd; 23 sts.
Row 7: Knit.
Row 8: Rm's. K2tog, k8, cdd, pm, knit to last 2 sts, ssk – 4 sts dec'd; 19 sts.
Row 9: Knit.
Row 10: K2tog, knit to 2 sts bef m, rm, cdd, pm, knit to last 2 sts, ssk – 4 sts dec'd; 15 sts.
Row 11: Knit.
Rows 12–15: Rep [Rows 10 & 11] twice – 8 sts dec'd; 7 sts.
Row 16: Rm, cdd, k1, cdd – 4 sts dec'd; 3 sts.
Row 17: Cdd – 2 sts dec'd; 1 st.

Left roof (Lr) – 18 sts dec'ing to 1 st

Row 1 (WS): Knit.
Row 2 (RS): Knit to 2 sts bef m, ssk, knit to last 2 sts, ssk – 2 sts dec'd; 16 sts.
Rows 3–8: Rep [Rows 1 & 2] 3 times – 6 sts dec'd; 10 sts.
Row 9: Knit.
Row 10: Rm. K2tog, knit to last 2 sts, ssk – 2 sts dec'd; 8 sts.
Row 11: Knit.
Rows 12–15: Rep [Rows 10 and 11] twice – 4 sts dec'd; 4 sts.
Row 16: K2tog, ssk – 2 sts dec'd; 2 sts.
Row 17: K2tog – 1 sts dec'd; 1 st.

ROOFS

See Figure 2 for construction and Figure 3 for color schemes. Charts are on page 118.

Right roof (Rr)

In each space labeled "Rr," pu&k 13 sts from red triangle to next corner, pm, pu&k 5 sts to next corner – 18 sts. Work [Rr]. Cut yarn and fasten off.

Roof full (Rf)

In each space labeled "Rf," pu&k 13 sts from red triangle to next corner, pm, pu&k 9 sts to next corner, pm, pu&k 13 sts to next corner – 35 sts. Work [Rf]. Cut yarn and fasten off.

Left roof (Lr)

In each space labeled "Lr," pu&k 5 sts from red triangle to next corner, pm, pu&k 13 sts to next corner – 18 sts. Work [Lr]. Cut yarn and fasten off.

ASSEMBLY

Arrange Sky and House Strips 1–11 as shown in Figure 3. Using long tails from Houses, sew Strips tog using mattress st, aligning corners.

BORDERS

Stitch counts per shape are in italics in Figure 3.

RIGHT BORDER

On RS, starting at the right-bottom corner of blanket, with C, pu&k 333 sts to next corner. Knit 17 rows. BO loosely leaving last st on needle and do not cut yarn.

TOP BORDER

Pu&k 9 sts on left edge of Right Border and 243 sts on top edge of blanket – 253 sts. Knit 17 rows. BO loosely, leaving last st on needle and do not cut yarn.

LEFT BORDER

Pu&k 9 sts on left edge of Top Border. Knit sts off holders on edges of Houses, and pu&k sts on edges of Roofs – 343 sts. Knit 17 rows. BO loosely, leaving last st on needle and do not cut yarn.

BOTTOM BORDER

Pu&k 9 sts on bottom edge of Left Border, 243 sts on bottom edge of blanket, and 10 sts on the edge of Right Border – 263 sts. Knit 17 rows. BO loosely. Cut yarn and fasten off.

FINISHING

Weave in ends.

CHARTS

House, Star, and Moon charts are rotated 90 degrees clockwise from blanket orientation. In charts, the width of a House, Star, and Moon appear elongated because in garter stitch the height of 2 rows equals the width of 1 stitch.

Each area worked with a separate strand for intarsia contains a yardage estimate. Use this estimate to work the first House then adjust as needed for subsequent Houses.

House

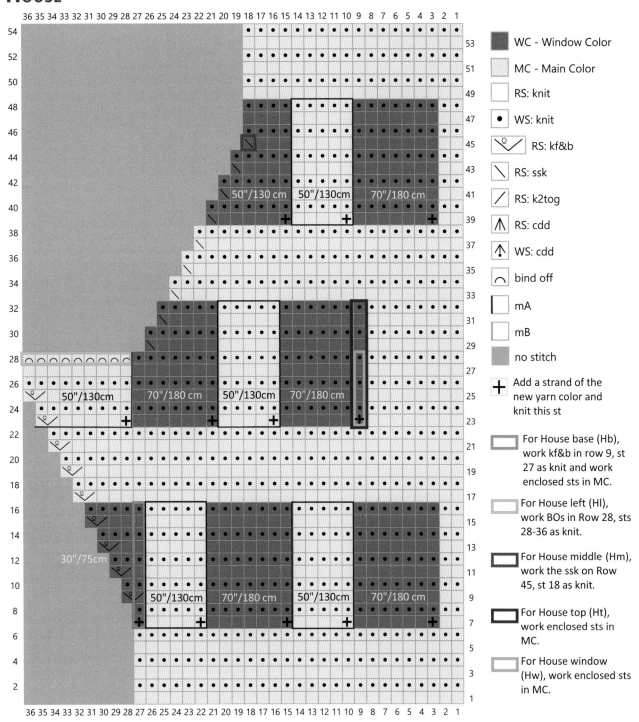

■	WC - Window Color
▨	MC - Main Color
□	RS: knit
•	WS: knit
◩	RS: kf&b
\	RS: ssk
/	RS: k2tog
⋀	RS: cdd
⋀	WS: cdd
⌒	bind off
▢	mA
▢	mB
▨	no stitch
✛	Add a strand of the new yarn color and knit this st

For House base (Hb), work kf&b in row 9, st 27 as knit and work enclosed sts in MC.

For House left (Hl), work BOs in Row 28, sts 28-36 as knit.

For House middle (Hm), work the ssk on Row 45, st 18 as knit.

For House top (Ht), work enclosed sts in MC.

For House window (Hw), work enclosed sts in MC.

MOON

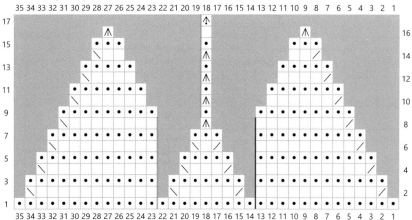

520"/1320 cm

36"/90 cm

192"/490 cm

■ black (Q)
■ blue (C)
□ yellow (M)

ROOF (RF)

RIGHT ROOF (RR)

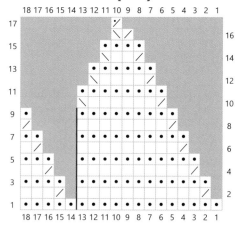

LEFT ROOF (LR)

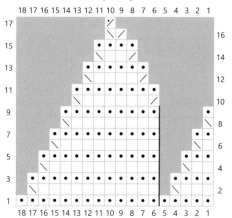

STAR

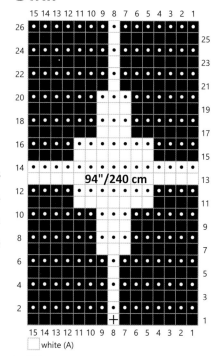

94"/240 cm

□ white (A)
■ black (Q)

Make a Safe in the City pillow to try out the pattern!

This pillow is worked by making a Sky Strip and 2 House Strips and then sewing them together.

See the blanket pattern for yarn colors and abbreviations, needle size, notions, Roof pattern stitches, Sky, House and Part House charts, Roof charts, and notes.

SIZE

18"/45 cm square Pillow Cover

SUPPLIES

18"/45 cm square pillow form
18"/45 cm zipper
Sewing thread matching yarn color A
Sewing needle and safety pins

PILLOW FRONT

Yarn Requirements

The yarn requirements for working the front side only are:

	yds	meters		yds	meters		yds	meters
A	6	6	B	2	2	C	3	3
D	6	6	E	13	12	F	2	2
G	10	10	H	2	2	J	2	2
K	2	2	L	10	10	M	3	3
N	6	6	O	2	2	P	2	2
Q	158	145						

Instructions

Strip 1

Hf1 With MC for right-most House on Strip, CO 27 sts and work [Hf] – 18 sts rem.

Hf2 – Hf3 With MC, turn and CO 9 sts – 27 sts. Work [Hf] – 18 sts. After Hf3, BO loosely.

Strip 2

Ht With MC for Ht, CO 9 sts, work [Ht].

Hm With MC for Hm, turn and CO 9 sts – 18 sts. Work [Hm].

Hb With MC for Hb, turn and CO 9 sts, work [Hb], working Rows 1–28 of House chart only. BO loosely.

Illustration of Safe in the City Pillow

Sky see Figure 7

Cut moon and star yarns after completing each intarsia shape.

With Q, CO 45 sts.

1st Rep (45 sts dec'ing to 36 sts)
　　Rows 1–18: Work [Sky, Rows 36–53] – 9 sts dec'd; 36 sts.

2nd Rep (36 sts inc'ing to 45 sts dec'ing to 27 sts)
　　Row 19: K18, work [Star chart Row], k3, work [Star chart Row], k3.
　　Rows 20–72: Work [Sky].

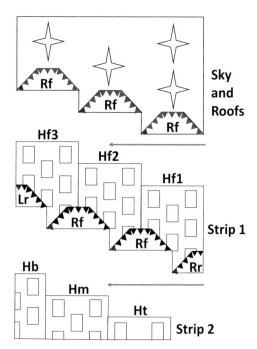

Figure 5: Construction of House Strips and Sky

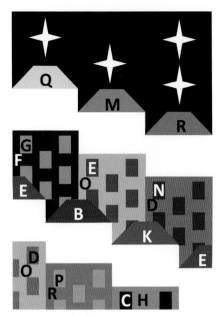

Figure 6: Color Schemes for Pillow

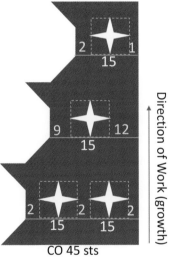

Left edge of pillow
BO loosely

Right edge of pillow

Figure 7: Sky Construction

3rd Rep (27 sts inc'ing to 36 sts dec'ing to 18 sts)
   Row 73: K12, work [Star chart Row], k18.
   Rows 74–126: Work [Sky].

4th Rep (18 sts inc'ing to 27 sts)
   Row 127: K12, work [Star chart Row], k18.
   Rows 128–161: Work [Sky, Rows 1–34] – 9 sts inc'd 27 sts.
   Row 162: Knit.
BO loosely. Cut yarn and fasten off.

Roofs

See Figure 5 for construction and Figure 6 for colors.

Right roof (Rr) In space labeled "Rr" on Strip 1, pu&k 13 sts from red triangle to next corner, pm, and 5 sts to next corner – 18 sts. Work [Rr]. Cut yarn and fasten off.

Roofs full (Rf) In each of the spaces labeled "Rf," in Figure 5, pu&k 13 sts from red triangle to next corner, pm, 9 sts to next corner, pm, and13 sts to next corner – 35 sts. Work [Rf]. Cut yarn and fasten off.

Left roof (Lr) In each of the spaces labeled "Lr" in Figure 5, pu&k 5 sts from red triangle to next corner, pm, and 13 sts to next corner – 18 sts. Work [Lr]. Cut yarn and fasten off.

Pillow Front Assembly

Arrange Sky and Strips 1 and 2 as shown in Figure 6. Using Q and mattress st, sew Strips tog, aligning corners.

PILLOW BACK

Either repeat the Pillow Front (yarn amounts for the Pillow Front should be doubled), or work a plain garter stitch back (instructions below).

Yarn Requirements

365 yds/333 m of Q for a solid color back.

Instructions

CO 81sts. Knit 161 rows (81 ridges). BO loosely.

PILLOW FRONT/BACK ASSEMBLY

See "Assembling Pillows with a Zipper Closure" on page 192.

Design Variations and Ideas

Work all the windows in different colors for a more scrappy, randomized look.

Work striped Roofs by changing colors at the beginning of all RS rows.

Work the Sky in a medium or light blue and omit the Stars. Include some puffy clouds and work the Moon as a yellow sun.

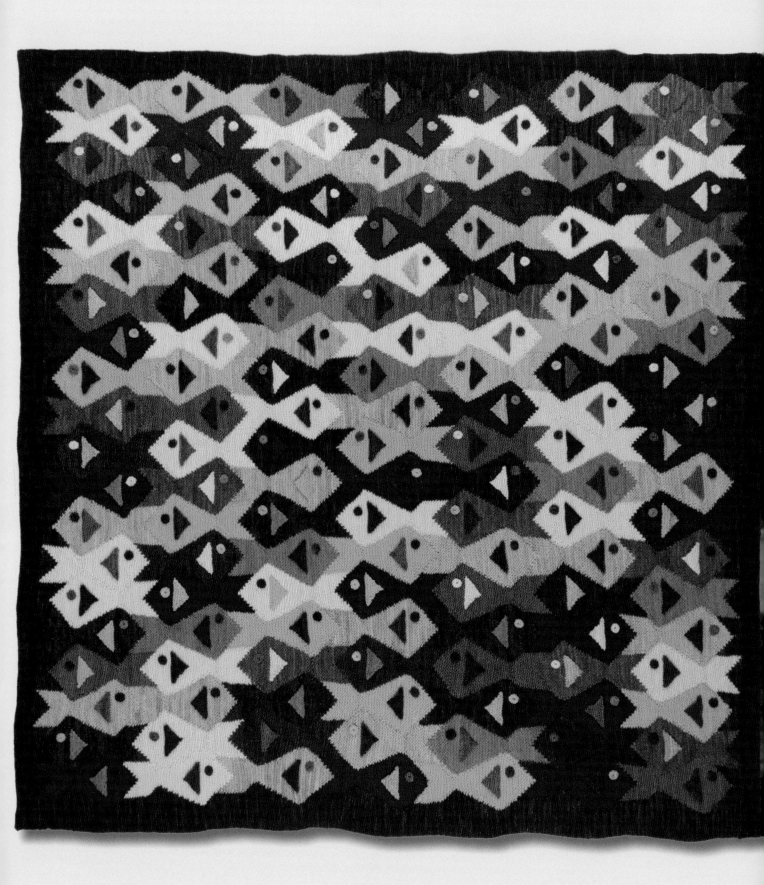

SOMETHING FISHY

Brighten up a room with this school of colorful fish.

TECHNIQUES

Intarsia, sewing, provisional CO, single crochet

SIZE

60 x 67.5"/152 x 171 cm

YARN

Malabrigo Rios, worsted (100% superwash merino wool; 210 yds/192 m; 3.5 oz/100 g):

Pattern color ID	Color swatch	Color ID	Color name	Color description	# Hanks
A		063	Natural	off-white	2
B		096	Sunset	bright yellow	2
C		896	Living Coral	orange-red	2
D		035	Frank Ochre	dark gold	2
E		016	Glazed Carrot	burnt orange	2
F		093	Fucsia	fuchsia	2
G		689	Valentina	light, dusty purple	2
H		148	Hollyhock	purple	1
I		211	Syrah Grapes	darkest purple	5
J		708	Cucumber	mint green	2
K		011	Apple Green	yellow-green	2
L		725	Kris	teal	2
M		213	Pines	dark teal green	2

NEEDLES

US Size 7/4.5 mm 40"/100 cm circular needles

NOTIONS

Tapestry needle, US Size 7/4.5 mm crochet hook, 3 medium bobbins, stitch holders or scrap yarn

GAUGE

18 sts x 36 rows = 4"/10 cm in garter st

NOTES

This blanket is worked in horizontal Strips with a small amount of intarsia. Strips are sewn together. Right and Left Borders are picked up from the edge of the blanket.

BLANKET INSTRUCTIONS

Charts are on page 127.

TOP AND BOTTOM (OUTER) STRIPS

With I, provisionally CO 13 sts.
Knit 8 rows.
Work [OS] 7 times (from chart or st pattern in the green box).
Knit 12 rows.
Place rem 13 sts on holder for Border.

Outer Strip (OS)
Rows 1 (RS)–14: Knit.
Row 15: Knit to last st, kf&b – 1 st inc'd; 14 sts.
Row 16: Knit.
Rows 17–24: Rep [Rows 15 & 16] 4 times – 4 sts inc'd; 18 sts.
Row 25: Knit to last st, k2tog – 1 st dec'd; 17 sts.
Rows 26–28: Knit.
Rows 29–56: Rep [Rows 25 –28] 7 times – 7 sts dec'd; 10 sts.
Row 57: Rep Row 25 – 1 st dec'd; 9 sts.
Row 58: Knit.
Rows 59–66: Rep [Rows 15 & 16] 4 times – 4 sts inc'd; 13 sts.
Rows 67–74: Knit.

FISH STRIPS

Notes for Fish Strips

Refer to the Fish chart. Strip Construction and colors are shown in Figure 1. Fish colors are specified as [MC][EC][FC], defined as:

> **MC:** Main Fish Color
> **EC:** Eye Color
> **FC:** Fin Color

The Previous Main Color (PMC) is the MC of the prev fish. For the first fish of a Strip, PMC is color I. Work MC directly from the skein.

The Eye and Fin (worked in colors EC and FC, respectively) are worked after a Fish is complete. They can be worked after each Fish is complete or after the Strip is complete; however, they should be worked before Assembly of the Strips.

When cutting the right PMC strand (from the skein) after Row 12, leave a 40"/110 cm tail for sewing. Wind up tail and pin to back of Strip to prevent tangling.

Trim remaining yarn ends to 6"/15 cm for weaving in.

STRIPS 1–20

With I, CO 13 sts using a provisional CO.

Knit 8 rows. Work [Fish chart] 7 times, and with I, work [Fish chart, rows 1–12] once more. Place 13 rem sts on holder for Border.

Eye Make 1 per Fish
Wrap EC for Fish twice around L index finger. Slide wraps off finger and pinch circle between thumb and index finger of L hand.

With crochet hook, draw working yarn through center of circle, ch1, make 8 sc through center of circle, then slip st in first sc. Cut yarn leaving 10"/25 cm tail. Pull short yarn to close hole. Fasten off securely.

Thread long tail onto tapestry needle and sew to Fish at location indicated on Fish chart, making stitches around the edges. Fasten off securely on WS.

Fin Make 1 per Fish
With FC for Fish, and working on RS, pull loop through front "bump" identified on Fish chart. This is on Ridge 13. Pull 12 more loops through on subsequent bumps of the row as indicated on Fish chart, and add these loops to needle – 13 sts.

Row 1 (WS): Knit.
Row 2: (RS): K2tog, knit to last 2 sts, ssk – 2 sts dec'd; 11 sts.
Row 3: Knit.
Rows 4–11: Rep [Rows 2 & 3] 4 times – 8 sts dec'd; 3 sts.
Row 12: Cdd – 2 sts dec'd; 1 st.
Cut yarn, leaving 10"/25 cm tail. Weave in the short tail on WS of Fin. With long tail, make several stitches to attach point of Fin to Fish at ridge 19 at location shown on Fish chart. Weave in ends on WS of Fin.

ASSEMBLY

Lay out completed Strips as shown in Figure 1, orienting OS and Fish Strips according to arrows. Using matching colored long PMC tails, where available, and mattress stitch, sew Strips tog matching corners as shown in Figure 2, where red dotted lines show alignment for corners of adjacent tails and green dotted lines show alignment for corners of the fish body.

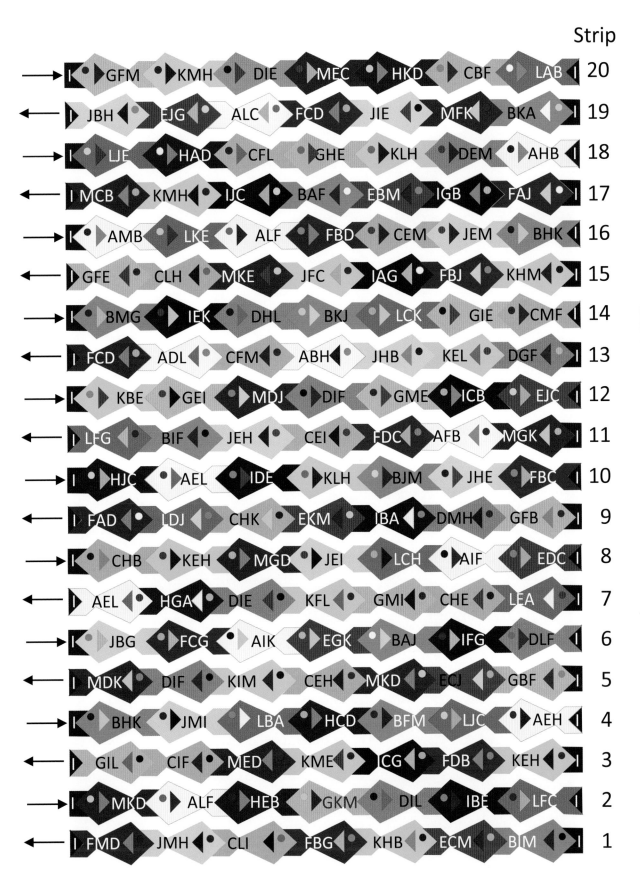

Figure 1: Colors [MC][EC][FC] and Construction for Strips

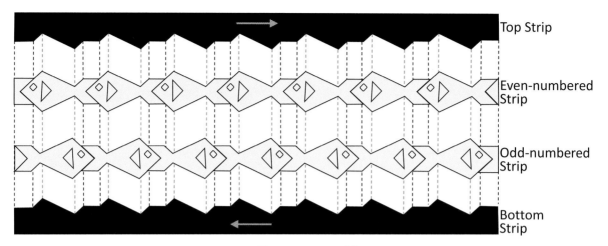

Figure 2: Assembly

BORDERS

RIGHT BORDER

Transfer provisionally CO sts or sts on holder from Bottom Strip, Strips 1–20, and Top Strip to needle – 308 sts. Starting on RS, with I, knit 16 rows. BO loosely.

LEFT BORDER

Work as for Right Border, attaching I at top left corner of blanket.

FINISHING

Weave in ends and block to measurements.

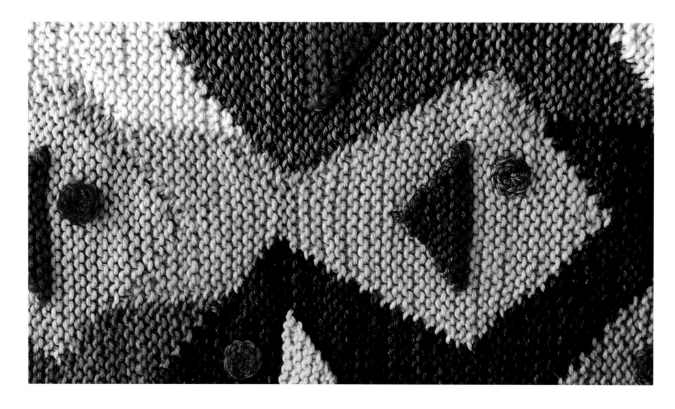

OUTER STRIP (OS)

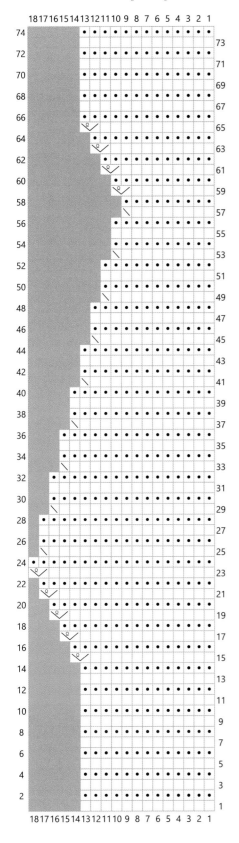

FISH

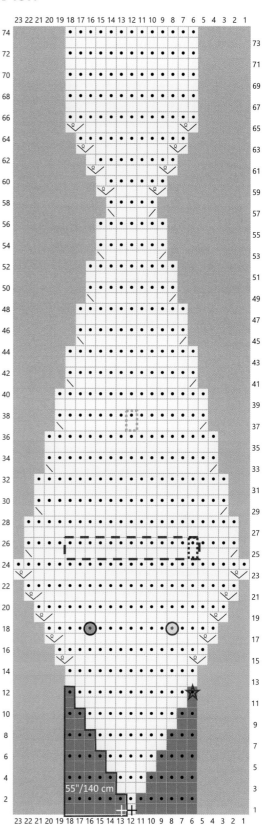

	RS: knit
•	WS: knit
╱	RS: k2tog
╲	RS: ssk
⌄	RS: kf&b
	no stitch
	Previous Main Color (PMC)
	Main Color (MC)
	Eye Color (EC)
	Fin Color (FC)
✚	Add yarn strand
⌐¬	Sts on which to pu&k for fin (ridge 13)
⌐⌐	1st st on which to pu&k for fin (ridge 13)
	Location to attach end point of Fin
●	Location to attach eye for even-numbered Strips
○	Location to attach eye for odd-numbered Strips
☆	When cutting off PMC yarn, leave long tail of 40"/110 cm for sewing strips

55"/140 cm

Make a Something Fishy pillow to try out the pattern!

This pillow is worked by making 4 Fish Strips and 2 Outer Strips, then sewing the Strips together.

See the blanket pattern for yarn colors and abbreviations, needle size, notions, charts, instructions for Fins and Eyes, and notes.

SUPPLIES

20"/50 cm square pillow form
20"/50 cm zipper
Sewing thread matching yarn color A
Sewing needle and safety pins

PILLOW FRONT

Yarn Requirements

	yds	meters		yds	meters		yds	meters
A	40	40	B	40	40	C	40	40
F	40	40	G	40	40	J	40	40
K	40	40	L	40	40	M	200	190

Instructions

Fish Strips 1–4 see "Notes for Fish Strips" on page 124.

Provisionally CO 13 sts.
Knit 8 rows. Work [Fish chart] twice sequentially, then work [Fish chart, rows 1–12] once more in colors specified in Figure 3. BO loosely.

Eye – Make 1 per Fish

See instructions for "Eye" on page 124.

Fin - Make 1 per Fish

See instructions for "Fin" on page 124.

Top and Bottom Strips

With I, provisionally CO 3 sts, pm, CO 13 sts. Knit 8 rows. Work [OS chart] twice as follows: On RS, knit to m, then work chart. On WS, work chart to m, then knit to end. Knit 12 rows. BO loosely.

Assembly

Lay out completed Strips as shown in Figure 3, orienting according to arrows. Using long PMC tails and mattress stitch, sew Strips tog matching corners as shown in Figure 2, where red dotted lines show alignment for corners of adjacent tails and green dotted lines show alignment for corners of the fish.

Illustration of Something Fishy Pillow

PILLOW BACK

Either repeat the Pillow Front (yarn amounts for the Pillow Front should be doubled) or work a plain garter stitch back (instructions below).

Yarn Requirements

365 yds/333 m of Q for a solid color back.

Instructions

CO 81 sts. Knit 161 rows (81 ridges). BO loosely.

FRONT/BACK ASSEMBLY

See instructions for "Assembling Pillows with a Zipper Closure" on page 192.

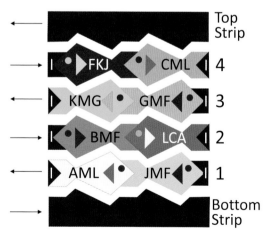

Figure 3: Colors and Layout for Strips

Something Fishy Top
A loose-fitting drop-shoulder top

Illustration of Something Fishy Top

SIZES

Finished Chest Measurement for S, (M, L, 1X, 2X):
38"/97 cm (42"/107 cm; 46"/117 cm; 50"/127 cm;
54"/137 cm)

5"/13 cm ease through chest. Length is 23.5"/60 cm.

YARN REQUIREMENTS

For both Front and Back
Color M: 650 yds/600 m (730 yds/670 m; 840 yds/770;
950 yds/870 m; 1,050 yds/970 m; 1,160 yds/1070 m)

	yds	meters		yds	meters		yds	meters
A	80	80	**B**	80	80	**C**	80	80
F	80	80	**G**	80	80	**J**	80	80
K	80	80	**L**	80	80			

INSTRUCTIONS

Front see Figure 4

Center Panel

Make "Fish Strips 1-4" on page 128, placing sts on
holder at the end of each Strip.

Top and Bottom Strips

CO 12 sts, pm, CO 13 sts – 25 sts. Knit 8 rows. Work
[OS chart,] twice as follows: On RS, knit to m, then
work chart. On WS, work chart to m, then knit to end.
Knit 12 rows. Place sts on holder.

Assembly of Strips see "Assembly" on page 128

Right Panel for Sizes M (L, 1X, and 2X)

With RS facing, transfer sts from right edge of Center
Panel to circular needle. Knit 5 (10, 14, 19) ridges. BO.

Left Panel for Sizes M (L, 1X, and 2X)

With sts on left edge of Center Panel, rep as for Right
Panel.

Back

Work as for "Front." Block Front and Back to
measurements. Lay Front and Back on flat surface.
Using measurements in Figure 4, pm's for openings.

FRONT/BACK ASSEMBLY

Working on the RS, with tapestry needle and Y, using
mattress st, sew shoulders tog along red dashed
lines. Sew left edges tog from bottom corner to
marked beg of armhole opening along red dashed
line. Repeat for right edges.

Note: For best results, sew on a flat surface.

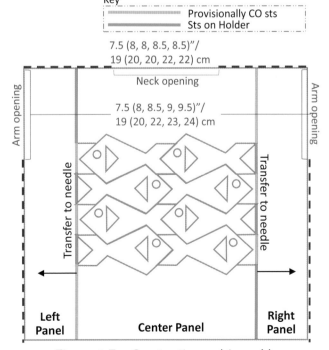

Figure 4: Top Construction and Assembly

STAY PAW-SITIVE

Take a lesson from our canine friends and greet each new day with joy!

TECHNIQUES

Sewing, crochet

SIZE

Small (Large): 41.5 x 55"/105 x 140 cm (55 x 82"/140 x 208 cm)

YARN

Ella Rae, Classic Superwash, worsted (100% superwash wool; 219 yds/200 m; 3.5 oz/100 g):

Pattern color ID	Color swatch	Color ID	Color name	Color description	# Skeins for Size	
					Small	Large
A		1	Vanilla	off-white	4	5
B		4	Yellow	light yellow	2	3
C		69	Sunflower	goldenrod	2	3
D		78	Lime	yellow green	1	2
E		130	Bermuda Heather	light aqua	2	3
F		66	Emerald City	jade green	1	2
G		139	Deep Blue Sea Heather	dark teal	1	2
H		6	Light Blue	light blue	2	3
I		92	Blueberry	medium blue	1	1
J		28	Deep Navy	dark navy	2	4
K		85	Medium Violet	medium violet	2	2
L		3	Pink	pink	1	2
M		76	Fuchsia	magenta	2	3

NEEDLES

US Size 7/4.5 mm 40"/100 cm circular needles

NOTIONS

Tapestry needle, locking stitch markers or safety pins, stitch holders

GAUGE

19 sts and 38 rows = 4"/10 cm in garter st

NOTES

The blanket is worked in Blocks that are sewn together. Blocks are worked in a series of shapes, then nose and eye details are added after each Block is completed. The nose is knitted and sewn on and the eyes are worked

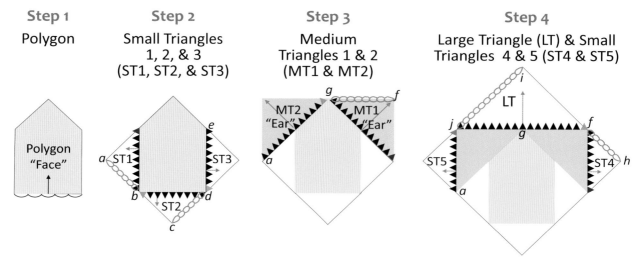

Step 1
Polygon

Step 2
Small Triangles
1, 2, & 3
(ST1, ST2, & ST3)

Step 3
Medium
Triangles 1 & 2
(MT1 & MT2)

Step 4
Large Triangle (LT) & Small
Triangles 4 & 5 (ST4 & ST5)

Figure 1: Block Construction

in slip st crochet. Triangular edge shapes are worked from sts picked up on edges of the assembled blanket. Borders are picked up and knit on the edges of the blanket.

Tip 1: Before beginning see "Single Crochet for Edging" on page 189.

Tip 2: Some shapes require leaving a long tail that is used later for sewing Blocks together. To avoid tangling, wind long tails into a small ball and secure to edge with a locking stitch marker until needed.

Tip 3: When using slip st to move yarn to a new starting location, insert hook in each garter st bump (last st on a ridge) and every other "leg" (the outermost yarn strand of the edge st bet two ridges).

BLANKET INSTRUCTIONS

BLOCK – MAKE 18 (39)

See Figure 1 for construction, Figure 2 for color key, and Figure 4 (page 134) for color schemes. Each Block is worked in a series of shapes: Polygon, Small Triangles 1, 2, and 3 (ST1, ST2, and ST3), Medium Triangles 1 and 2 (MT1 and MT2), Large Triangle (LT), and Small Triangles 4 and 5 (ST4 and ST5). Starting stitches for each shape after the Polygon are generated by pu&k from the edges of previously completed shapes.

Color schemes have 5 colors: [BC][FC][EC][NC][LC], defined as:

    BC: Background Color
    FC: Face Color
    EC: Ear Color
    NC: Nose Color
    LC: Lash Color (for eyes)

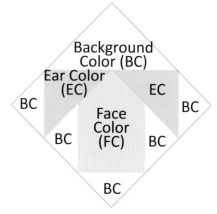

Figure 2: Block Parts and Color Identification

Polygon

See Figure 1, Step 1 for construction.
With FC, CO 21 sts. Knit 41 rows (21 garter st ridges, including CO row). On RS, pm's on 3rd (m1), 9th (m2), 13th (m3), and 19th (m4) sts, marking lash locations.
Work [DT] (page 133), starting on Row 2. Cut yarn and fasten off.

SMALL TRIANGLES 1, 2, AND 3

See Figure 1, Step 2 for construction.

Small Triangle 1 (ST1)

In space labeled "ST1," with BC, pu&k 21 sts (1 st per garter st ridge) from red triangle to **b**.

Work [DT]. Do not cut yarn. With crochet hook and starting with rem st on needle, work slip st from **a** to **b**. Transfer rem loop to needle.

Small Triangle 2 (ST2)

In space labeled "ST2," pu&k 20 sts from blue triangle at **b** to **d** – 21 sts.

Work [DT]. Do not cut yarn. With crochet hook and starting with rem st on needle, work slip st from **c** to **d**. Transfer rem loop to needle.

Small Triangle 3 (ST3)

In space labeled "ST3," pu&k 20 sts from green triangle at **d** to **e** – 21 sts.

Work [DT]. Do not cut yarn. Place rem st on marker for ST4.

MEDIUM TRIANGLES 1 AND 2

See Figure 1, Step 3 for construction.

Medium Triangle 1 (MT1)

In space labeled "MT1," with EC, pu&k 29 sts from red triangle to **g**.

Work [DT]. Do not cut yarn. With crochet hook, and starting with rem st on needle, work slip st loosely from **f** to **g** in Figure 1, Step 3. Transfer rem slip loop to needle.

Medium Triangle 2 (MT2)

In space labeled "MT2," starting at blue triangle at **g**, pu&k 28 sts to **a** – 29 sts. Work [DT]. Cut yarn, and fasten off.

SMALL TRIANGLES 4 AND 5 AND LARGE TRIANGLE

See Figure 1, Step 4 for construction.

Small Triangle 4 (ST4)

Transfer rem st from ST3 from marker to needle, and in space labeled "ST4," with uncut BC yarn still attached, pu&k 20 sts from red triangle to **f** – 21 sts.

Work [DT]. Do not cut yarn. With crochet hook, and starting with rem loop on needle, work slip st loosely from **h** to **f**, as shown in Figure 1, Step 4, to move yarn to starting position for Large Triangle.

Large Triangle (LT)

Transfer last slip st to needle and starting at blue triangle, pu&k 20 sts along MT1 to **g**, bli, pu&k 21 sts

Decreasing Triangle (DT) – odd sts dec'ing to 1 st
Row 1 (WS): Knit.
Row 2 (RS): K2tog, knit to last 2 sts, ssk – 2 sts dec'd.
Row 3 (WS): Knit.
Rep [Rows 2 & 3] until 3 sts rem, ending after a WS row.
Next row (RS): Cdd – 2 sts dec'd; 1 st.

along MT2 from **g** to **j** – 43 sts. Work [DT]. Do not cut yarn. With crochet hook, and starting with rem loop on needle, slip st loosely from **i** to **j**, shown in Figure 1, Step 4, to move yarn to starting position for ST5.

Small Triangle 5 (ST5)

Transfer last slip st to needle and pu&k 20 sts from orange triangle at **j** to **a** – 21 sts. Work [DT]. Cut yarn and fasten off, leaving 40"/100 cm tail.

Eyelashes See Figure 3 and Figure 5 on page 135 (page 135)

Cut 25"/60 cm of LC. On WS tie one end of yarn to bump next to m1. Holding yarn on WS, use crochet hook to draw a loop of yarn through to RS through red dot (st marked by m1). *Make 6 slip sts by inserting crochet hook from RS in sts marked by yellow dots in Figure 3. Work last slip st of Right eye in m2 st; pull yarn all the way through to RS, then pull all the way to WS*, weave in on WS to starting position of Left Lash at green dot at m3 st. Begin Left Lash by using crochet hook to pull loop through to RS at green dot at m3 st.

Rep bet * and * for m3 and m4. Cut yarn and fasten off. Trim ends and weave in on WS of Lash stitches.

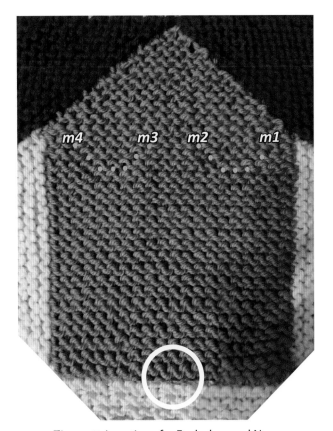

Figure 3: Locations for Eyelashes and Nose

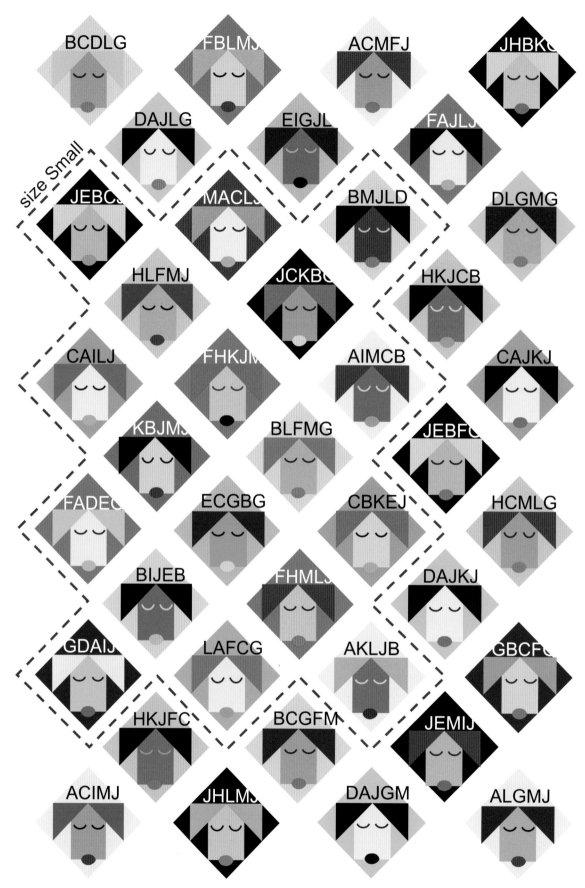

Figure 4: Layout and Colors for Blanket (Size Small enclosed in dashed lines)

Nose

With NC, CO 1 st, leaving 10"/25 cm tail. Work [Nose]. Cut yarn and fasten off, leaving 15"/40 cm tail.

Thread long CO tail onto tapestry needle and, with mattress st, sew tog edges to form a circle.

Thread BO tail onto tapestry needle. On RS of Block, position Nose as shown in Figure 3 and sew around edge of Nose to attach to Block. On WS, fasten off.

Nose – 1 st inc'ing to 9 sts, dec'ing to 1 st

Row 1: (K1, yo, k1, yo, k1, yo, k1) in same st – 6 sts inc'd; 7 sts.
Row 2: Knit.
Row 3: Kf&b, knit to last st, kf&b – 2 sts inc'd; 9 sts.
Rows 4 – 6: Knit.
Row 7: K2tog, knit to last 2 sts, ssk – 2 sts dec'd; 7 sts.
Row 8: Knit.
Row 9: Slip 6 sts, 1-by-1, to R needle, knit last st. Pass slipped sts 1-by-1 over knitted st – 6 sts dec'd; 1 st.

Figure 6: Completed Eyelashes

ASSEMBLY OF BLOCKS

Arrange Blocks as in Figure 6. On RS, using long tails of matching color (when available), sew Blocks together along red dashed lines to form diagonal Strips, matching corners and aligning tips of ears to corner of face at black dots as shown in Figure 7. Sew Strips together along blue lines. When sewing a garter stitch edge to a garter stitch edge, use mattress st, when sewing a slip stitched edge, insert needle through the front loop.

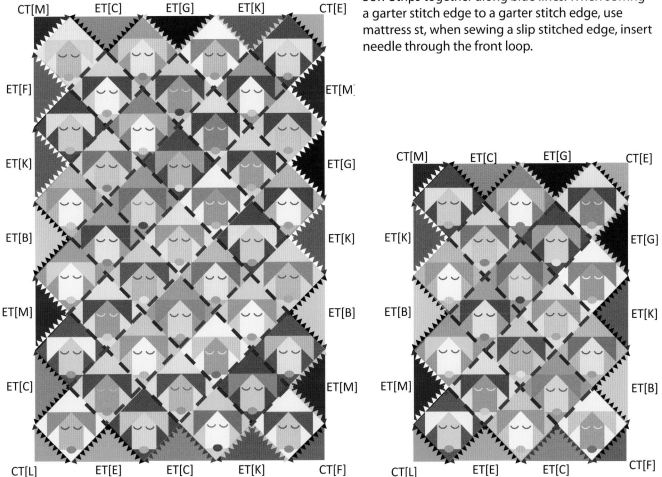

Figure 5: Edge and Corner Triangles

Edge Triangles (ET)

On RS, in each of the 10 (16) edge shapes labeled "ET[<color>]" in Figure 6 (page 135), with yarn color indicated in the square brackets, pu&k 45 sts from red triangle to next corner, pm, pu&k 45 sts to next corner – 90 sts. Work [ET]. Cut yarn and fasten off.

> **Edge Triangle (ET)** – 90 sts dec'ing to 2 sts
>
> **Row 1 (WS):** Knit.
> **Row 2 (RS):** K2tog, knit to 2 sts bef m, ssk, sm, k2tog, knit to last 2 sts, ssk – 4 sts dec'd; 86 sts.
> **Row 3:** Knit.
> **Rows 4–43:** Rep [Rows 2 & 3] 20 times – 80 sts dec'd; 6 sts.
> **Row 44 (RS):** Cdd twice – 4 sts dec'd; 2 sts. Pass 1st st over 2nd st.

Corner Triangles (CT)

On RS, in each of the 4 corner shapes labeled "CT[<color>]" with yarn color indicated in square brackets of label in Figure 6 (page 135) and starting at red triangle, pu&k 45 sts to next corner. Work [DT] (page 133). Cut yarn and fasten off.

Figure 7: Alignment Points for Assembly

BORDERS

Right Border

On RS, starting at the bottom right corner of blanket, with A, pu&k 256 (384) sts (32 sts per CT edge and 64 sts per ET edge) on right edge of blanket.

Knit 11 rows. BO loosely, leaving last st on needle for Top Border.

Top Border

On RS, pu&k 6 sts on edge of Right Border and 192 (256) sts on top edge of blanket – 199 (263) sts.

Knit 11 rows. BO loosely, leaving last st on needle.

Left Border

Pu&k 6 sts on left edge of Top Border and 256 (384) sts on left edge of blanket – 263 (391) sts.

Knit 11 rows. BO loosely, leaving last st on needle.

Bottom Border

Pu&k 6 sts on bottom edge of Left Border, 192 (256) sts on bottom edge of blanket, and 7 sts on bottom edge of Right Border – 206 (270) sts.

Knit 11 rows. BO loosely. Cut yarn and fasten off.

FINISHING

Weave in ends.

Make a Stay Paw-sitive pillow to try out the pattern!

This pillow is worked by making Block and adding 4 corners. A short seam is sewn to join the corners. See the blanket pattern for yarn colors, abbreviations, needle size, notions, pattern stitches, and notes.

SIZE

16"/40 cm square Pillow Cover

SUPPLIES

16"/40 cm square pillow form
16"/40 cm zipper
Sewing thread matching yarn color B
Sewing needle and safety pins

PILLOW FRONT

Yarn Requirements

The Block is worked in colors BFENL [background] [face][ears][nose][lash]

The yarn requirements for working the front side only are:

	yds	meters		yds	meters		yds	meters
B	220	200	E	40	40	F	30	30
L	10	10	N	10	10			

Instructions

Block

Using color scheme BFENL, make one Block (instructions on page 132)

Corners

In each space labeled "Bd" in Figure 8, leave a 10"/25 cm tail, and pu&k 41 sts from red triangle to next corner.

Row 1(WS): Knit.
Row 2: Kf&b, knit to last st, kf&b – 2 sts inc'd; 43 sts.
Rows 3–10: Rep [Rows 1 & 2] 4 times – 8 sts inc'd; 51 sts.
Work [DT] (Instructions on page 133).

Using long tails and mattress st, sew edges of adjacent corners tog along blue-dashed lines.

Illustration of Stay Paw-sitive Pillow

PILLOW BACK

Either repeat the Pillow Front (yarn amounts for the Pillow Front should be doubled) or work a plain garter stitch back (instructions below).

Yarn Requirements

330 yds/300 m of B for a solid color back.

Instructions

CO 76 sts. Knit 151 rows (76 ridges). BO loosely.

FRONT/BACK ASSEMBLY

See instructions for "Assembling Pillows with a Zipper Closure" on page 192.

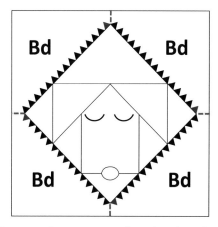

Figure 8: Construction of Borders for Pillow

Stay Paw-sitive Poncho

This poncho is made from 12 Blocks and 4 Truncated Blocks. Blocks are sewn together and a ribbed neck is worked from stitches picked up and knitted around the center opening. A garter stitch border is added by picking up and knitting sts around outer edge.

See the blanket pattern for yarn colors and abbreviations, needle size, notions, notes, pattern stitches, and instructions for Eyes and Noses.

SIZE

Length from front/back tip to top of neckband: 23.5"/60 cm

YARN REQUIREMENTS

	yds	meters		yds	meters		yds	meters
A	300	280	B	170	160	C	250	230
D	90	90	E	160	150	F	190	180
G	80	80	H	140	130	J	90	90
K	120	110	L	140	130	M	70	70

NEEDLES

US 7/4.5 mm straight or circular needles for working Blocks

US 7/4.5 mm circular needle of 16"/40 cm for working neckband and borders

INSTRUCTIONS

Using Figure 1 and the Block instructions (both are on page 132) make 12 Blocks (Bk) and 4 Truncated Blocks (TB) in color schemes shown in Figure 10. TB is a Block from which the Large Triangle (LT) is omitted.

ASSEMBLY

Arrange Bks and TBs into four groups as shown in Figure 10. On RS, using long tails of matching color (when available), sew Blocks tog along blue dashed lines in Figure 9, matching corners and aligning tips of ears to corner of face at black dots in Figure 7 (page 136). Arrange groups as shown in Figure 9, orienting according to arrows. Sew groups together along red dashed lines. When sewing a slip stitched edge, insert needle through the front loop.

Illustration of Stay Paw-sitive Poncho

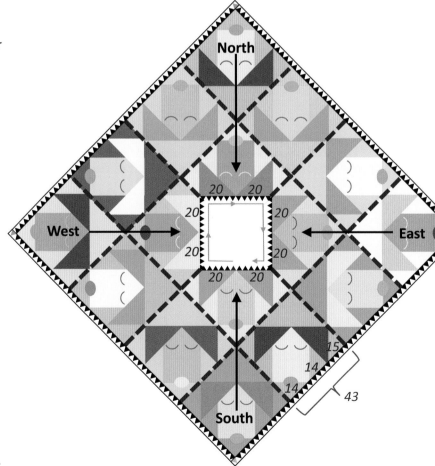

Figure 9: Layout and Assembly of Poncho

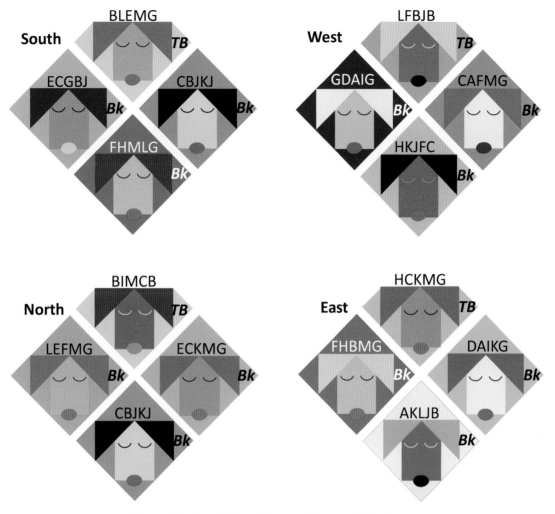

Figure 10: Block Color Schemes, Arranged into Groups

Neckband

With A and circular needle, start at red triangle on top edge of the South group (Figure 9), and pu&k 20 sts to next corner, *40 sts to next corner (20 sts on each "Ear"); rep from * twice more, then pu&k 20 sts from corner to beg of pu&k – 160 sts. Join in the round.

Rnd 1: *K1, p1; rep from * to end.
Rnds 2–8: Rep Rnd 1.

BO using Cable BO (see "Cable BO" on page 189).

Border

North-East Border

With A and circular needle, pu&k 172 sts from red triangle at the corner of the East group (Figure 9) to the end of the edge (43 per Block, which can be divided into sets of 14, 14, and 15 on edges of STs). Knit 3 rows. BO loosely, leaving last st on needle for next Border.

North-West Border

Starting at green triangle at North corner of Figure 9, pu&k 1 st on left edge of North-East Border, and 172 sts to the end of the edge – 174 sts. Knit 3 rows. BO loosely.

South-West Border

Rep as for North-West Border.

South-East Border

Starting at yellow triangle at South corner (Figure 9), pu&k 1 st on the left edge of the South-West Border, then 172 sts to the end of the edge, then 2 sts on the right edge of the North-East Border – 176 sts. Knit 3 rows. BO loosely.

FINISHING

Weave in ends and block to measurements.

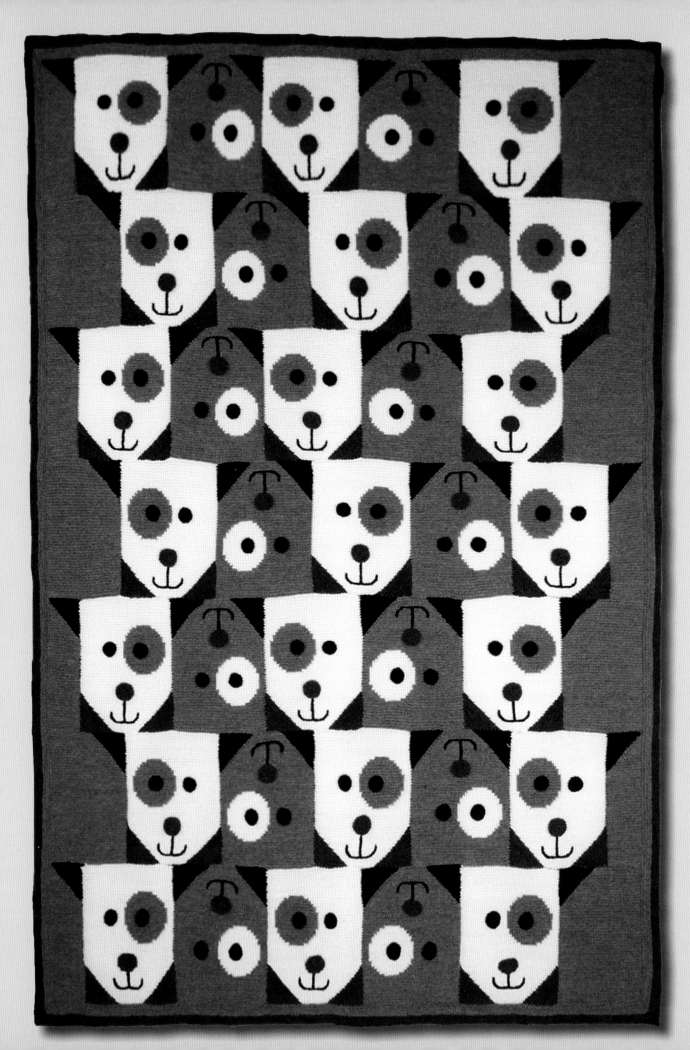

UPSIDE DOWG

**This topsy-turvy pack of dogs worked in monochromes
will keep you (and the dog?) warm and comfortable.**

TECHNIQUES

Intarsia, sewing

SIZE

55.5 x 77"/141 x 196 cm

YARN

Valley Yarns, Northampton, worsted (100% wool; 247 yds/226 m; 3.5 oz/100g):

Pattern color ID	Color swatch	Color ID	Color name	Color description	# Skeins
A		02	Natural	off-white	7
B		50	Medium Gray	medium gray	9
C		06	Dark Gray	almost black	3
D		07	Black	black	3

NEEDLES

US 7/4.5 mm circular of minimum length 40"/100 cm

GAUGE

19 sts x 38 rows = 4"/10 cm

NOTES

- The blanket is worked in individual Blocks that are sewn together. The Dog Blocks have a small amount of intarsia for the eye patch. The Eyeball and Nose are knitted separately and tacked on. The Mouth is embroidered. Stitches for new shapes are generated using pick up and knit.

- Stitch generation (pu&k or CO) is counted as Row 1, and the pattern stitch or row-by-row instructions that follow starts with Row 2, so that all RS rows are odd-numbered, and all WS rows are even-numbered. An exception to this convention is the instructions for the Nose.

- A ridge in garter stitch knitting is a distinctive feature created by two rows of knitting. To determine the number of rows knitted, after completing a WS row, turn the work to the RS and count the number of ridges, then divide by 2.

- See "Single Crochet for Edging" on page 189.

BLANKET INSTRUCTIONS

Dog Block - make in colors/ quantities specified in Figure 1

Face

With color for Face (either A or B), CO 12 sts. Work [Face].

> **Face** – 12 sts inc'ing to 40 sts
> Instructions are for Dog Right (DR) with changes for Dog Left (DL) in square brackets.

Row 2: Knit.
Row 3: Kf&b, knit to last st, kf&b – 2 sts inc'd; 14 sts.
Row 4: Knit.
Rows 5–30: Rep [Rows 3 &4] 13 times – 26 sts inc'd; 40 sts.
Rows 31–44: Knit 14 rows (adds 7 ridges).
Row 45 : K3 [19], work [Eye Patch chart, row 1, on page 146] over next 18 sts, knit to end.
Rows 46–80: Knit, working next row of established Eye Patch Chart.
Note: Last row of Eye Patch Chart is worked on Row 80, so Eye Patch yarn color may be cut after that row.
Rows 81–100: Knit. BO loosely. Cut yarn and fasten off, leaving 40"/100 cm tail. Wind up tail and pin to corner of Block to avoid tangling.

Corners

See Figure 2.

Cr1 In space labeled "Cr1," with color for Corner, working on RS, and starting at the red triangle, pu&k 21 sts to next corner. Work [Cr].

Cr2 In space labeled "Cr2," with color for Corner, working on RS, and starting at the green triangle, pu&k 21 sts to next corner. Work [Cr].

> **Corner (Cr)** – 21 sts dec'ing to 0 sts

Row 2 (WS): Knit.
Row 3 (RS): K2tog, knit to last 2 sts, ssk – 2 sts dec'd;
Row 4: Knit.
Rep [Rows 3 & 4] until 3 sts rem, after working RS row.
Next WS row: Cdd – 2 sts dec'd; 1 st.
Cut yarn and fasten off, leaving 20"/45 cm tail.

Make **4**
Large Rectangle
Left (LL) in BD

Make **3**
Large Rectangle
Right (LR) in BD

Make **3**
Small Rectangle
Left (SL) in BD

Make **4**
Small Rectangle
Right (SR) in BD

Make **7** Dog-Left (DL)

Make **7** Dog-Right (DR)

Make **10** Dog-Left (DL)

Make **11** Dog-Right (DR)

For DL and DR, color D is used for eye and mouth

Figure 1: Block Colors and Quantities

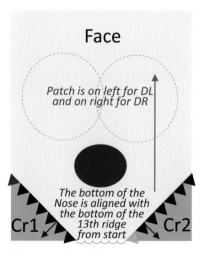

Figure 2: Dog Block Construction

Nose

The Nose is worked separately and tacked on. With C, using long-tail method, CO 22 sts, leaving 12"/30.5 cm tail. Work [Nose].

Nose – 22 sts dec'ing to 10 sts
Row 2 (WS): Knit. **Row 3: (RS):** K1, (k2tog, k1) 3 times, k3, (k2tog, k1) 3 times – 6 sts dec'd; 16 sts. **Row 4:** Knit. **Row 5:** K1, k2tog 3 times, k2, k2tog 3 times, k1 – 6 sts dec'd; 10 sts. **Row 6:** Knit. Cut yarn leaving 12"/30 cm tail. Thread tail onto tapestry needle and insert tail through 10 sts on needle. Pull taut and fasten off securely. On RS, with mattress st, seam edges together to form an oval. Weave in end on reverse side.

Tack Nose as shown in Figure 3, with the bottom of the Nose aligned with the 13th ridge of the Face. See "Tacking Embellishments" on page 189.

Eyeballs - Make 2

The Eyeballs are worked separately and tacked on. With D, CO 18 sts (CO is Row 1). Work [Eyeball].

Tack Eyeballs to the Block at locations shown. See "Tacking Embellishments" on page 189.

Eyeball – 18 sts dec'ing to 0 sts
Row 2 (WS): Knit. **Row 3 (RS):** K2tog 9 times – 9 sts dec'd; 9 sts. **Row 4:** Knit. Cut yarn leaving 12"/30 cm tail. Thread tail onto tapestry needle and insert tail through 9 sts on needle. Pull taut and fasten off securely. On RS, with mattress st, seam edges together to form an oval. Weave in end on reverse side.

Mouth

Cut 30"/75 cm of D and thread onto tapestry needle. Using embroidery *chain stitch,* and using Figure 3 as a guide, embroider a curved line from *a* to *b* to *c*. Pull the needle and thread to the WS of the work and travel the yarn (make stitches into the threads of existing embroidery) to *b*. Bring the yarn up to the RS, around left index finger and back down to the WS to make the first loop of the vertical part of the mouth. Continue the *chain stitch,* making 7 more loops, to the bottom center of the nose at *d*.

Tips for positioning of Nose and Mouth Embroidery

Center the Nose on the vertical line. Point *a* of the Mouth in Figure 3 is 6 sts to the right of the center of the Block and 10 ridges up from the bottom of the Block. Use scrap yarn and a tapestry needle to create a temporary vertical line between stitches 20 and 21 of the Block to mark the center vertical line, then count over 6 stitches from the vertical and up 10 rows from the bottom to *a*.

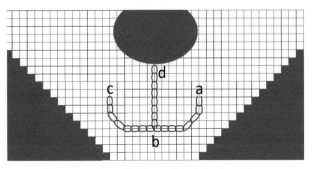

Figure 3: Mouth Chain-Stitch Embroidery

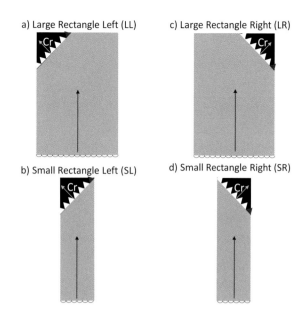

a) Large Rectangle Left (LL) c) Large Rectangle Right (LR)

b) Small Rectangle Left (SL) d) Small Rectangle Right (SR)

Figure 4: Rectangle Blocks Construction

LARGE RECTANGLE RIGHT (LR) [AND SMALL RECTANGLE RIGHT (SR)]

Make in colors/quantities specified in Figure 1.

Directions are for LR, with changes for SR in square brackets.

With B, CO 34 [15] sts. *Note:* CO is Row 1.

Rows 2–72: Knit (adds 36 ridges).

Work [RD] (adds 14 ridges) – 14 sts dec'd; 20 [1] sts. End of SR.

Right Decrease (RD)
Row 1: K2tog, knit to end – 1 st dec'd. **Row 2:** Knit. **Rows 3–28:** Rep [Rows 1 & 2] 13 times – 13 sts dec'd. End of SR.

For LR only: BO loosely.

Cut yarn and fasten off, leaving 40"/100 cm tail.

With D, and starting at the red triangle in Figure 4.c [4.d], pu&k 21 sts to end of edge.

Work [Cr] on page 142.

LARGE RECTANGLE LEFT (LL) [AND SMALL RECTANGLE LEFT (SL)]

Make in colors/quantities specified in Figure 1.

Directions are for LL, with changes for SL in square brackets.

With B, CO 34 [15] sts.

Note: CO is Row 1.

Rows 2–72: Knit (36 ridges, including CO row).

Work [LD] (adds 14 ridges) – 14 sts dec'd; 20 [1] sts.

Left Decrease (LD)
Row 1: Knit to last 2 sts, ssk – 1 st dec'd. **Row 2:** Knit. **Rows 3–28:** Rep [Rows 1 & 2] 13 times – 13 sts dec'd. End of SL.

For LL only: BO loosely.

Cut yarn and fasten off, leaving 15"/40 cm tail.

With D, and starting at the red triangle in Figure 4.a [4.b], pu&k 21 sts to end of edge.

Work [Cr].

ASSEMBLY

Lay out completed Blocks as shown in Figure 5. Orient Blocks as shown. With long tails of matching color (when available) and mattress stitch, sew Blocks into horizontal Strips along red dashed lines, then sew Strips together, aligning the center of the top of each Dog Block with the seam of the two Blocks above, as shown by the blue dotted lines. Use pins or stitch markers to keep Strips aligned when sewing.

BORDERS

RIGHT BORDER

With B, and starting at the bottom-right corner of the blanket on the RS, pu&k 350 sts (50 sts per dog block) to right-top corner of blanket. Work [MB].

> **Mitered** Border (MB)
>
> **Row 2 (WS):** Knit.
> **Row 3:** Kf&b, knit to last st, kf&b – 2 sts inc'd.
> **Row 4: Knit.**
> **Rows 5–8:** Rep [Rows 3 & 4] twice – 4 sts inc'd. Cut B, leaving 10"/25 cm tail.
> **Rows 9–16:** With C, rep [Rows 3 & 4] 4 times – 8 sts inc'd.
> BO loosely. Cut C, leaving 10"/25 cm tail.

LEFT BORDER

Work as for Right Border beg pu&k on top-right corner of Blanket.

TOP BORDER

With B, and starting at the top-right corner of the blanket on the RS, pu&k 249 sts (40 sts per dog Block, 34 sts per LR [or LL] and 15 sts per SR [or SL]). Work [MB].

BOTTOM BORDER

Work as for Top Border beg pu&k on bottom-left corner of blanket.

FINISHING

Using matching long tails from Borders, working on RS, with mattress st, sew corner seams.

Weave in ends.

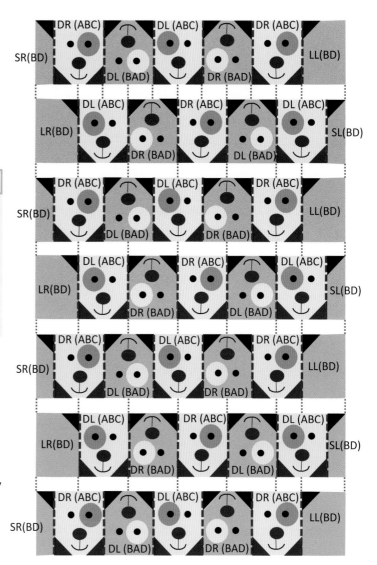

Figure 5: Assembly

CHART

Eʏᴇ Pᴀᴛᴄʜ

Worked on Rows 46–80 of Dog Face.

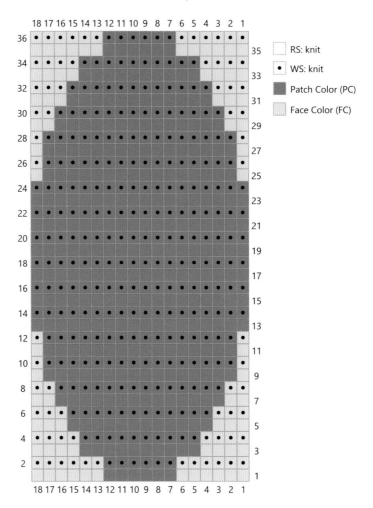

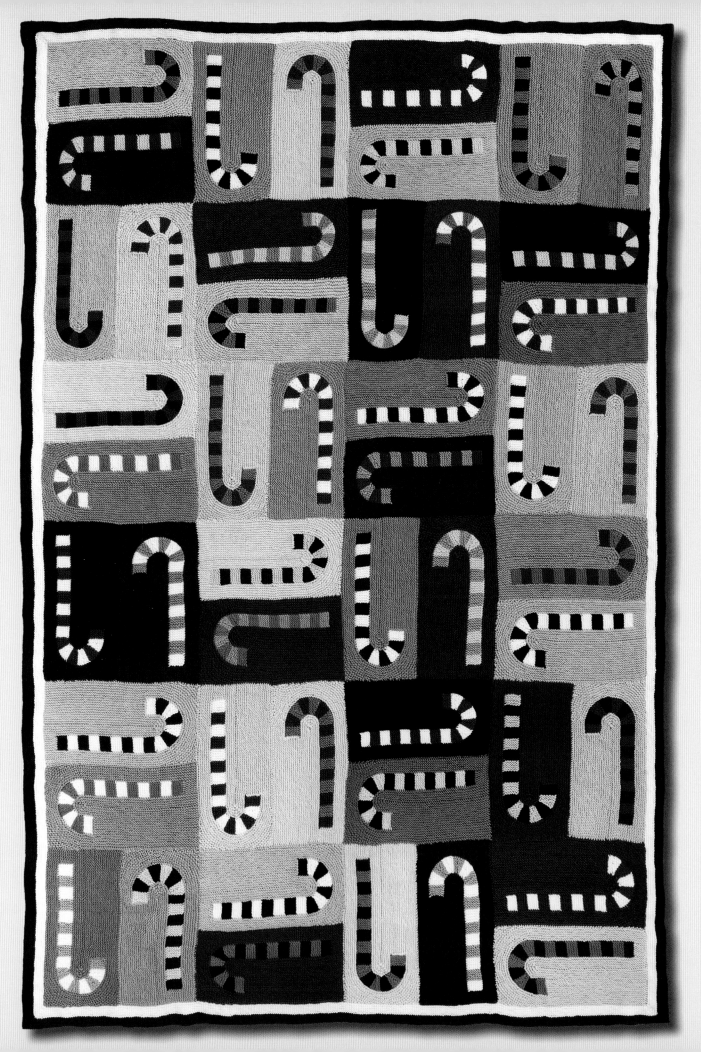

CANDY CANES

Sweet, brightly striped, and festive, these candy canes
will add a delightful flavor to your holiday home.

TECHNIQUES

Wrap & turn, 3-needle BO, sewing, provisional CO

SIZE

Small (Large): 47 x 61"/119 x 155 cm (61 x 90"/155 x 229 cm)

YARN

Valley Yarns, Valley Superwash (100% extra fine merino; 97 yds/89 m; 1.75 oz/50 g):

Pattern color ID	Color swatch	Color ID	Color name	Color description	# Balls for Size	
					Small	Large
A		260	White	white	5	9
B		600	Forest	dark green	2	4
C		612	Grass	medium green	2	4
D		694	Spring Leaf	avocado green	3	6
E		303	Daquiri Ice	mint	2	4
F		522	Teal	teal	4	6
G		302	Sriracha	bright red	3	6
H		968	Crimson	red	4	8
I		022	Pink	light pink	3	6
J		913	Mauve	mauve	3	5
K		304	Manic Panic	bright magenta	1	2
L		321	Mulberry	dark purple	2	5
M		571	Classic Navy	navy blue	3	5
N		021	Light Blue	light blue	2	4
O		023	Soft Yellow	light yellow	1	1
P		300	Golden Girl	strong yellow	1	2

NEEDLES

US Size 7/4.5 mm 40"/100 cm circular needle, US Size 10/6 mm straight or circular needle (for BOs)

NOTIONS

Stitch markers, stitch holders, tapestry needle, US 7/4.5 mm crochet hook

GAUGE

20 sts x 40 rows = 4"/10 cm in garter st

NOTES

- The blanket is offered in two sizes. Instructions are for Small, with changes for Large in parentheses.
- The blanket is worked in Blocks that are sewn together. Borders are picked up from the edges of the completed blanket.
- Long tails are left when cutting yarn after completing Corners. To keep these manageable, wind up yarn and use safety pins or stitch markers to attach wound yarn to the edge of Blocks until assembly.
- To obtain a loose edge, use larger needle for 3-needle BOs, and optionally for other BOs.

BLANKET INSTRUCTIONS

BLOCK

Make 24 (48) Blocks in color schemes shown in Figure 1.

For size Large, work all blocks shown in Figure 1, and for size Small, work only the Blocks within the dashed line.

A Block consists of a Cane and its Background. Block parts are worked in 3 steps:

    1) Base and Cane,
    2) Rectangle, Frame, Right Corner, and Left Corner,
    3) Arch.

The Color Schemes for Blocks in Figure 1 are given as [MC][CC][BC], defined as:

MC: Main Color (used to cast on for the Cane)
CC: Contrast Color (for Canes)
BC: Background Color (for all background pieces).

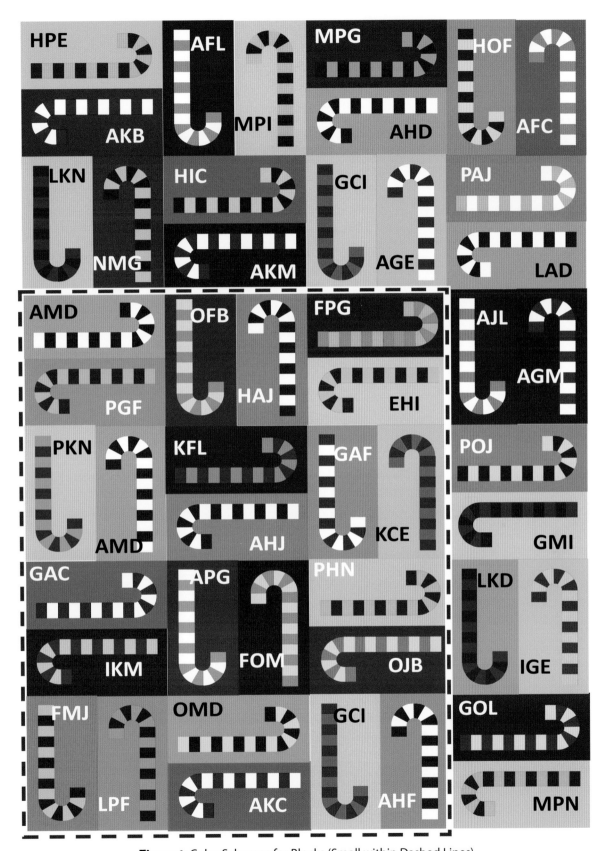

Figure 1: Color Schemes for Blocks (Small within Dashed Lines)

See Figure 2 for construction steps.

1) Base and Cane

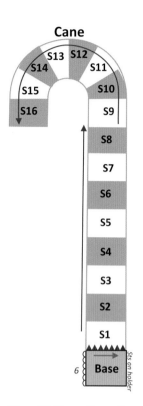

Cane

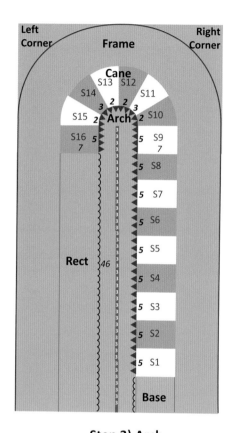

Step 1) Base then Cane

Step 2) Rect, Frame, Right Corner, then Left Corner

Step 3) Arch

Figure 2: Construction of Block

Base

With BC, CO 6 sts provisionally.

Rows 1 (WS)-14: Knit. Place 6 sts on holder for Frame. Pm on RS. Do not cut BC.

Cane

A Cane has 16 Stripes worked alternatingly in MC and CC. Do not cut yarn after use. Carry nonworking yarn on right edge of work, by draping it to the beginning of the next Stripe where it is needed, leaving a small amount of slack yarn. The drape will be tacked to the WS of the Block in a later step (see "Tacking Draped Yarn" on page 202).

On RS, attach MC at red triangle at the top of Base and pu&k 7 sts to next corner.

Color Key

 MC   CC   BC

Stripe 1 (S1) With MC, knit 9 rows.

Stripe 2 (S2) With CC, knit 10 rows.

Stripe 3 (S3) With MC, knit 10 rows.

Stripes 4 – 9 (S4 – S9) Rep [Stripes 2 and 3] 3 more times.

Stripe 10 (S10) With CC, work [Wedge].

Strip 11 (S11) With MC, work [Wedge].

Stripes 12 – 15 (S12 – S15) Rep [Stripes 10 and 11] twice. Cut MC and fasten off.

Stripe 16 (S16) With CC, knit 10 rows. Place sts on holder. Cut CC and fasten off.

2) Rect, Frame, Right Corner, Left Corner

Rectangle (Rect)

Note: Directions that follow work a perpendicular join on the right edge of the Rect to the end of S16.

With BC, provisionally CO 46 sts (Left needle). Transfer 7 sts from S16 from holder to second needle (Right needle) with RS facing.

> **Row 1 (RS):** Bring yarn forward, sl 1 st from S16 (Right needle) to Left needle, k2tog (S16 st and Rect st), knit to end, turn.
>
> **Row 2 (WS):** Knit 46 Rect sts, turn.
>
> Rep [Rows 1 & 2] 6 more times. Place rem 46 sts on holder. Cut yarn and fasten off.

Frame

With RS of Base facing, transfer 6 sts on holder to needle, then, starting at yellow triangle in Figure 2, Step 2, pu&k 86 sts around outer edge of completed Cane (*Note:* Stitch counts per stripe are provided in Figure 2). With RS of Rect facing, knit 46 sts from holder for Rect – 138 sts. Pm's after 51st and 69th sts. Work [Frame].

Right Corner (RC) – 24 sts dec'ing to 1 st

Work [Corner].

Left Corner (LC) – 24 sts dec'ing to 1 st

Transfer 24 sts from holder to needle. On RS, attach BC.

Work [Corner].

Wedge – 7 sts

Row 1 (RS): Knit.
Row 2 and all even (WS) rows to 12: Knit.
Row 3: K5, w&t.
Row 5: K4, w&t.
Row 7: K2, w&t.
Rows 9 & 11: Knit.

Frame – 138 sts dec'ing to 48 sts

Row 1 and all odd (WS) rows to 9: Knit.
Row 2: Knit to 1st m, k4, (bli, k6) 5 times, bli, knit to end – 6 sts inc'd; 144 sts.
Row 4: Knit.
Row 6: Knit to 1st m, k1, (bli, k7) 5 times, bli, knit to end – 6 sts inc'd; 150 sts.
Rows 8 & 10: Knit.
Row 11: BO first 51 sts, k24 to 2nd m, then place worked sts on holder for Left Corner, knit to end – 75 sts rem on needle.
Row 12: BO first 51 sts to 1st m. Rm – 24 sts on needle.

Corner – 24 sts dec'ing to 1 st

Rows 1 (RS) & 2 (WS): BO first 3 sts loosely, knit to end – 6 sts dec'd; 18 sts.
Row 3: BO 2, knit to end – 2 sts dec'd; 16 sts.
Row 4–6: Rep [Row 3] 3 times – 6 sts dec'd; 10 sts.
Row 7: K2tog, knit to last 2 sts, ssk – 2 sts dec'd; 8 sts.
Row 8: Knit.
Rows 9–12: Rep [Rows 7 & 8] twice – 4 sts dec'd; 4 sts.
Row 13: Rep [Row 7] once – 2 sts dec'd; 2 sts.
Row 14: K2tog – 1 st dec'd; 1 st.
Cut yarn and fasten off leaving 60"/152 cm tail for sewing Blocks.

3) Arch

Transfer 46 provisionally CO sts from Rect to needle with RS facing and starting at red triangle at the bottom-right corner of S16 in Figure 2, Step 3, pu&k 5 sts along edge of S16, pm, pu&k 59 sts along inner edge of Cane and knit 6 provisionally CO sts from Base – 116 sts. (*Note:* Stitch counts per piece are shown in Figure 2 in italics.)

Work [Arch].

ASSEMBLY

Arrange Blocks as shown in Figure 3 (Figure 4). With long tails of Corners and mattress st, sew along blue dashed lines shown in Figure 3 (Figure 4) to make squares, then along red dashed lines to make horizontal Strips, then along black dashed lines to join Strips.

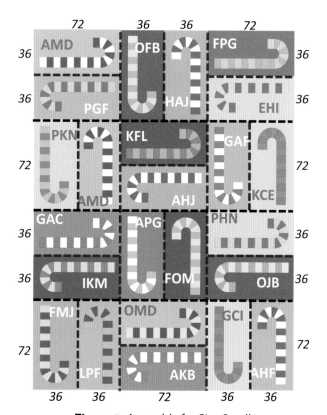

Figure 3: Assembly for Size Small

> **Arch** – 116 sts dec'ing to 1 st.

Row 1 and all odd (WS) rows to 7: Knit.
Row 2 (RS): Knit to m, k1, (k2tog, k3) 3 times, knit to end – 3 sts dec'd; 113 sts.
Row 4: Knit to m, k1, (k2tog, k1) 3 times, knit to end – 3 sts dec'd; 110 sts.
Row 6: Knit to m, k2tog 4 times, knit to end – 4 sts dec'd; 106 sts.
Row 8: Knit to 1 st bef m, rm, cdd, pm, cdd, knit to end – 4 sts dec'd; 102 sts
Row 9: Knit. Turn needles so that they are parallel with tips aligned, and right sides of work are together. Split stitches at m pushing 51 to one tip and 51 to the other. Rm. With 3rd needle and yarn already attached, 3-needle BO remaining sts – 102 sts dec'd; 1 st. Cut yarn and insert yarn end through last st to fasten off sts.

BORDERS

See Figure 3 (Figure 4) for pu&k stitch counts on individual pieces.

RIGHT BORDER

On RS, attach A at bottom-right corner of blanket and pu&k 288 (432) sts along edge. Work [Border] – 18 sts inc'd; 306 (450) sts.

TOP BORDER

Attach A at top-right corner, and pu&k 216 (288) sts. Work [Border] – 18 sts inc'd; 234 (306) sts.

LEFT BORDER

Attach A at top-left of blanket and pu&k 288 (432) sts along edge to next corner. Work [Border] – 18 sts inc'd; 306 (450) sts.

BOTTOM BORDER

Attach A at bottom-left corner of blanket and pu&k 216 (288 sts). Work [Border] – 18 sts inc'd; 234 (306) sts.

FINISHING

Using long tails of matching color and mattress st, sew Border corner seams. Weave in ends. Block to measurements.

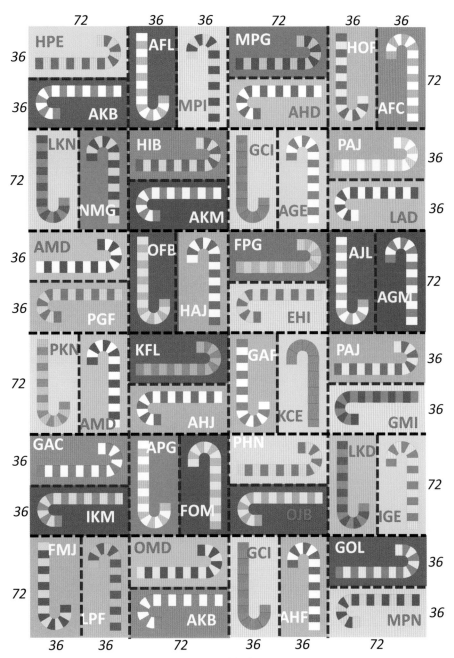

Figure 4: Assembly for Size Large

Border

Row 1 (WS): Knit.

Row 2 (RS): Kf&b, knit to last st, kf&b – 2 sts inc'd.

Row 3: Knit.

Rows 4–9: Rep [Rows 2 & 3] 3 times – 6 sts inc'd. Cut A leaving 10"/25 cm tail. Attach H.

Rows 10–19: Rep [Rows 2 & 3] 5 times – 10 sts inc'd.

BO loosely. Cut yarn and fasten off, leaving 10"/25 cm tail.

CHRISTMAS TREE LOT

Picking out a Christmas tree with the family is an honored tradition that inspired this blanket.

TECHNIQUES

Sewing, intarsia

SIZE

61 x 71"/155 x 180 cm

YARN

Valley Yarns, Valley Superwash, worsted (100% extra fine merino; 97 yds/89 m; 1.75 oz/50 g):

Pattern color ID	Color swatch	Color ID	Color name	Color description	# Skeins
A		261	Natural	off-white	17
B		600	Forest	forest green	18
C		694	Spring Leaf	yellow-green	5
D		306	Wine Time	dark red	6
E		968	Crimson	bright red	2
F		419	Biscuit	tan	2

NEEDLES

US Size 7/4.5 mm 40"/100 cm circular needles

NOTIONS

Stitch markers, stitch holders, tapestry needle, 3 bobbins

GAUGE

18 sts x 36 rows = 4"/10 cm in garter st

NOTES

The blanket is worked in Strips that are sewn together. Strips are formed from Blocks where each Block has a "Frame" piece and a "Tree." The Frame piece of each Block uses intarsia and simultaneous edge increases and decreases. It can be worked from a chart or written instructions. Stitches for Tree are picked up and knit from the edges of the diagonals of the Frame.

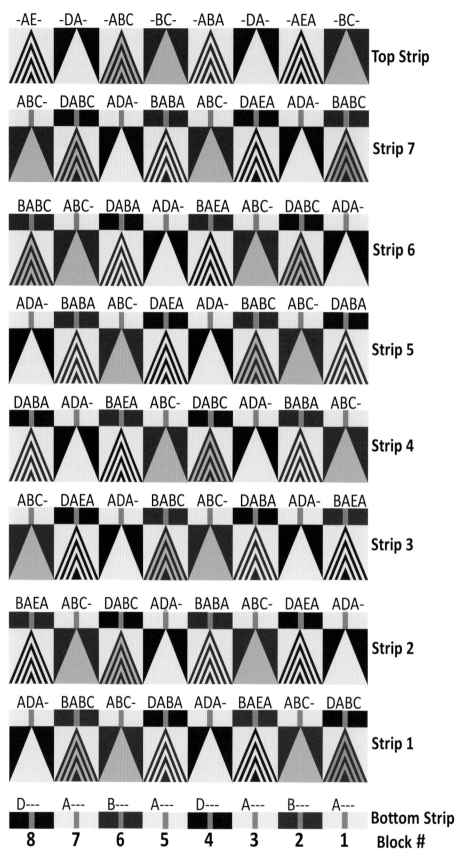

Figure 1: Colors

BLANKET INSTRUCTIONS

STRIPS 1–7

A Strip is composed of 8 Blocks, worked from right to left. A Block is worked in two steps, first the Frame, then the Tree, as shown in Figure 2.

A Tree is either Striped or Plain. See Figure 1 for the color schemes for the Blocks in each Strip. Colors are listed above the Block and are interpreted as follows: [UC][LC][T1][T2]:

UC: Upper Frame color
LC: Lower Frame color
T1: 1st color for Tree striping if a Striped Tree or color for Plain Tree
T2: 2nd (alternate) color for Tree striping if a Striped Tree
- -- - No color for that shape (i.e., no T2 for Plain Trees or no UC for Top Strip)

Color F is used for the Trunk Color (TC) for all Blocks.

Directions are for working a Frame, placing rem sts on a holder and working the Tree for that Frame before working the next Frame. However, all the Frames of the Strip may be worked in sequence, and the Trees added last.

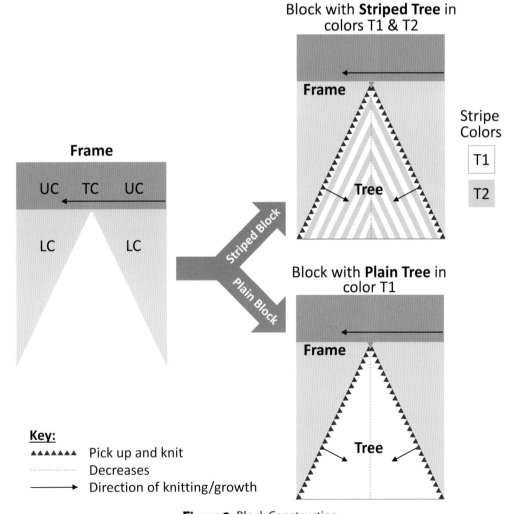

Figure 2: Block Construction

Block 1

Frame

Wind yarn amounts specified for UC, LC, and TC in Table 1 onto bobbins.

Table 1: Yarn amounts to wind onto bobbins

	Yarn length (yd/m)
UC	11/10
LC	22/20
TC	2/1.8

With LC for Block, CO 28 sts, pm, with UC for Block, CO 9 additional stitches – 37 sts.

Work [Frame chart on page 162] or work [Frame] (pattern st in light green box).

Place sts on holder.

Tree (Plain or Striped)

In each Frame, in space labeled "Tree" in Figure 2, attach T1 at red triangle, pu&k 31 sts to next corner, 1 st in corner, pm, and 31 sts to next corner – 63 sts. Work [Tree chart on page 162] or work [Tree] (pattern st in light green box).

Blocks 2–8

With sts on holder from prev Block and colors for next Block (Figure 1), work as for Block 1. Place sts on holder after completing Block 8.

Bottom Strip

CO 9 sts.

Block 1

Work [Upper Frame]. Cut yarn but do not BO.

Blocks 2–8

With colors for Block in Figure 1 on page 158 and sts rem from prev Block, work as for Block 1 in Bottom Strip. Place sts on holder after completing Block 8. Cut yarn and fasten off.

Top Strip

With LC, CO 28 sts.

Block 1

Frame

Work [Frame chart, Rows 1–56, sts 10–37] or work [Lower Frame] (pattern st in light green box). Cut yarn and fasten off and place sts on holder. In each

---

> **Frame** – 37 sts dec'ing to 10 sts inc'ing to 37 sts.

Row 1 (RS): With UC, knit to m, with LC, knit to end.

Row 2 (WS): With LC, k2tog, knit to m, with UC, knit to end – 1 st dec'd; 36 sts.

Row 3: With UC, knit to m, with LC, knit to last 2 sts, ssk – 1 st dec'd; 35 sts.

Row 4: Rep [Row 2] – 1 st dec'd; 34 sts.

Rows 5–24: Rep [Rows 3 & 4] 10 times – 20 sts dec'd; 14 sts.

Drop UC but carry along the edge twisting together with working yarn at the beg of RS rows.

Row 25: With TC, knit to m, with LC, knit to last 2 sts, ssk – 1 st dec'd; 13 sts.

Row 26: With LC, k2tog, knit to m, with TC, knit to end – 1 sts dec'd; 12 sts.

Rows 27 & 28: Rep [Rows 25 & 26] – 2 sts dec'd; 10 sts.

Row 29: With TC, knit to m, with LC, knit to end.

Row 30: With LC, CO 1, knit to m, with TC, knit to end – 1 st inc'd; 11 sts.

Row 31: With TC, knit to m, with LC, knit to last 2 sts, k1 tbl, kf&b – 1 st inc'd; 12 sts.

Row 32: Rep [Row 30] – 1 st inc'd; 13 sts. Cut TC.

Row 33: With UC, knit to m, with LC, knit to last 2 sts, k1 tbl, kf&b – 1 st inc'd; 14 sts.

Row 34: With LC, CO 1 st, knit to m, with UC, knit to end – 1 st inc'd; 15 sts.

Rows 35–56: Rep [Rows 33 & 34] 11 times – 22 sts inc'd; 37 sts.

Frame in space labeled "Tree" work as for Tree for Strips 1–7.

Tree

Work as for Tree in Strip 1, Block 1.

Blocks 2–8

With colors for Block in Figure 1, work as for Block 1 in Top Strip. Place sts on holder after completing Block 8. Cut yarn and fasten off.

ASSEMBLY

Arrange Bottom Strip, Strips 1–7, and Top Strip as shown in Figure 1. With matching long tails, sew Strips together using mattress st, aligning corners of Strips.

Tree – 63 sts dec'ing to 1 st

Row 1 (WS): Knit to 2 sts bef m, rm, cdd, pm, knit to end – 2 sts dec'd; 61 sts.
Rows 2 & 3: With T2 (striped Tree) or T1 (plain Tree) rep [Row 1] twice – 4 sts dec'd; 57 sts.
Row 4: With T1, k2tog, knit to 2 sts bef m, rm, cdd, pm, knit to last 2 sts, ssk – 4 sts dec'd; 53 sts.
Row 5: Rep [Row 1] – 2 sts dec'd; 51 sts.
Rows 6–25: Rep [Rows 2 – 5] 5 times – 50 sts dec'd; 1 st.
Cut yarn and fasten off.

BORDERS

RIGHT BORDER

On RS, attach B at bottom-right corner of blanket, pu&k 296 sts to top-right corner of blanket, 37 sts per Block, 28 sts along Top Strip and 9 sts along Bottom Strip (1 st per CO/BO st).

Row 1 (WS): Knit.
Row 2 (RS): Kf&b, knit to last st, kf&b – 2 sts inc'd; 298 sts.
Row 3: Knit.
Rows 4–7: Rep [Rows 2 & 3] twice – 4 sts inc'd; 302 sts.
Cut B leaving 10"/25 cm tail, attach C.
Rows 8–15: Rep [Rows 2 & 3] 4 times – 8 sts inc'd; 310 sts.
Cut A leaving 10"/25 cm tail, attach B.
Rows 16–23: Rep [Rows 2 & 3] 4 times – 8 sts inc'd; 318 sts.
Cut B leaving 10"/25 cm tail.

LEFT BORDER

On RS, attach yarn at top-left corner of blanket and knit the 296 sts on holders. Work as for Right Border.

TOP BORDER

Attach B at top-right corner of blanket, and pu&k 28 sts per Block (1 st per garter st ridge, or CO st) – 224 sts. Work as for Right Border, ending with 246 sts.

BOTTOM BORDER

Work as for Top Border, attaching yarn at bottom-left corner of blanket.

Using long tails and mattress st, sew together Border corners.

Upper Frame – 9 sts

Rows 1 (RS)-24: With UC, knit.
Rows 25–32: With TC, knit, twisting UC with TC at the beginning of each RS (odd) row.
Cut TC.
Rows 33–56: With UC, knit.

Lower Frame – 28 sts dec'ing to 1 st inc'ing to 28 sts

Row 1 (RS): With LC, knit to end.
Row 2 (WS): K2tog, knit to end – 1 st dec'd; 27 sts.
Row 3: Knit to last 2 sts, ssk – 1 st dec'd; 26 sts.
Row 4: Rep [Row 2] – 1 st dec'd; 25 sts.
Rows 5–28: Rep [Rows 1 & 2] 1twice – 24 sts dec'd; 1 st.
Row 29: K1.
Row 30: CO 1, knit to end – 1 st inc'd; 2 sts.
Row 31: Knit to last 2 sts, k1 tbl, kf&b – 1 st inc'd; 3 sts.
Row 32: Rep [Row 30] – 1 st inc'd; 4 sts.
Row 33–56: Rep [Rows 31 & 32] 1twice – 24 sts inc'd; 28 sts.

CHARTS

FRAME

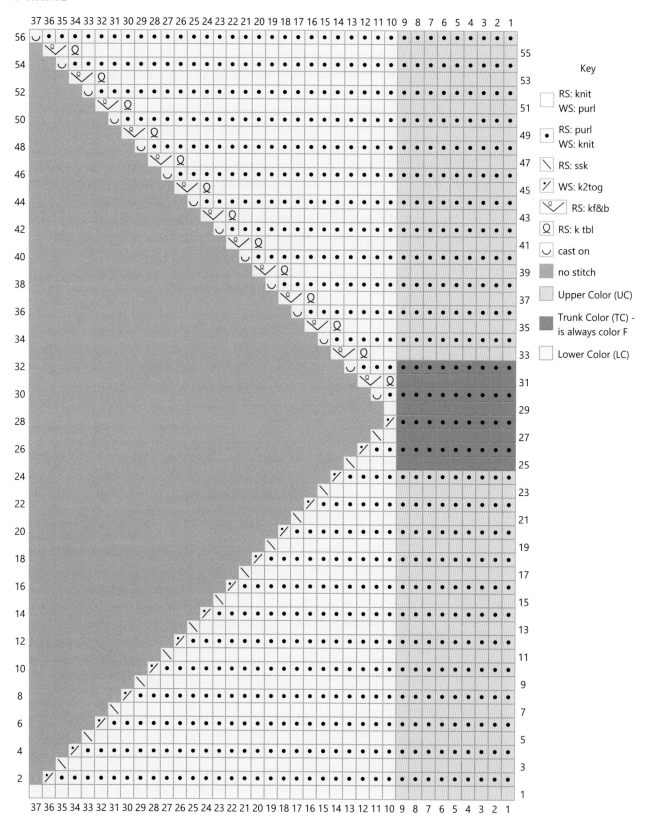

Key

☐ RS: knit
WS: purl

• RS: purl
WS: knit

\ RS: ssk

/ WS: k2tog

☑ RS: kf&b

Ω RS: k tbl

⌣ cast on

☐ no stitch

☐ Upper Color (UC)

☐ Trunk Color (TC) -
is always color F

☐ Lower Color (LC)

TREE

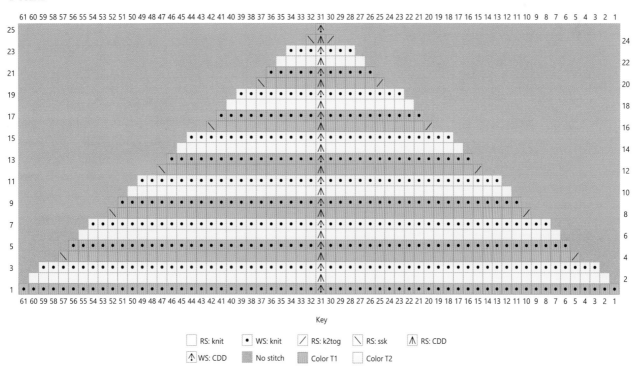

Key

☐ RS: knit   • WS: knit   ╱ RS: k2tog   ╲ RS: ssk   ⋀ RS: CDD

⋀ WS: CDD   ▨ No stitch   ▨ Color T1   ☐ Color T2

FESTIVE FOREST

A forest of enchanting trees is a fine place to stroll on a winter's day.

TECHNIQUES

Sewing, crochet slip stitch

SIZE

58.5 x 75"/149 x 191 cm

YARN

Valley Yarns, Northampton, worsted (100% wool; 247 yds/226 m; 3.5 oz/100 g):

Pattern color ID	Color swatch	Color ID	Color name	Color description	# Skeins
A		02	Natural	off-white	5
B		03	Fawn	taupe	2
C		47	Rust	rust	2
D		43	Denim Heather	dusty medium blue	2
E		42	Lake Heather	medium green-blue	2
F		54	Nebula	dark teal	3
G		58	Caribbean Heather	medium green	2
H		23	Dark Green Heather	dark green	2
I		59	Lilac	dusty pink	2
J		17	Red	true red	2
K		21	Dahlia	magenta	1
L		26	Raspberry Heather	light magenta	1

NEEDLES

US Size 7/4.5 mm 40"/100 cm circular needles

NOTIONS

Tapestry needle, US G-6/4 mm crochet hook

GAUGE

18 sts x 36 rows = 4"/10 cm in garter st

NOTES

The blanket is worked in Tree Blocks and Edge Blocks that are sewn together into vertical Strips. Strips are then sewn together. The Borders are picked up and knit from the edges of the completed blanket.

BLANKET INSTRUCTIONS

TREE BLOCK (TB) – MAKE 85

A Tree Block is composed of a Tree (isosceles triangle) and three Frame shapes: Right (RF), Left (LF), and Trunk (TF) as shown in Figure 1. TF is worked first, then sts are picked up & knit on the top edge TF for the Tree. Stitches are pu&k on the diagonal edges of the Tree for RF and for LF. The final step is a crochet edge worked around the entire Block to smooth out edges and make seaming easier.

See Figure 1 for construction and Figure 2 for Block colors which are specified as follows: [FM][FC][TM][TS], where:

- **FM:** Frame's Main Color – this is the color used to CO for the Trunk frame, for LF, and for RF.
- **FC:** Trunk Frame's Contrast Color – this is the color used for the Trunk.
- **TM:** Tree's Main color – this is the main or first Tree color, used for pu&k of sts.
- **TS:** Tree's Stripe color – this is used for the striping pattern (denoted as a dash: "-" if the Tree does not have stripes).

Trunk Frame (TF)

With FM specified in Figure 2, CO 8 sts.

Rows 1 (RS)–16 (16 rows): With FM, knit. Attach FC and do not cut FM.

Rows 17–22 (6 rows): With FC, knit, twisting together FM with FC at the beginning of each RS row. Cut FC and fasten off.

Rows 23–38 (16 rows): With FM, knit. BO loosely, do not cut FM.

Tree

There are four styles of Trees that differ only in whether they have stripes and how stripes are arranged.

The instructions for the Tree are provided in Table 1. Row by row instructions are in the left two columns. The columns on the right are the instructions for a particular Tree style. The color of the cell and the abbreviation "TM" or "TS" indicates the color to use for the row, where TM is the main color of the Tree and TS is the stripe color.

For Trees with stripes, do not cut yarn until after the final stripe of that color is completed. Drape yarn between uses then tack to edge during the pu&k of Right Frame and Left Frame by alternately inserting the needle below and above the draped yarn.

See "Tacking Draped Yarn" on page 202.

Attach TM specified in Figure 2 at yellow triangle in Figure 1 and pu&k 19 sts (one st per garter st bump). Work [Tree table] following color substitutions in the column for the Tree style being worked.

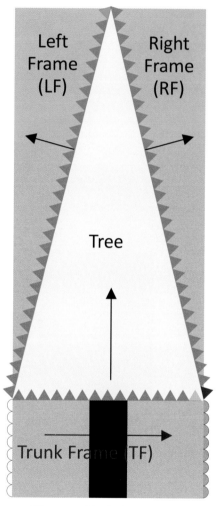

Figure 1: Block Construction

Table 1: Tree Table
Row by row instructions for the Tree with color substitutions for the four Tree styles

Row Instructions for Tree		No Stripe	Big Stripe	Pin Stripe	Mini Stripe
Row 1 (WS)	Knit.	TM	TM	TM	TM
Row 2 (RS)	Knit.	TM	TM	TM	TS
Row 3	Knit.	TM	TM	TM	TS
Row 4	Knit.	TM	TM	TM	TM
Row 5	Knit.	TM	TM	TM	TM
Row 6	K1, k2tog, knit to last 3 sts, ssk, k1 – 2 sts dec'd; 17 sts.	TM	TM	TS	TS
Row 7	Knit.	TM	TM	TS	TS
Row 8	Knit.	TM	TM	TM	TM
Row 9	Knit.	TM	TM	TM	TM
Row 10	Knit.	TM	TM	TM	TS
Row 11	Knit.	TM	TM	TM	TS
Row 12	Knit.	TM	TS	TM	TM
Row 13	Knit.	TM	TS	TM	TM
Row 14	K1, k2tog, knit to last 3 sts, ssk, k1 – 2 sts dec'd; 15 sts.	TM	TS	TS	TS
Row 15	Knit.	TM	TS	TS	TS
Row 16	Knit.	TM	TS	TM	TM
Row 17	Knit.	TM	TS	TM	TM
Row 18	Knit.	TM	TS	TM	TS
Row 19	Knit.	TM	TS	TM	TS
Row 20	Knit.	TM	TS	TM	TM
Row 21	Knit.	TM	TS	TM	TM
Row 22	K1, k2tog, knit to last 3 sts, ssk, k1 – 2 sts dec'd; 13 sts	TM	TS	TS	TS
Row 23	Knit.	TM	TS	TS	TS
Row 24	Knit.	TM	TM	TM	TM
Rows 25–48	Rep [Rows 1–24] once – 6 sts dec'd; 7 sts.				
Rows 49–61	Rep [Rows 1–13] once – 2 sts dec'd; 5 sts.				
Row 62	K2tog, k1, ssk, in established color – 2 sts dec'd; 3 sts.				
Rows 63–69	Knit, in established color sequence.				
Row 70	With TM, cdd – 2 sts dec'd; 1 st. Cut yarn and fasten off.	TM	TM	TM	TM

Right Frame (RF)

With FM for Block, attach yarn at red triangle in Figure 1 and pu&k 36 sts to tip of Tree.

Knit 1 row. Work [Fr]. Cut yarn and fasten off.

Left Frame (LF)

With FM for Block, attach yarn at green triangle and pu&k 36 sts to corner as for RF.

Work [Fr]. Do not cut yarn.

Frame (Fr) – 36 sts dec'ing to 1 st

Note: Row 1 is the WS for LF and the RS for RF.
Row 1: BO 4, knit to end – 4 sts dec'd; 32 sts.
Row 2: Knit.
Rows 3–6: Rep [Rows 1 & 2] twice – 8 sts dec'd; 24 sts.
Row 7: BO 4 sts, knit to last 2 sts, ssk – 5 sts dec'd; 19 sts.
Row 8: Knit.
Rows 9–16: Rep [Rows 1–8] once – 17 sts dec'd; 2 sts.
Row 17: Ssk.

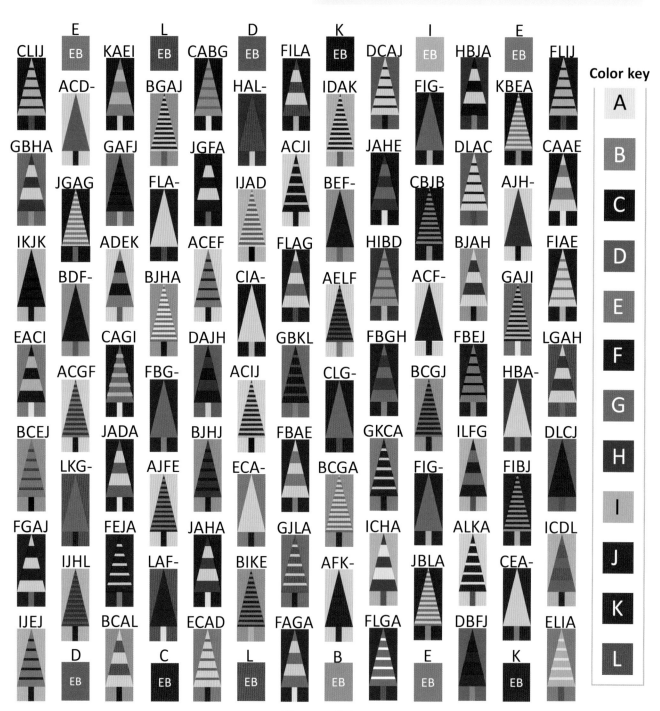

Figure 2: Colors

Crochet Edge

With crochet hook, sl st loosely around entire Block. Make 1 st in each CO or BO st, and 1 st in each garter stitch ridge and 2 sl sts to turn corner. Sl st in first sl st to close round. Cut yarn leaving 55"/140 cm tail.

Note: Sl st should not pull in edge. If needed use a larger crochet hook or add more slip sts to achieve a loose edge.

Edge Block (EB) – make 12

In color for EB in Figure 2, CO 19 sts.

Knit 40 rows. BO loosely.

ASSEMBLY

Arrange 85 TBs and 12 EBs as shown in Figure 2. Using long tails of matching color and mattress st, sew Blocks together to form 13 vertical Strips. Using remaining long tails, sew Strips together. Align EB to center of long edge of adjacent Tree, and align the midpoint of each Tree with the seam between Trees on the adjacent strip as shown in Figure 3.

BORDERS

Right Border

On RS, attach A at bottom-right corner of blanket, pu&k 322 sts to top-right corner of blanket, 46 sts per Block. Knit 15 rows. BO loosely, leaving last st on needle for Top Border.

Top Border

On RS, pu&k 7 sts along edge of Right Border, then 19 sts on top edge of each EB or Tree Block – 255 sts. Knit 15 rows. BO loosely, leaving last st on needle for Left Border.

Left Border

On RS, pu&k 7 st along edge of Top Border, then 46 sts on edge of each Tree Block – 330 sts. Knit 15 rows, BO loosely leaving last st on needle for Bottom Border.

Bottom Border

On RS, pu&k 7 sts along edge of Left Border, then 19 sts on top edge of each EB or Tree Block, then 8 sts along edge of Right Border – 263 sts. Knit 15 rows. BO loosely.

FINISHING

Weave in ends and Block to measurements.

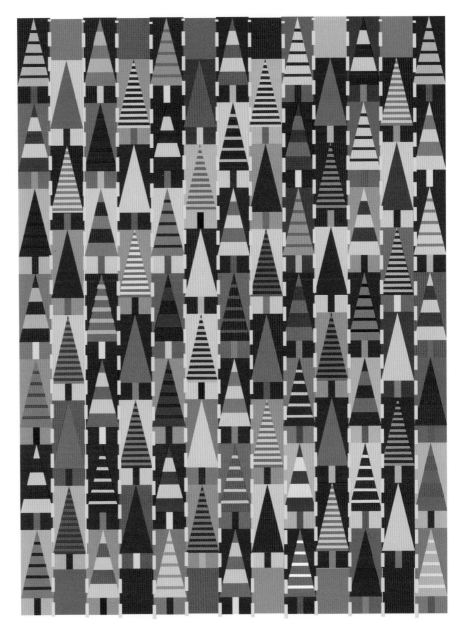

Figure 3: Sewing Together Strips

SNOWFLAKES

On a cold winter's night you will want to snuggle up under this blanket of delicate, melt-on-your-nose snowflakes.

TECHNIQUES

Sewing, intarsia, provisional CO (optional), embroidered chain st or crocheted slip stitch

SIZE

67"/170 cm square

YARN

Valley Yarns, Becket, bulky (50% superfine alpaca, 50% wool; 141 yds/129 m; 3.5 oz/100 g):

Pattern color ID	Color swatch	Color ID	Color name	Color description	# Balls
MC		11	Denim Heather	navy blue heather	20
CC		01	Natural	off-white	7
BC		25	Storm Cloud	light gray-blue	5

NEEDLES

US Size 9/5.25 mm circular needles of minimum length 40"/100 cm

NOTIONS

Stitch markers, tapestry needle, US I-9/5.5 mm crochet hook for adding lines to snowflakes, 2 bobbins

GAUGE

13 sts x 26 rows = 4"/10 cm in garter st

NOTES

The blanket is worked in 9 Blocks that are sewn together. Blocks begin with four Arms, then Mitered Squares are worked from stitches picked up on the edges of completed Arms. Mitered Squares can be worked from written instructions (pattern stitch) or chart at the back of the pattern. Embroidered chain st or crocheted slip st is used to add the thin stripes to Arms of the Snowflakes.

BLANKET INSTRUCTIONS

BLOCK – MAKE 9

Arms

See Figure 1 for construction. There are four striped arms, worked in order: East, North, West, and South. While working an Arm, do not cut yarn between stripes. Either drape nonworking yarn or twist it with working yarn at the beginning of RS rows. For a pu&k on an edge with a draped yarn, secure the draped yarn by alternating between inserting needle (or crochet hook) over and under the draped yarn.

Use a knitted CO when CO is required. A provisional CO may be used, optionally, in which case, transfer provisionally CO sts to needle instead of generating sts by pu&k.

Arm East

With CC, CO 7 sts, pm, CO 6 sts – 13 sts.

Work [Arm].

Arm North

Attach CC at red triangle and pu&k 7 sts on edge of Arm East, pm, turn to WS and CO 6 sts – 13 sts.

Work [Arm].

Arm West

Work as for Arm North, attaching yarn at green triangle on corner of Arm North.

Arm South

Attach CC at yellow triangle, pu&k 6 sts on edge of Arm West, 1 st in corner, pm, 6 sts to next corner on edge of Arm East – 13 sts.

Work [Arm].

Weave in short ends on all Arms. Leave long ends for sewing Blocks together.

Arm – 13 sts dec'ing to 1 st

Row 1 (WS): Knit.
Row 2 (RS): Kf&b, knit to 2 sts bef m, rm, cdd, pm, knit to last st, kf&b.
Row 3: Knit.
Rows 4–13: Rep [Rows 2 & 3] 5 times. Drop CC, attach MC.
Rows 14–23: Rep [2 & 3] 5 times. Drop MC.
Rows 24–31: With CC, rep [Rows 2 & 3] 4 times. Drop CC.
Rows 32–41: With MC, rep [Rows 2 & 3] 5 times. Cut MC.
Rows 42 & 43: With CC, rep [Rows 2 & 3] one time.
Row 44: K2tog, knit to 2 sts bef m, rm, cdd, pm, knit to last 2 sts, ssk – 4 sts dec'd; 9 sts.
Row 45: Knit.
Rows 46 & 47: Rep [Rows 44 & 45] once – 4 sts dec'd; 5 sts.
Row 48: Cdd-2 – 4 sts dec'd; 1 st. Cut CC leaving 15"/40 cm tail.

Figure 1: Arm Construction

Mitered Squares

See Figure 2 for construction.

Cut yarns in amounts indicated in Mitered Square chart on page 176 and wind them onto bobbins for working smaller sections of Mitered Squares. Areas on chart that do not include precut yarn length should be worked from the skein.

In each of the four spaces between Arms, labeled "MS," attach MC at red triangle and pu&k 29 sts to corner, 1 st in corner, 29 sts to next corner – 59 sts.

Work [MS chart] or work [MS] (pattern st in light green box). Trim bobbin yarns and weave in. Cut MC at final corner, leaving a 50"/155 cm tail for sewing Blocks.

*Note: T*he numbers in italics along the Arms are the number of sts to pu&k per color section of the Arm.

Figure 2: Mitered Square Construction

Mitered Square (MS) – 59 sts dec'ing to 1 st

Pm after 30th st on RS.
Row 1 (and all odd/WS rows to 57): Knit, working stitches in same color as prev RS row.
Row 2 (RS): With MC, knit to 2 sts bef m2, rm, cdd, pm, knit to end – 2 sts dec'd; 57 sts.
Row 4: Rep [Row 2] – 2 sts dec'd; 55 sts.
Row 6: Knit to 11 sts bef m, drop MC, add CC, knit to 2 sts bef m, rm, cdd, pm, k9, drop CC, add a separate strand of MC, knit to end – 2 sts dec'd; 53 sts.
Rows 8 & 10: Rep [Row 6] twice – 4 sts dec'd; 49 sts.
Rows 12, 14, & 16: Rep [Row 2] 3 times – 6 sts dec'd; 43 sts.
Rows 18, 20, 22, 24, 26, & 28: Rep [even Rows 6–16] once – 12 sts dec'd; 31 sts.

Row 30: Rep [Row 6] – 2 sts dec'd; 29 sts.
Row 32: Knit to 2 sts past beg of CC section, drop MC, with CC knit to 2 sts bef m, rm, cdd, pm, knit to 2 sts bef end of CC section, drop CC, with MC knit to end – 2 sts dec'd; 27 sts.
Rows 34, 36, & 38: Rep [Row 32] 3 times – 6 sts dec'd; 21 sts.
Cut CC and separate strand of MC after WS Row 39.
Rows 40, 42, 44, 46, 48, 50, 52, 54, & 56: with MC, rep [Row 2] 9 times – 18 sts dec'd; 3 sts.
Row 58: Cdd – 2 sts dec'd; 1 st.

SLIP STITCH STRIPES

On each Arm and MS shape, add a stripe of CC-colored slip sts between each green and red dot shown in Figure 3. Use one of these methods:

(1) With a crochet hook and a double strand of CC, create slip stitches as follows:

Draw a loop to the front at the green dot. Make a total of 15 sl sts for the diagonal stripes (see details in Figure 4) and 14 sts for the horizontal/vertical stripes (see details in Figure 5) by drawing up a loop between each ridge along the line of cdd's to the red dot. Adjust tension so that the slip sts lie flat without causing work to either bulge or pucker. After the last sl st at the red dot, cut the double strand and draw through the last loop, then draw to the back of the work and tie off.

(2) Thread a double strand of CC onto a tapestry needle. Draw needle up at the green dot, leaving a tail on the WS of the work, loop thread and hold it down with left thumb. Insert the needle where it first emerged, and bring the tip out at the ending point for the stitch and inside the loop, and pull the needle through. To make the next stitch, insert the needle into the hole from which thread has just emerged.

Figure 3: Slip Stitch Stripes

Figure 4: Details of Stripes Added to MS

Figure 5: Details of Stripes Added to Arms

ASSEMBLY

Arrange Blocks as shown in Figure 6. With long tails of matching color and mattress st, sew along red dashed lines to make Strips, then along green dashed lines to join Strips.

BORDERS

See italic numbers in Figure 6 for pu&k stitch counts on edges of individual Block shapes.

RIGHT BORDER

On RS, attach BC at lower-right corner of blanket and pu&k 198 sts along right side of blanket. Knit 17 rows. BO loosely, leaving last st on needle. Do not cut yarn.

TOP BORDER

Pu&k 9 sts on edge of Right Border and 198 sts across the top of blanket – 208 sts. Knit 17 rows. BO loosely, leaving last st on needle. Do not cut yarn.

LEFT BORDER

Work as for Top Border, picking up and knitting sts on left edge of Top Border, then left side of blanket.

BOTTOM BORDER

Pu&k 9 sts on edge of Left Border, 198 sts across the bottom of blanket then 10 sts on the bottom of the Right Border – 218 sts. Knit 17 rows. BO loosely. Cut yarn and fasten off.

Weave in ends.

Figure 6: Assembly

CHART

MITERED SQUARE (MS)

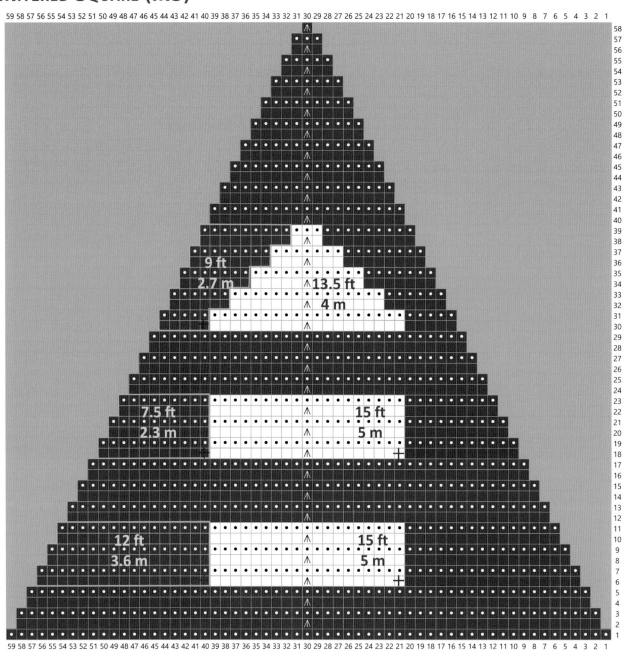

RS: knit

• WS: knit

Λ central double decrease

╋ Add yarn color
Precut yarn amounts indicated in shape and
wind onto bobbins. If no precut amount is
specified, area is to be worked from skein

grey no stitch

white (CC)

blue (MC)

TREE OF LIGHT

A magical blanket made from chevrons and mitered squares.

TECHNIQUES

Sewing, 3-needle BO

SIZE

Small (Large): 47 x 54.5"/119 x 138 cm (57 x 64"/145 x 163 cm)

YARN

Cascade, 220 Superwash, worsted (100% superwash wool; 220 yds/200 m; 3.5 oz/100 g):

Pattern color ID	Color swatch	Color ID	Color name	Color description	# Balls	
					Small	Large
A		228	Frosted Almond	dark cream	5	6
B		1926	Doeskin Heather	light tan	4	5
C		871	White	white	2	2
D		296	Myrtle Heather	dark spruce green	2	2
E		352	Verdant Green	true green	2	2
F		802	Green Apple	green-yellow	2	3
G		809	Really Red	true red	1	1
H		263	Gold Fusion	yellow-gold	1	1
I		907	Tangerine Heather	pure orange	1	1
J		914A	Tahitian Rose	strong pink	1	1
K		814	Hyacinth	periwinkle blue	1	1
L		862	Walnut Heather	muted brown	1	1
M		905	Celery	muted green	2	3

NEEDLES

US Size 7/4.5 mm 40"/100 cm circular needles

NOTIONS

Tapestry needle, 2 stitch markers

GAUGE

18 sts x 36 rows = 4"/10 cm in garter stitch

NOTES

- The blanket is worked in two sections: Background and Tree. The Background starts with a Foundation Strip. Additional Strips are worked by generating stitches on the bottom edge of the prev Strip using pick up & knit (pu&k). The Tree is also worked in Strips. When Background and Tree are complete they are seamed together. Borders are pu&k on edges of the blanket.

- When shapes include striping, do not cut yarn between uses. Drape yarn along edge to next use and cut yarns only when instructed.

- Leave a 25"/60 cm tail of B for sewing when cutting yarns after completing Mitered Square (MS) shapes along the inner edge of the Background (where the Tree shape will be sewn) Wind up each yarn and secure to the edge of the Background to prevent tangling.

- All pu&k is performed on the RS of the work.

BLANKET INSTRUCTIONS

BACKGROUND

Foundation Strip

Increasing Triangles see Figure 1

*With B, CO 1 st. Work [IT], pm, and leave 32 sts on needle and do not remove center marker. With RS facing, rep from * 8 (10) more times, aggregating stitches onto the Left needle – 288 (352) sts.

Mitered Squares see Figure 2

Starting on RS, work [W1] over next 16 sts to 1st marker. Cut yarns and fasten off.

*Starting on the RS, work [MS; using B for C1, A for C2, and C3 from Figure 2] over the next 32 sts to 2nd m. Rm. Rep from * 7 (9) more times, then work [W2] over last 16 sts of row.

> **Increasing Triangle (IT)** – 1 st inc'ing to 32 sts

CO counts as Row 1.
Row 2 (WS): With **B**, kf&b – 1 st inc'd; 2 sts.
Row 3 (RS): Kf&b, pm, kf&b– 2 sts inc'd; 4 sts.
Row 4 (WS): Knit.
Row 5: Kf&b, knit to 1 st bef m, kf&b, sm, kf&b, knit to last st, kf&b – 4 sts inc'd; 8 sts.
Row 6: Knit.
Drop **B** but do not cut.
Rows 7–10: With **A**, rep [Rows 5 & 6] twice – 8 sts inc'd; 16 sts. Drop **A** but do not cut.
Rows 11–14: With **B**, rep [Rows 5 & 6] twice – 8 sts inc'd; 24 sts.
Rows 15–18: With **A**, rep [Rows 5 & 6] twice – 8 sts inc'd; 32 sts.
Cut yarns and fasten off.

> **Mitered Square (MS)** – 32 sts dec'ing to 0 sts

Row 1 (RS): With **C1**, k8, bli, knit to 2 sts bef m, rm, cdd, pm, knit to end – 1 st dec'd; 31 sts.
Row 2 (WS): Knit.
Row 3: Knit to 2 sts bef m, rm, cdd, pm, knit to end – 2 sts dec'd.
Row 4: Knit.
Drop **C1**, cont with **C2**.
Rows 5–8: With **C2**, rep [Rows 3 & 4] twice – 4 sts dec'd; 25 sts.
Rows 9–12: With **C1**, rep [Rows 3 & 4] twice – 4 sts dec'd; 21 sts.
Rows 13–16: With **C2**, rep [Rows 3 & 4] twice – 4 sts dec'd; 17 sts.
Cut **C1** and **C2**.
Note: If working the Background pieces, if C1 and C3 are the same color, do not cut C1.
Rows 17–30: With **C3**, rep [Rows 3 & 4] 7 times – 14 sts dec'd; 3 sts.
Row 31: Rm. Cdd – 2 sts dec'd; 1 st. Cut yarns and fasten off.

Areas enclosed in red dashed lines are included for Large and excluded for Small

Foundation Strip:
Increasing Triangles (IT)

Figure 1: Foundation Strip

W1 and W2 – 16 sts dec'ing to 0 sts

Row 1 (RS): With B,
for shape **W1**: K2tog, knit to end
for shape **W2**: Knit to last 2 sts, ssk – 1 st dec'd; 15 sts.
Row 2 (WS): Knit.
Rows 3 & 4: Rep [Rows 1 & 2] – 1 st dec'd; 14 sts.
Drop B, cont with A.
Rows 5–8: With A, rep [Rows 1 & 2] twice – 2 sts dec'd; 12 sts.

Rows 9–12: With B, rep [Rows 1 & 2] twice – 2 sts dec'd; 10 sts.
Rows 13–16: With A, rep [Rows 1 & 2] twice – 2 sts dec'd; 8 sts.
Cut **A**.
Rows 17–30: With B, rep [Rows 1 & 2] 7 times – 7 sts dec'd; 1 st.
Cut yarns and fasten off.

Areas enclosed in red dashed lines are included for
Large and excluded for Small

Foundation Strip:
Wedges (W1 & W2),
Mitered Squares (MS)

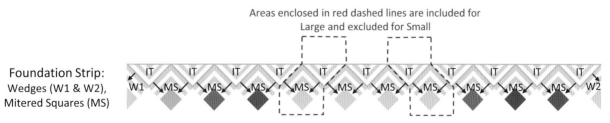

Figure 2: Foundation Strip: Triangles and Mitered Squares

Left Background (Strips LB1– LB8 [LB10 for Large])

See Figure 3 for construction and colors. Stitch counts for Strips are provided in Table 1 on page 183. Work Strips in ascending number order.

Strip LB1

On RS, with B, and starting at red triangle at the tip of left-most W1 of the prev Strip, *pu&k 15 sts to next corner, 1 st in the tip of the IT (in the leg bet the center 2 sts of the IT), pm; pu&k 15 sts to next corner, 1 st in the tip of MS, pm; rep from * until end of edge at blue triangle. Work [Ch1, using B for C1 and A for C2].

*Work [MS, using B for C1, A for C2, and C3 from Figure 3] over next 32 sts to 2nd m. Cut yarns and fasten off. Rep from * across rem groups of 32 sts, reattaching yarns as required.

Strip LB2

On RS, with B, and starting at the green triangle on the edge of the prev Strip, *pu&k 15 sts to next corner, 1 st in tip of MS†, pm, 15 sts on next edge, 1 st in the tip of the prev Ch1, pm; rep from * to end of edge at pink triangle, ending the last rep at †.

Work [Ch2, using B for C1, A for C2].

Over the first 16 sts, work [W1]. *Over next group of 32 sts, work [MS, using B for C1, A for C2, and C3 from Figure 3]; rep from * across rem groups of 32 sts.

Strips LB3, LB5, LB7 (LB9 for Large)

Work as LB1, but when working the pu&k, for the 16th stitch and every 32nd st thereafter, work the pu&k bet adjacent MS (in the tip of the Ch2).

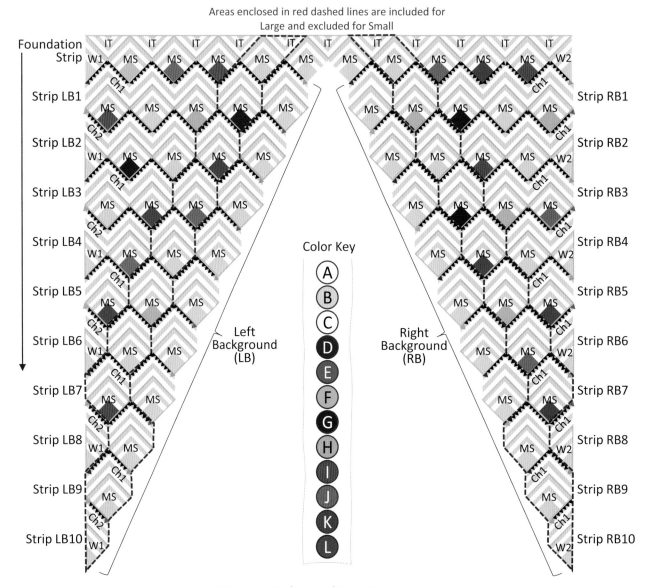

Figure 3: Background Strip Construction

Strips LB4, LB6 (LB8 for Large)

Work as for LB2.

Strip LB8 (LB10 for Large)

On RS, with B, and starting at the green triangle on the prev Strip, pu&k 16 sts. Work [Ch2, using B for C1, and A for C2] working Row 3 as follows:

> **Row 3:** K2tog, knit to last st, kf&b.

Work [W1].

Right Background (Strips RB1 - RB8 [RB10 for Large])

See Figure 3 for construction and colors. Stitch counts for Strips are provided in Table 1 on page 183. Work Strips in ascending number order.

Strip RB1

Work as for LB1, beg pu&k at the red triangle at the tip of the 5th (6th) Foundation Strip's MS, and ending at the tip of the W2.

Strips RB3, RB5, RB7 (RB9 for Large)

Work as for LB1, beg pu&k at the point of the left-most MS of the prev Strip, and ending at the tip of the W2.

Strips RB2, RB4, RB6 (RB8 for Large)

On RS, with B, and starting at green triangle at the point of left-most MS of the prev Strip, *pu&k 15 sts to next corner, 1 st in the tip of the prev Ch1†, pm; pu&k 15 sts to next corner, 1 st in the tip of MS, pm; rep from * until end of edge at pink triangle, ending the last rep at †. Work [Ch1, using B for C1, and A for C2] and working Row 3 as follows:

> **Row 3:** Kf&b, knit to 2 sts bef m, rm, *cdd, pm, knit to 1 st bef m, rm, kyok, pm after center st of kyok, knit to 2 sts bef m, rm; rep from * to last 2 sts, k2tog.

*Work [MS, using B for C1, A for C2, and C3 from Figure 3] over next 32 sts to 2nd m. Cut yarns and fasten off. Rep from * across rem groups of 32 sts until 16 sts rem, reattaching yarns as required. Work [W2] over last 16 sts.

Strip RB8 (RB10 for Large)

Note: for size Large, work only RB10.

On RS, with B, and starting at the green triangle at the point of the MS of the prev Strip, pu&k 16 sts. Work [Ch1, using B for C1, and A for C2], working Row 3 as follows:

> **Row 3:** Kf&b, knit to last 2 sts, k2tog.

Work [W2].

Chevron 1 (Ch1) – multiple of 16 sts

Row 2 (WS): Cont with C1, knit.
Row 3: Kf&b, knit to 2 sts bef m, rm, cdd, pm, *knit to 1 st bef m, rm, kyok, pm after center st of kyok, knit to 2 sts bef m, rm, cdd, pm; rep from * until no m's rem, knit to last st, kf&b.
Row 4: Knit.
Drop C1.
Rows 5–8: With C2, rep [Rows 3 & 4] twice.
Drop C2.
Rows 9–12: With C1, rep [Rows 3 & 4] twice.
Drop C1.
Rows 13–16: With C2, rep [Rows 3 & 4] twice.

Chevron 2 (Ch2) – multiple of 16 sts

Row 2 (WS): Cont with C1, knit.
Row 3: K2tog, *knit to 1 st bef m, rm, kyok, pm after center st of kyok, knit to 2 sts bef m, rm, cdd, pm; rep from * until no m's rem, knit to last st, kf&b.
Row 4: Knit.
Drop C1.
Rows 5–8: With C2, rep [Rows 3 & 4] twice.
Drop C2.
Rows 9–12: With C1, rep [Rows 3 & 4] twice.
Drop C1.
Rows 13–16: With C2, rep [Rows 3 & 4] twice.

Table 1: Stitch Counts for Strips

Strip Name	Blanket Size	
	Small	Large
LB1 and RB1	128	160
LB2 and RB2	112	144
LB3 and RB3	96	128
LB4 and RB4	80	112
LB5 and RB5	64	96
LB6 and RB6	48	80
LB7 and RB7	32	64
LB8 and RB8	16	48
LB9 and RB9		32
LB10 and RB10		16

TREE: STRIPS T1–T8 (T10) See Figure 4

Strip T1

With C, CO 16 sts, pm, CO 16 sts – 32 sts. Work [Ch3, using C for C1, E for C2, and F for C3], working Row 3 as follows:

> **Row 3:** Kf&b, knit to 2 sts bef m, rm, cdd, pm, knit to last 1 st, kf&b.

Work [MS, using E for C1, F for C2, and C3 from Figure 4].

Strip T2

With C, CO 16 sts, pm, starting at green triangle on corner of prev Strip, pu&k 15 sts to corner, 1 st in tip

of MS, pm, pu&k 15 sts on next edge, 1 st in prev Ch3, pm; rep from * to end of bottom edge of prev Strip, turn and CO 16 sts.

Work [Ch3, using C for C1, C2 from Figure 4, and F for C3].

*Over next 32 sts to 2nd m, work [MS, with C1 from Figure 4, F for C2, and C3 from Figure 4]; rep from * across row.

Strips T3 - T8 (T10)

Work as for T2.

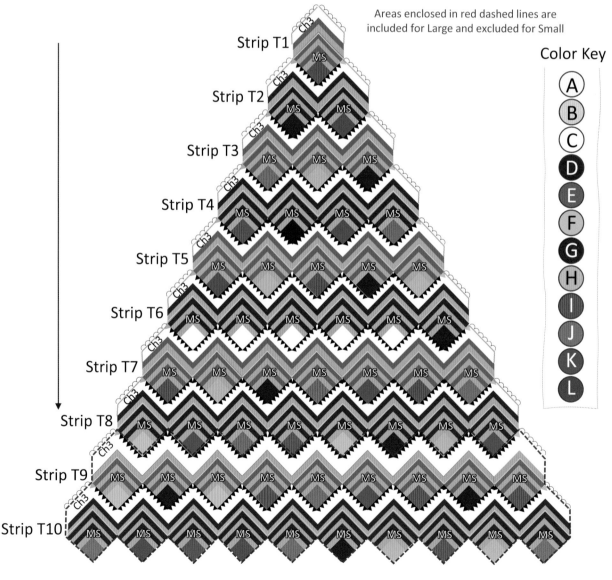

Figure 4: Colors and Construction for Tree Strips

UNDER THE TREE See Figure 5

Strip UL1

With B, CO 16, pm, then starting at green triangle at edge of MS on prev Strip, *pu&k 15 sts to next corner, 1 st in tip of MS, pm, pu&k 15 sts along next edge, pm in tip of prev Ch3; rep from * 2 (3) more times, pu&k 16 sts on edge to blue triangle – 128 (160) sts.

Work [Ch1, using B for C1, and A for C2].

*Work [MS, using B for C1, and A for C2, and C3 from Figure 5] over next 32 sts to 2nd m. Cut yarns and fasten off. Rep from * across rem groups of 32 sts, reattaching yarns as required.

Strip UR1

With B, starting at green triangle at the edge of the MS adjacent to opening for the Trunk, *pu&k 15 sts to next corner, 1 st in tip of prev Ch3, pm, pu&k 15 sts to next corner, 1 st in tip of MS, pm; rep from * 2 (3) more times, pu&k 16 sts to blue triangle, pm, turn and CO 16 sts – 128 (160) sts.

Work [Ch1, using B for C1, and A for C2].

*Work [MS, using B for C1, and A for C2, and C3 from Figure 5] over next 32 sts to 2nd m. Cut yarns and fasten off. Rep from * across rem groups of 32 sts, reattaching yarns as required.

Chevron 3 (Ch3) – multiple of 32 sts

Row 2 (WS): Cont with C1, Knit.
Row 3: Kf&b, knit to 2 sts bef m, rm, cdd, pm, *knit to 1 st bef m, rm, kyok, pm after center st of kyok, knit to 2 sts bef m, rm, cdd, pm; rep from * until no m's rem, knit to last st, kf&b.
Row 4: Knit.
Rows 5–8: Cont with C1, rep [Rows 3 & 4] twice. Drop C1.
Rows 9–12: With C2, rep [Rows 3 & 4] twice. Drop C2.
Rows 13–16: With C3, rep [Rows 3 & 4] twice.

Strip UL2 and UR2

Starting at the green triangle at the bottom of the prev Strip, *pu&k 15 sts to next corner, 1 st in point of MS, pm, 15 sts on next edge, 1 st in tip of prev Ch1, pm; rep from * 3 (4) more times, omitting pm at end of last rep.

Work [Ch4, using B for C1, A for C2].

Chevron 4 (Ch4) – multiple of 32 sts

Note: Pu&k counts as Row 1.
Row 2 (WS): Cont with C1, knit.
Row 3: K2tog, knit to 1 st bef m, rm, kyok, pm after center st of kyok, *knit to 2 sts bef m, rm, cdd, pm, knit to 1 st bef m, rm, kyok, pm after center st of kyok; rep from * until no m's rem, knit to last st, ssk.
Row 4: Knit.
Drop C1.
Rows 5–8: With C2, rep [Rows 3 & 4] twice.
Drop C2.
Rows 9–12: With C1, rep [Rows 3 & 4] twice.
Drop C1.
Rows 13–16: With C2, rep [Rows 3 & 4] twice.

Small Triangle (ST) – 16 sts dec'ing to 0 sts

Row 1 (RS): Cont with Figure 3, k2tog, knit to last 2 sts, ssk – 2 sts dec'd.
Row 2 (WS): Knit.
Row 3: Rep Row 1 – 2 sts dec'd; 12 sts.
Row 4: Knit. Drop C1.
Rows 5–8: With C2, rep [Rows 1 & 2] twice – 4 sts dec'd; 8 sts. Drop C2.
Rows 9–12: With C1, rep [Rows 1 & 2] twice – 4 sts dec'd; 4 sts. Drop C1.
Rows 13–14: With C2, rep [Rows 1 & 2] once – 2 sts dec'd; 2 sts.
Row 15: K2tog – 1 st dec'd; 1 st. Cut yarns and fasten off.

Areas enclosed in red dashed lines are included for Large and excluded for Small

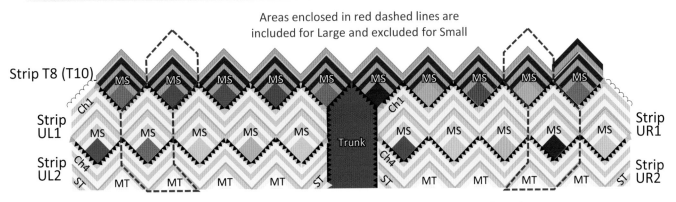

Figure 5: Colors and Construction for Strips Under the Tree and Trunk

Mitered Triangle (MT) – 32 sts dec'ing to 0 sts

Row 1 (RS): Cont with C1, k2tog, knit to 1 st bef m, rm, k2tog, pm, knit to last 2 sts, ssk – 3 sts dec'd; 29 sts.

Row 2 (WS): Knit.

Row 3: K2tog, knit to 2 sts bef m, rm, cdd, pm, knit to last 2 sts, ssk – 4 sts dec'd; 25 sts.

Row 4: Knit.
Drop C1.

Rows 5–8: With C2, rep [Rows 3 & 4] twice – 8 sts dec'd; 17 sts. Drop C2.

Rows 9–12: With C1, rep [Rows 3 & 4] twice – 8 sts dec'd; 9 sts. Drop C1.

Rows 13–14: With C2, rep [Rows 3 & 4] once – 4 sts dec'd; 5 sts.

Row 15: Cdd2 – 4 sts dec'd; 1 st. Cut yarns and fasten off.

STs and MTs on the bottom of UL2

Starting on RS on the bottom edge of Strip UL2, work [ST, using B for C1, and A for C2] over the 1st 16 sts to m. *Reattach yarns, work [MT, using B for C1, and A for C2] over next 32 sts; rep from * 2 (3) more times. Work [ST, using B for C1, and A for C2] over last 16 sts.

STs and MTs on the bottom of UR2

Work as for STs and MTs on the bottom of UL2.

Trunk - see Figure 5

With L, and starting at the yellow triangle on the bottom-right edge of Strip UL2, pu&k 33 sts to corner (11 sts on each of ST, Ch2, and Ch1 pieces), pm, (pu&k 16 sts to next corner, pm) twice, then 33 sts along next edge – 98 sts (33–16–16–33).

Row 2 and all even-numbered (WS) rows to 20: Knit.

Row 3 (RS): *Knit to 2 sts bef m, ssk, sm, k2tog; rep from * 2 more times, knit to end – 6 sts dec'd (32–14–14–32).

Row 5: Knit to 2 sts bef 2nd m, ssk, sm, k2tog, knit to end – 2 sts dec'd.

Figure 6: Assembly of Tree and Background for Size Large

Row 7: Rep Row 3 – 6 sts dec'd; 84 sts (31–11–11–31).
Row 9: Rep Row 5 – 2 sts dec'd; 82 sts (31–10–10–31).
Row 11: Rep Row 3 – 6 sts dec'd; 76 sts (30–8–8–30).
Row 13: Rep Row 5 – 2 sts dec'd; 74 sts (30–7–7–30).
Row 15: Rep Row 3 – 6 sts dec'd; 68 sts (29–5–5–29).
Row 17: Rep Row 5 – 2 sts dec'd; 66 sts (29–4–4–29).
Row 19: Rep Row 3 – 6 sts dec'd; 60 sts (28–2–2–28).
Row 21: Rep Row 5 – 2 sts dec'd; 58 sts (28–1–1–28).
Row 22: Rm 1st and 3rd m only. Knit to 1 st bef m, rm, cdd.

Turn needles so that tips are parallel and RS are together. With 3rd needle, 3-needle BO all sts. Insert yarn end through rem loop on needle and pull to tighten.

ASSEMBLY

Using long ends from MS's from the Background and mattress stitch, sew Tree to Background along dashed lines in Figure 6, matching corners.

Note: Figure depicts size Large.

BORDERS

Right Border

With K and circular needle, working on RS and starting at bottom-right corner of blanket, pu&k 231 (275) sts on edge (22 sts per Wedge, 11 sts per Ch and ST). Knit 11 rows. BO loosely leaving last st on needle.

Top Border

Starting at right corner of Right Border, pu&k 6 sts on edge of Border, then 198 (242) sts (22 sts per IT) on top edge of Blanket – 205 (249) sts. Knit 11 rows. BO loosely leaving last st on needle.

Left Border

Starting at left corner of Top Border, pu&k 6 sts on edge of Border, then 231 (275) sts on left edge of blanket (22 sts per Wedge, and 11 sts per Ch and ST) – 238 (282) sts. Knit 11 rows, BO loosely leaving last st on needle.

Bottom Border

Start at left corner of Left Border, pu&k 6 sts on edge of Border, then 198 (242) sts (22 sts per MT) on bottom edge of blanket, and 7 sts on the right edge of Right Border – 212 (256) sts. Knit 11 rows. BO loosely. Cut yarn and fasten off.

FINISHING

Weave in yarn ends and block if desired.

RESOURCES

ABBREVIATIONS

Bef	Before	**Pm**	Place marker
Beg	Begin(ning)	**Prev**	Previous
Bet	Between	**Psso**	Pass 1 slipped stitch over
Bli	Backwards loop increase	**Pu&k**	Pick up & knit
BO	Bind off	**Pwise**	Purlwise
Cdd	Central double decrease: slip 2 sts as if to k2tog, k1, pass slipped sts over (2 sts dec'd)	**R**	Right, right hand
		Rem	Remain(ing)
		Rep(s)	Repeat(s) (ing)
Cdd2	Slip 3 sts as if to k3tog, k2tog, pass slipped sts over (4 sts dec'd)	**Rm**	Remove marker
		Rnd(s)	Round(s)
CO	Cast on	**RS**	Right side
Cont	Continu(e)(ing)	**Sk2po**	Slip 1 st knitwise, knit 2 sts together; pass slipped stitch over (2 sts dec'd)
Dec('d)(ing)	Decrease(d)(ing)		
Dpns	Double-pointed needles	**Sl**	Slip
Inc('d)(ing)	Increase(d)(ing)	**Sm**	Slip marker
K	Knit	**Ssk**	Slip 2 sts knitwise, knit these 2 sts together through back loops (1 st dec'd)
K2tog	Knit 2 sts together (1 st dec'd)		
K2togBO	Knit 2 sts together then bind off the resulting stitch (2 sts dec'd)		
Kf&b	Knit into the front leg of the next st, leaving it on the Left needle, then knit into the back leg of the same st, then transfer the st to the Right needle (1 st inc'd)	**St(s)**	Stitch(es)
		Tbl	Through back loop(s)
		Tog	Together
		W&T	Wrap & turn
		WS	Wrong side
		WYIF	With yarn in front
		YO	Yarn over
Koh	Knit off holder		
Kwise	Knitwise		
Kyok	(k1, yo, k1) into 1 st (2 sts inc'd)		
L	Left, left hand		
M	Marker		
P	Purl		
P2sso	Pass 2 slipped stitches over		
P2tog	Purl 2 together (1 st dec'd)		
Patt	Pattern stitch		

GLOSSARY

Common knitting techniques are on this page, and less common techniques are covered in more depth on the pages that follow.

Techniques that have a camera icon after the title have an instructional video. See page 206 for access to videos.

Backwards Loop Increase (bli)

*With yarn in back, wrap yarn around left index finger, back to front, once with yarn exiting to right. Insert R needle, right to left, under the front leg of the loop and slip loop off finger and onto R needle. Tighten yarn (1 st inc'd).

Cable BO

K1, bring yarn to front, sl st to L needle, p2tog, *yarn to back, sl 1 st kwise to R needle, sl both sts to L needle, p2tog, yarn to front, sl1 pwise to R needle, sl both sts to L needle, P2tog; rep from *.

Knitted Cast-On

6 inches from end of yarn, make a slipknot and slide loop onto L needle. *Insert R needle left-to-right through front leg of last-made loop (i.e., kwise), wind working end of yarn around R needle counterclockwise and pull new loop through existing loop. Transfer new loop on R needle to the L needle. Pull yarn to adjust tension. Rep from * to add more sts.

Provisional Cast-on

Method 1: Traditional Crochet Chain: Using a crochet hook and contrasting yarn of the same weight as working yarn, make a chain with twice the number of sts as need to be CO plus 1. Using crochet hook and working yarn, insert hook into the back "bump" of the 2nd chain st, draw yarn through and transfer to needle. Rep in every 2nd back bump until the number of sts needed for the CO are on the needle. Begin knitting from these sts.

When provisionally CO sts need to become "live," undo the crochet chain from the end, one stitch at a time, and transfer sts to needle as they become free.

Method 2: Wrapping a Yarn: Use a piece of scrap yarn about 3 times the length of the edge to be cast on. With working yarn, make a slipknot on one end of the scrap yarn, then lay scrap yarn parallel to the needle used for casting on, with the slip knotted end furthest from the needle tip. Wind the working yarn around both the needle and the scrap yarn snugly until there are the same number of winds on needle as needed for the cast-on. Tie ends of the scrap yarn tog. With working yarn, begin work. *Note:* It may be easier to use the cable of an interchangeable needle set or a stitch holder in place of the scrap yarn.

Single Crochet for Edging

*Insert hook through next edge st. Yarn over the hook and draw a yarn loop through the edge stitch. Yarn over the hook again and draw through rem loop(s) on hook. Rep from *.

Slip Stitch (Crochet) for Edging

Insert hook through next edge st. Bring yarn over hook from back to front. Draw the yarn through to the front, then through existing loop on the hook. Repeat.

Tacking Embellishments

When fastening off, leave a long tail. Pin the embellishment to the RS of the work as instructed, inserting pin on the WS so that sewing yarn doesn't get tangled around the pin. Starting at the location where the tail begins, *take a stitch in the front bump of the blanket, just under the edge of the embellishment. To locate this bump, lift the edge of the embellishment slightly to peak underneath. Then take a stitch in the edge (outermost leg) of the embellishment. Rep from * around the entire embellishment, to the starting point. Tie off, then insert the needle back and forth between the embellishment and blanket until the yarn end is ½"/1 cm long, to bury the yarn underneath the embellishment. Carefully trim yarn end flush with the edge of the embellishment.

TECHNIQUE TUTORIALS
3-NEEDLE BIND-OFF 📹

The 3-needle bind-off is used to join 2 sets of live stitches and is a great modular method for making a geometric shape.

How to

A 3-needle BO used for joining and shaping is generally commenced after working part or all of a right side row, as follows:

1) On the next (a WS) row, knit half the stitches on the row only.

2) Rotate needles so that tips are parallel, RS are tog, WS facing out. Pull working yarn out from bet needles. The needle closer to you is the front needle, and the one behind is the back needle.

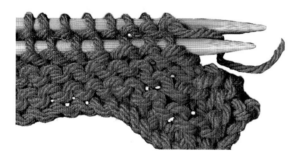

3) Insert third needle, as if to knit, through 1st st on front needle, then 1st st on back needle. Wrap yarn around third needle, as if to knit.

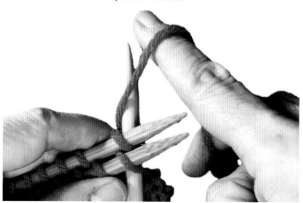

4) With third needle, draw yarn loop through the 1st loop on the back needle, then through 1st loop on the front needle.

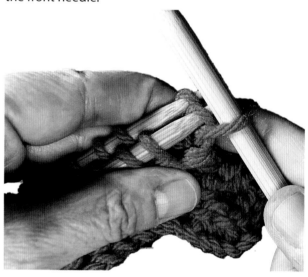

5) Slip both stitches off the two needles. There is now one loop on the third needle.

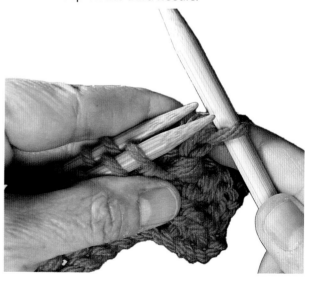

6) Repeat Steps 3 through 5 with the next pair of stitches on the front and back needles.

7) There are now 2 sts on the third needle. Insert the back needle into 2nd (right-most) st on third needle, and pull over the 1st stitch on the third needle, to bind off.

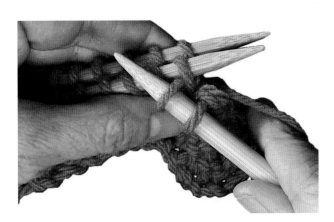

Now there is just 1 stitch remaining on the third needle. Repeat Steps 6 and 7 until there are no stitches remaining on the front and back needles and 1 st remaining on the third needle. Follow pattern instructions for handling the remaining stitch.

Hints for Success

- Avoid dropping stitches by keeping the front and back needle tips aligned and working near needle tips.

- If there are too many stitches on the front needle, decrease during the BO by inserting the third needle through 2 stitches on the front needle, instead of just 1 st. Likewise, if there are too many stitches on the back needle, insert the third needle through 2 sts on the back needle. Space out multiple decreases evenly over the BO.

- A BO that is too tight will distort the shape. If your BO tends to be tight, choose a larger size needle as your third needle.

ASSEMBLING PILLOWS WITH A ZIPPER CLOSURE

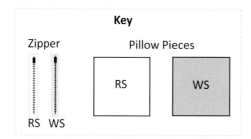

Key

Zipper — Pillow Pieces — RS — WS

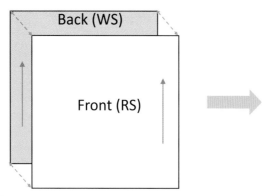

1) Place Front and Back, wrong sides together, aligning corners. Pin.

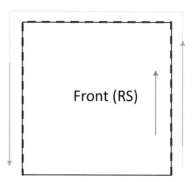

2) With matching yarn and tapestry needle, hand sew the right, top, and left edges. Leave bottom edge open.

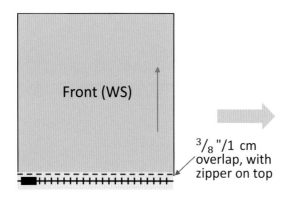

$^3/_8$ "/1 cm overlap, with zipper on top

3) Turn pillow cover so RS are together and WS are facing out. Close zipper. Orient zipper with tab facing down. Center zipper on bottom edge of Front, overlapping edges by $^3/_8$ "/1 cm. Zipper is on top of Front piece. Pin. With matching colored thread, hand sew along red dashed line. Open zipper.

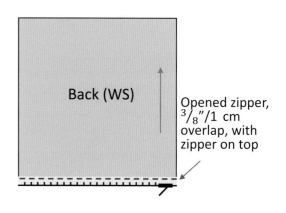

Opened zipper, $^3/_8$ "/1 cm overlap, with zipper on top

4) With zipper open, center free zipper edge to bottom edge of Back, overlapping edges by $^3/_8$ "/1 cm. Pin. With matching colo red thread, hand sew along red dashed line.

5) Turn pillow cover right side out and insert pillow form into cover. Optional: With safety pins, pin form to inside of cover at the four corners to prevent the form from floating around in the cover.

BORDERS AND BACKINGS

Adding borders and an optional backing to your blanket will produce a blanket that shines.

BORDERS

Each blanket in this book has a border selected to complement the blanket. This section has ideas and how-to's for alternate border treatments.

A border provides a consistent and flat edging that doesn't curl or distort. It terminates the pattern by framing the design elements. Audition different colors for the border to see what the blanket needs to look complete. Using a dominant color from the blanket makes the border part of the design. A more muted version of a color in the blanket or a neutral color will frame the blanket without drawing attention or competing with the design.

LOG CABIN see Figure 1

A Log Cabin border is used when the Border is worked in a single color. It is used in most of the blankets in this book. "Nr," is the number of complete ridges knitted in the Border. The number of stitches to pu&k on the short edge of a completed border is 1 + Nr.

Figure 1: Construction of a Log Cabin Border

JOIN-AS-YOU-GO BORDER (JAYG)

If you don't have a circular needle, a JAYG border can be worked counterclockwise around the blanket starting at a corner, with two dpns. CO 5 to 10 stitches. Knit all rows, making a join to the blanket edge at the end of every RS row by inserting the R needle through the back loop of the last Border stitch and the edge of the blanket. Use the original instructions from the blanket's Border for the number of Joins to make per shape along the blanket's edge.

At corners, use the following pattern stitch to **turn the corner** (See "Wrap & Turn (w&t)" on page 203):

> **Row 1 (RS):** Knit to last st, wrap & turn (w&t) last st.
>
> **Row 2 (WS):** Knit.
>
> **Row 3:** Knit to 1 st before prev wrap, w&t next stitch.
>
> **Row 4:** Knit.
>
> Rep [Rows 3 and 4] until the 2nd st from the beginning of the RS row is wrapped.
>
> **Next RS row:** K1, w&t.
>
> *Note:* In this phase, we are wrapping stitches for the second time.
>
> **Next WS row:** Knit.
>
> **Row 5:** Knit to end including the stitch that was wrapped on the prev RS row, w&t next stitch.
>
> **Row 6:** Knit.
>
> Repeat [Rows 5 & 6] until the last st on a RS row is wrapped.
>
> **Next WS Row:** Knit.

Points

To make a JAYG border with points, make an increase at the beginning of, for example, each of the next 7 RS rows, then a decrease at the beginning of each of the following 7 RS rows, and repeat this pattern.

Turning Corners: When approaching a corner, plan out where joins will be made so that the pattern stitch completes exactly at the corner. Use the **turn the corner** instructions at corners. After turning the corner, restart the pattern stitch along the next edge.

Petals

To make a JAYG border with Petal shapes, work as follows:

CO 1 to 7 sts.

> **Row 1 (RS):** CO 2 sts, knit to end – 2 sts inc'd.
> **Row 2 and all WS rows to Row 20:** Knit.
> **Row 3:** Repeat Row 1 – 2 sts inc'd.
> **Row 5:** Kfb, knit to end – 1 st inc'd.
> **Row 7:** Repeat Row 5 – 1 st inc'd.
> **Rows 9 & 11:** Knit.
> **Row 13:** K2tog, knit to end – 1 st dec'd.
> **Row 15:** Repeat Row 15 – 1 st dec'd.
> **Row 17:** BO 2 sts, knit to end – 2 sts dec'd.
> **Row 19:** Repeat Row 17 – 2 sts dec'd.

Use the **turn the corner** instructions at corners.

CROCHET BORDER

A scalloped crocheted edge is fast and attractive. With yarn and crochet hook, on RS, attach yarn to center of right edge of blanket face by pulling loop up from back of work. Ch1. *Skip 2 garter st ridges/CO/BO sts and make 7 double crochet (dc) in next ridge/st, skip 2 garter st ridges/CO/BO sts and make sl st in next ridge/CO/BO st.*

Rep between * and *, to end of edge making adjustments if needed to end the scallop exactly at the corner. Sl st in the blanket corner, ch3, sl st in same corner location, and continue scallops on the next border. When the starting point is reached, sl st in the initial chain stitch. Cut yarn, fasten off and weave in ends. If there are diagonal pieces on the blanket edge, you may first work a single crochet around the entire blanket, making 1 sc for each st that would have otherwise been pu&k on the pieces.

BACKING A BLANKET

A fabric backing can add a nice finish to a knitted blanket. It makes the blanket warmer and eliminates the stretch for a blanket that will be used as a coverlet on a bed. If planning to back a blanket you can just fasten off the yarn ends and skip the weaving in.

Select a fabric for the backing. One good option for a non-stretch backing is double-brushed flannel. It can be machine or hand washed. It is warm, strong, affordable, and easy to work with. Some flannels have a flat woven surface on the wrong side. Double-brushed flannels are thicker and fuzzy on both sides. The fuzzy surface helps the WS of the flannel to stick to the knitted blanket, requiring less tacking in the middle of the blanket to keep the knitted blanket and backing together. Another option is fleece, which is thicker and stretchier than flannel. Fleece is only available as a synthetic. It does not need to be prewashed. If the blanket is wool, or extra warmth is desired, use a woven wool fabric for the backing. For the lightest weight backing, use double gauze.

Prepare the blanket by blocking the blanket, following the washing and drying instructions on the yarn label.

Mark the center of the blanket with a stitch marker by folding it into quarters with right sides together and corners aligned.

On a large surface, spread out and flatten the blanket, right side down, so it lays flat and is not skewed. Using masking or painter's tape, tape edges to the work surface so they don't move.

Measure the width of the blanket in several places, average, and record. Do the same for the length.

Determine the fabric requirements. If the width of the fabric, after selvages are removed, is smaller than the width of the blanket, the amount of fabric needed will be 2 times the length of the blanket.

If the width of the fabric is the same or more than the width of the blanket then the amount of fabric needed is the same as the length of the blanket.

Prepare the fabric. Cotton fabric should be washed, dried, and pressed to remove wrinkles, following manufacturer's instructions. Before washing the fabric, cut off all the selvage edges (where the printing is) because they shrink at a faster rate than the fabric.

Construct the fabric backing. The backing will be the same size as the blanket.

Measure the fabric. If the blanket is wider than the fabric, two widths of fabric need to be sewn together to span the width. It will be easiest with a sewing machine but it can be done by hand. With right sides of the fabric together, sew a vertical seam, leaving a ½"/1.25 cm seam allowance. Press the seam out flat. When seaming together two lengths of fabric, it is more asthetically pleasing to cut one in half along the vertical, and center the uncut piece between the two cut halfs. You may use several different fabric patterns for design interest, or even piece together a backing from smaller pieces of fabric.

You may use a bedsheet as a backing to avoid seaming. However, the high thread count of most sheets makes it very tiring to sew by hand.

Mark the center of the backing by folding it in half twice, matching corners exactly, then inserting a safety pin through the corner of the folds.

Center the fabric, right side up, on top of the blanket using this approach:

> With the backing folded in quarters with right sides together, place it on the blanket, matching the marked center of the backing with the marked center of the blanket, then unfold the backing carefully, maintaining alignment of the centers of the fabric and blanket.

Trim the backing almost even with the blanket edge, cutting ⅛"/0.3 cm to ¼"/0.6 cm outside the blanket edge. Be careful not to cut the blanket.

Proceed in one of the following ways:

1) With safety pins, lift the backing edge slightly and turn in a ½"/1.25 cm hem and finger press, then insert a safety pin through the turned hem and the knitted blanket edge to secure. Continue around the blanket in this manner to pin the edge in place.

2) Separate the layers and with a hot iron, press a ½"/1.25 cm hem all around the edge of the backing. *Optional*: Using a 3 mm long straight stitch, sew the hem down ¼"/0.6 cm from the edge around entire perimeter of the fabric piece. Reassemble and align the center of the backing and blanket, wrong sides together, as they were initially, and use safety pins to pin them together.

Sewing the layers must be done by hand. With the fabric side facing up, a sewing needle and sewing thread that matches the border color, and using whipstitch, sew the hem of the fabric to the back of the border making a stitch about every ¼"/0.6 cm. The fabric hem will lie about ½"/1.25 cm in from the blanket edge. So that thread doesn't show on the knitted blanket side, take stitches into the bumps of the garter stitch ridges whenever possible.

Lay the blanket out flat again with the knitted side up. Take a few discrete stitches through both layers in about 8–10 different locations scattered around the blanket surface. Hide the thread ends between layers. This should be enough to keep the layers together during use and laundering.

Something Fishy won Best of the Knitting Division at the Los Angeles County Fair in 2023.

INTARSIA ◻️

Intarsia is used when a large one-color motif is to be added. For example, the large pink heart in the left of Figure 1 should be worked in intarsia. If you imagine knitting across a row in the heart area of the top, you first knit with the background (peach) color then the pink heart color, and finally with the background color. That row slice only has 3 colors.

Rule for Intarsia: When the row has a small number of colors compared to the number of stitches on the needle, and there are large numbers of contiguous stitches worked in each color of yarn, use intarsia.

Contrast that top with one in the center of Figure 1. Imagine you are knitting across one of the rows in the heart section and are alternating frequently between the background and heart colors.

Rule for Stranded: When switching between the background color and constrast color often and predictably (in a repeating pattern), use stranded (aka "fair isle").

What about the design on the far-right of Figure 1 with the hearts staggered diagonally? This is a murky situation. It doesn't meet the requirements for stranded because the heart pattern doesn't repeat across the row, but the hearts are very small so it doesn't meet the requirement for intarsia where the area of contrast color is large. For this area you could either work it in intarsia or in duplicate stitch or a combination of the two.

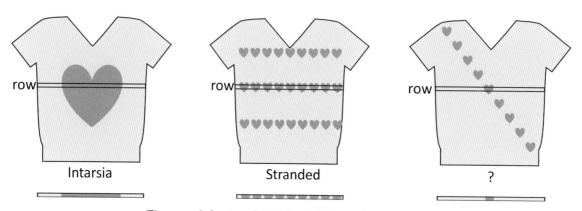

Figure 1: Selecting the Right Technique for Colorwork

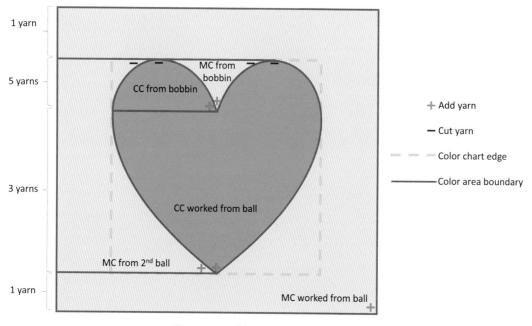

Figure 2: Adding and Cutting Yarn

HOW IT WORKS

With Intarsia, a separate yarn strand (ball) is needed for each noncontiguous area of color, as shown in Figure 2. In most of this Heart design there are 3 balls of yarn active at a time, but when we get to the row where the lobes split, 5 balls are needed until the heart is complete. Once the heart is complete, all four "extra" yarns that were added are cut, and the work continues with the main ball.

When knitting a row, each yarn is positioned at the right edge of the area to be worked in that color. When working across the row the yarn is dropped at the left edge of the color area, and the new color is picked up. Figure 4 shows the positions of the yarn balls at the beginning and end of a row. When the work is turned for starting the next row, the yarn ball positions are automatically at the right edge of each color area, just where they need to be to work the next row.

Intarsia designs are described via a color chart. The chart in Figure 3 contains 50 rows and is 25 stitches wide. For each row the chart specifies the stitch to use and the color to work the stitch. For instance, on Row 1, work sts 1–12 in MC, stitch 13 in CC, and stitches 14–25 in MC.

This chart is for garter stitch so it looks different than color charts you may have worked for stockinette stitch. A garter stitch chart will look elongated (stretched) when compared with the final knitted piece. On a chart, each stitch is represented by a square, but in garter stitch each ridge is 1 st wide and 2 sts tall. Every row is knitted so on WS rows there is a dot symbol indicating to knit on the WS. In some patterns, simple edge shaping is combined with intarsia, so there will be k2tog or ssk symbols on some rows. Some of the intarsia charts in this book only include RS rows. It is assumed the WS rows are knitted in the same color as the prev RS row.

In some patterns, there will be estimated yarn amounts for areas that should be worked from bobbins. Use those amounts as estimates then adjust

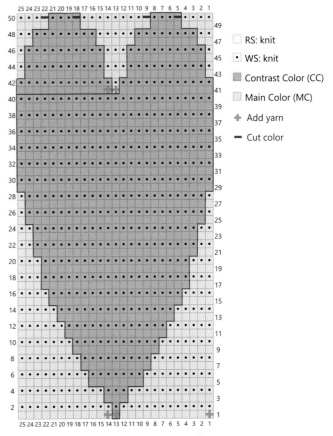

Figure 3: Heart Chart

Legend:
- RS: knit
- WS: knit
- Contrast Color (CC)
- Main Color (MC)
- Add yarn
- Cut color

At the beginning of each row, yarns are at right edge of their color sections.

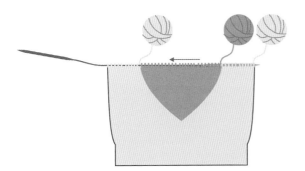

When the row is completed, yarns are now at the left edge of their color section. So, when work is turned, yarns are again at the right edge.

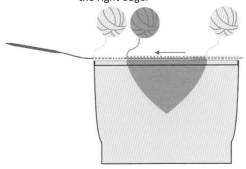

Note: A separate yarn strand (ball) is required for each noncontiguous color section.

Figure 4: Yarn Ball Positions for Intarsia at Beginning and End of Rows

yardage to actual use after the chart is worked the first time. Another way to estimate the length of yarn needed is to work an area from the ball, undo those rows, and measure how much yarn was used.

Added to this chart (Figure 3) are some additional symbols and outlines that show when to add and cut yarn. The dark gray lines enclose areas where separate yarns are used. The green plus sign indicates where to add yarn, and the red minus sign is where yarn is cut. A suggestion is made as to whether to work the yarn directly from the ball or to wind yarn onto a bobbin. It is not practical to put very long lengths of yarn onto a bobbin, but smaller areas that require less yardage may be knit from bobbins to help with yarn management.

Yarns are not cut until a color area is complete.

AVOIDING HOLES

When making color changes (dropping Old Yarn and continuing with New Yarn), we need to do something special to connect the yarns, otherwise we will have independent columns of stitches at the color transitions and holes in the knitting.

This *something* is to cross the yarns. How to cross depends on whether we're working a RS or WS row.

RS row yarn changes/crossing (see Figure 5): Yarns are already on the WS of the work because we are knitting. Take the Old Yarn (yarn that is about to be dropped) and cross it over and to the left of the New Yarn on the WS of the work, pick up the New Yarn color, draw up any extra slack yarn, and continue.

> ***Old Yarn over New Yarn,
> continue with New Yarn.***

WS row yarn changes/crossing (see Figure 6): A WS row is always knitted, which means that the Old Yarn (yarn that is about to be dropped) is away from you, on the RS of the work. Yarn crossing must always occur with both the yarns on the WS of the work, so move the Old Yarn (the yarn that is about to be dropped) between the needles and toward you (to the WS) and move it to the left so that it crosses over the New Yarn. Move the New Yarn between the needles to the RS of the work (away from you), draw up extra yarn and continue knitting with the New Yarn.

> ***Old Yarn forward, Old Yarn left over New Yarn,
> New Yarn to back,
> continue with New Yarn.***

Despite crossing yarns there will still be small holes next to locations where yarn was added and cut. Thread the yarn end onto a tapestry needle and on the WS, insert needle through the bump of the stitch of different color next to the hole, then back through the first stitch. On the WS, weave in yarn end (see "Weaving in Ends" on page 204).

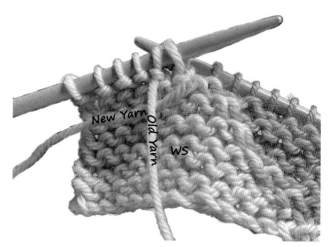

Figure 5: Yarn "cross" shown above. Crossing yarns is always done on the WS. New Yarn always goes under Old Yarn.

Figure 6: Color change when working a WS Row: Initially, the Old Yarn is away from you on RS. Bring Old Yarn forward (to WS) then cross as shown in Figure 5, then move only the New Yarn away from you (to the RS) and continue knitting with New Yarn.

MATTRESS STITCH 📹

Sewing garter stitch pieces together with mattress stitch produces the neatest and most invisible seam.

WHEN TO USE MATTRESS STITCH

Mattress stitch can be used to sew together: side edge to side edge, CO edge to CO edge, CO edge to BO edge, or side edge to CO/BO edge. We focus on side edge to side edge, which is the most common.

HOW TO SEAM WITH MATTRESS STITCH

1) Thread long CO/BO tail or yarn the color of one of the pieces onto tapestry needle.

Insert up through the first edge bump of the piece opposite where the yarn is emerging. In this example the yarn is emerging from the left piece so we insert first through the right edge, then through the first edge bump of the left edge.

Pull yarn to eliminate some but not all of the slack.

2) Insert needle upwards through the next bump on the right edge, and pull to eliminate slack.

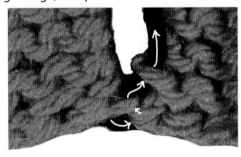

3) Continue inserting tapestry needle upwards through alternating left and right edge bumps.

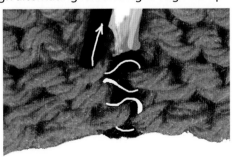

ALIGNING COLOR STRIPES

Aligning color transitions presents a challenge because the ridges of one edge will nest in the valleys of the other edge, causing striping to appear slightly misaligned (aka "jogging") along the seam. To align stripes, we will need to do an "around the world" maneuver as shown below.

1) Insert needle upwards through the last edge bump of the old color on the left edge.

On the right edge, insert needle downwards through the last edge bump of the old color.

2) Insert needle upwards through the last bump on the left edge, again. Draw up slack.

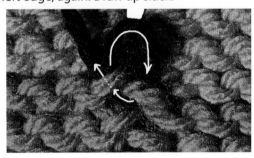

3) Unthread and trim current sewing yarn. Thread new yarn color onto needle, and continue.

Note: Sts before the "around the world" are blue, "around the world" sts are white, and sts in the new new yarn color are pink.

PICK UP AND KNIT (PU&K) 🎥

Pick up and knit (pu&k) is a technique used to generate live stitches on the edge of a previously completed piece (PCP) of knitting. It is used in modular knitting in place of sewing pieces together.

Pu&k differs from *picking up* stitches because a loop of working yarn is drawn through a small hole made by poking a knitting needle or crochet hook through the edge of the PCP. With *picking up,* the needle is loaded with loops of yarn that are *picked up* or *borrowed* from the PCP's edge.

When pu&k'ing on an edge perpendicular to (at right angles to) a CO/BO edge, as shown in Figure 3, 1 st is generated per every two rows of knitting. Two rows of knitting form an easily recognized surface feature on the knitting called a "ridge" as shown in Figure 1. The area between ridges is referred to as the "valley."

Start pu&k at location indicated in pattern. Hold the working yarn in your left hand and provide the proper tension by winding the yarn over and under your fingers.

For the neatest result, insert through bumps when available. A bump is the last st of a ridge. Working on the RS, and with a knitting needle, insert front to back through the next bump and draw a yarn loop to front of work. If working on the left or right edge that has no shaping, insert needle through each bump on the edge. If more sts are needed than there are bumps available, insert into the outside strand of the edge stitch bet ridges (aka, the "valley"). If working on a CO or BO edge, insert the needle through both strands of yarn.

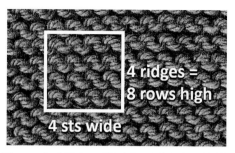

Figure 2: 4 Ridges High by 4 Stitches Wide

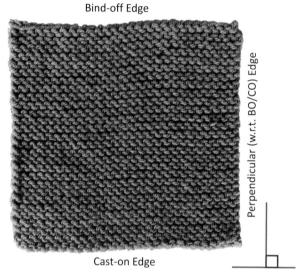

Figure 3: Identification of Edges

Bind-off Edge

Cast-on Edge

Perpendicular (w.r.t. BO/CO) Edge

When picking up on a 45 degree diagonal edge, as shown in Figure 1 *pu&k in two consecutive ridges, then in the valley bef the next ridge; rep from * cont this cadence. When close to the ending point, count the sts generated and plan out the remaining pu&k locations. If the stitch count is incorrect by a few sts, make increases (bli) or decreases (k2tog) on the next WS row. Place markers as a reminder, where a marker through 2 sts indicates a planned decrease (k2tog) and a marker through 1 st indicates a planned increase (bli).

A crochet hook may be used instead of a knitting needle. If using a crochet hook, use the same size (in mm) as the working knitting needle or up to 0.5 mm smaller than needle size. If working with a crochet hook, sts may be accumulated on the crochet hook's shaft, then transferred off the non-hook end to needle. The crochet hook must have a thin shank.

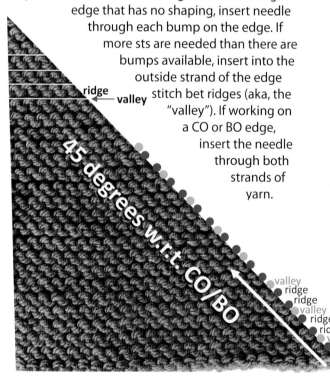

Figure 1: Pu&k on Diagonal Edge

SLIP STITCH TRAVELING

Slip stitch traveling is used to move the working yarn to a new location along an edge that will later be sewn to another piece. The purpose is to avoid cutting yarn, which generates more ends to weave in, and to produce a neat and regular edge to which other pieces may be sewn. The pattern's instructions will state how many stitches to work along an edge.

HOW TO

1) In this example we want to move the working yarn from point A to B.

3) Insert L needle, left to right, through the front leg of the right-most stitch on the R needle and slip stitch over the left-most stitch. 1 stitch remains on the R needle. Adjust tension so that edge does not pull in.

2) Using a crochet hook or knitting needle (latter shown here) and working on the RS, insert R needle front to back through the outer leg of the edge stitch of the first valley, yarn around counterclockwise, and pull a loop through. There are now 2 stitches on the needle.

4) Repeat Steps 2 and 3 along the edge to B, inserting R needle into the next valley.

Note: if ridges are perpendicular to edge, insert in every valley. If ridges are diagonal to edge, insert needle in every valley and in every other ridge in order to generate enough stitches. Stop occasionally to count stitches and plan out the remainder of the locations for inserting needle.

The slipped stitches should look like chaining.

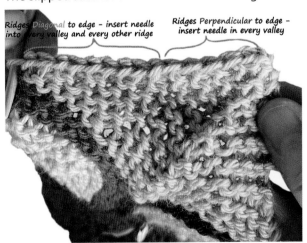

Ridges Diagonal to edge - insert needle into every valley and every other ridge

Ridges Perpendicular to edge - insert needle in every valley

TACKING DRAPED YARN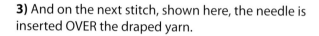

When an edge of knitting will later have stitches picked up and knitted (pu&k) along it, pattern instructions may say to drape yarn between uses instead of cutting and reattaching. Later, during a pu&k on the same edge, the draped yarn will be tacked to the edge. This reduces the number of yarn ends to weave in during finishing and saves yarn.

How to

1) When draping, leave about ½"/1.25 cm extra for every 1"/2.5 cm that yarn must be carried. Another way to get the right amount of drape is to stretch the edge of the garter stitch, and leave enough draped yarn to span the stretched edge.

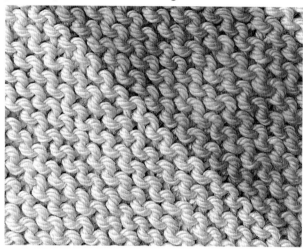

2) Later, when performing pu&k along an edge with a draped yarn, alternate inserting the R needle over and under the draped yarn. In the photo below, the needle is being inserted UNDER the draped yarn.

3) And on the next stitch, shown here, the needle is inserted OVER the draped yarn.

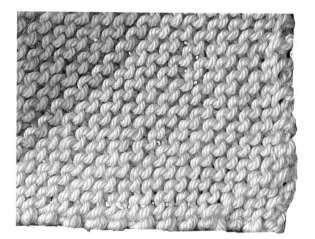

4) The WS of the completed pu&k shows that the mint green draped yarn is now neatly tacked to the edge of the orange stripe.

WRAP & TURN (W&T) 📹

Wrap & turn, aka short rows, is used to work only some of the stitches in a row. In apparel knitting it is used for shoulder shaping, sock heels, and bust darts. In geometric knitting it is used to create curved shapes.

How to Wrap & Turn

When instructed to wrap & turn you will be wrapping the next stitch on the L needle, and turning the work, leaving the remaining stitches unworked.

Whether working a RS or WS row, to wrap the next stitch, do as follows:

1. Work to the indicated turning point, slip the next stitch purlwise to the R needle.

2. Bring yarn forward.

3. Turn work (the slipped stitch is now on the L needle and the yarn is now at the back of the work), leaving rem sts of row unworked.

4. Insert R needle purlwise into the *slipped stitch* and slip it (again) back to the R needle.

5. Begin working the following row as instructed by the pattern.

Tensioning the Wrap

When wrapping the stitch do not leave a lot of loose yarn. Wrap it snugly.

What's Different about Garter Stitch?

In w&t for stockinette stitch, the wrap and the wrapped stitch are knitted together on the following row to avoid the little hole that normally forms.

But in garter stitch, we don't do this. On the following row, the wrapped stitch is just knitted. Nothing special needs to be done with the wrap. And there will not be a noticeable hole in the fabric because garter stitch is denser and the surface ridges hide the wraps that are in the *valleys* between ridges.

How to Determine Which Side Is the RS

All the turning of the work can cause you to lose track of which side is the RS. In garter stitch knitting, the front and back of the work look the same until color changes begin. Therefore, mark the RS of your work with a removable stitch marker. To determine

which is the RS, note the position of the CO tail, which is on the right-bottom corner of the RS. If it is on the bottom-left corner you are looking at the WS.

Perfect Opportunity to Purl Backwards

Also, so that you don't have to turn your work at all, you can purl backwards on WS rows. In this case you work Steps 1 and 2 of the w&t, with the current side still facing you, slip the slipped stitch back to the L needle then begin purling backwards the stitches on the R needle. Note that by purling backwards you are working a WS row with the RS facing you, so if there is a wrap & turn instruction on the RS row, you will do this:

1. Slip the stitch to be wrapped from R to L needle.

2. Move yarn from front to back of work.

3. Slip *slipped stitch* from L to R needle.

4. Begin knitting RS stitches.

Note: German short rows; don't worry if you don't know what that is . . . suffice it to say that it does not work well for garter stitch.

Figure 1: The flower petals in Flower Show use wrap & turn. The rows that use wrap & turn are the ones where the yellow ridges do not extend all the way to the magenta center.

WEAVING IN ENDS

When the wrong, or "private," side of the work will be seen, the best but not the fastest way to weave in ends is to work duplicate stitch on the WS of the work, The advantages are: 1) It is less visible on the WS, 2) it is more secure because the yarn ends are buried and won't poke out later, 3) there is no need to fasten off because the friction of the yarn will keep it securely in place, 4) it saves yarn because only 6"/15 cm of yarn is needed *if* you use a Susan Bates Finishing needle (recommended).

How to

If using a tapestry needle, leave a yarn end of 8"/20 cm, and if using a Susan Bates Finishing Needle, leave 6"/15 cm. Don't fasten off, unless the yarn is very slippery, like silk. Thread the yarn end onto the needle.

On the WS, near the place where the yarn emerges from the work, select a ridge of the same color yarn as the end to be woven in. Observe the smiley and frowny faces of the ridge. Now follow Steps 1–7.

1) Insert needle upwards through nearest smiley face, and pull yarn through.

3) Follow the yarn strand down and insert needle right to left underneath the stitch below the current smiley face and pull yarn through.

2) Following the yarn strand around the frowny face, insert needle downwards through next smiley face and pull yarn through.

4) Repeat Steps 1–3 following the strand until about 1"/2.5 cm of yarn remains (3"/7.5 cm if using tapestry needle).

5) Working from left to right, insert needle between the stitches being duplicated (orange) and the duplicate stitches (blue) and pull yarn through.

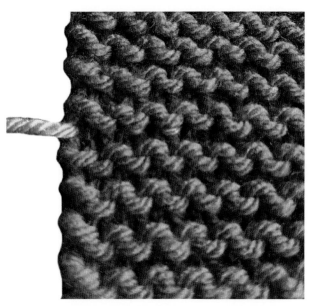

7) Turn work over and observe the slight shadow stitches on the RS. When worked in matching yarn color, these will not show.

6) Stretch knitting along ridges to see if end will nest. If necessary, trim yarn end flush with edge.

Final Tip: Tension of the duplicate stitches should match the tension of the stitches being duplicated.

This is the WS of the the Flower Show Block with 10 yarn ends woven in with duplicate stitch. Note that the interleaved stitches around the magenta center are from pu&k weaving of draped yarn not duplicate stitch weaving. The chaining around the Petals is from pu&k for the Edge and Corner pieces. The duplicate stitches cannot be found, which brings me to my final point: don't weave in using this method if there is any possibility you need to unravel your piece!

SUPPLEMENTAL MATERIAL

Technique videos, coloring pages for planning your own color schemes, and more can be found at:

http://www.theknitwit.org/dm3ffvpn8ovtnu49

or point your smartphone's camera at the QR code for access. See page 207 for a list of video topics.

YARN SUPPLIERS

The following yarn companies have generously provided yarn for the sample blankets in this book. Unless otherwise noted, each company provided yarn for one blanket.

Berroco
berroco.com
1 Tupperware Dr., Suite 4
N. Smithfield, RI 02896

Cascade Yarns (2 blankets)
cascadeyarns.com

Ella Rae Yarns
knittingfever.com/brand/ella-rae/yarns
Knitting Fever Inc.
315 Bayview Ave.
Amityville, NY 11701

Jagger Spun Yarn
jaggerspunyarn.com
5 Water Street
Springvale, ME 04083

Malabrigo Yarn (3 blankets)
malabrigoyarn.com
Montevideo, Uruguay

Plymouth Yarn
plymouthyarn.com
500 Lafayette St.
Bristol, PA 19007

Sugarbush Yarns*
*note, Sugarbush Yarns is closed

SweetGeorgia Yarns
sweetgeorgiayarns.com
Vancouver, BC, Canada

Valley Yarns (6 blankets)
yarn.com
Webs exclusive yarn collection

PHOTOGRAPHY

The photos for this book were taken by my husband Gerard Holzmann, aka: edsger-studio.com, at his studio in Monrovia, California.

TECHNICAL EDITING

Natalie Delbusso, Mary Rose, and Susan Hislop are gratefully acknowledged for their work to correct and improve these patterns.

SAMPLE KNITTING

Sample blankets were made by:

Julie Anderson (Oceanfront, Safe in the City, and Tree of Lights)

Jill Fauble (Stay Paw-sitive)

Marie Franzosa (More Than a Feline)

Linette Grayum (Snowflakes)

Phoebe Horton (Christmas Tree Lot)

Margaret Holzmann (Copycats, Love Bug, Safe at Home, Something Fishy, and Row Robin)

Vicki Noerdhoek (Festive Forest)

Sonia Savoulian (Upside Dowg)

Lori Veteto (Flower Show)

Thank you to each sample knitter for sharing their talents and time. They tested and helped me improve the clarity of the patterns.

INSTRUCTIONAL VIDEOS

Use the QR code for Supplemental Materials then select the "Videos" button.

TECHNIQUE VIDEOS

3-needle BO for Shaping
3-needle BO for Joining
Intarsia for Garter Stitch
Mattress Stitch for Garter Stitch
Pick Up and Knit
Pick Up and Knit on Diagonal Edge
Slip-Stitch Crochet Decoration
Weaving Draped Yarn during Pick Up & Knit
Wrap & Turn for Garter Stitch

VIDEOS FOR INDIVIDUAL PATTERNS

CAMP ALONG

Complete Tutorials for Camper and Tree Blocks

FLOWER SHOW

Tutorials for Edges, Corner, Petal

MORE THAN A FELINE, SOMETHING FISHY, STAY PAW-SITIVE

Crochet Eye

SOMETHING FISHY

Fin

REFERENCES

The inspiration for the Bird Block used in Row Robin is from *Sparrows* by Pen + Paper Patterns at penandpaperpatterns.com.

FURTHER KNITTING

Sign up for Margaret's newsletter to learn about new books and pattern releases:

theknitwit.org/news

Get Margaret's previously published books:

Geometric Knit Blankets: 30 Innovative and Fun-to-Knit Blankets

theknitwit.org/geometric-knit-blankets-book

At Home with Margaret Holzmann: 10 Knitted Blankets in Hayfield Bonus

theknitwit.org/at-home-with-margaret-holzmann-book

Indy patterns by Margaret on Ravelry:

ravelry.com/designers/margaret-holzmann

Indy patterns by Margaret at her store:

theknitwit.org/store

Margaret on Linked Tree: linktr.ee/mholzmann

Youtube channel: youtube.com/@knitwitme

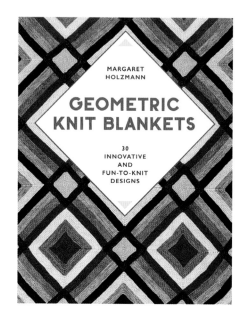

GROUP

Join Margaret's Facebook group to post about your project and see what others are making from Margaret's patterns:

Geometric Knit Blankets (for all designs)
facebook.com/groups/geometricknitblankets

CLASSES

Did you know that Margaret teaches classes?

Visit this webpage to learn more:

theknitwit.org/classes

NEWSLETTER

Be the first to learn about Margaret's new knitting patterns, contests and give-aways, pattern discounts, and the latest news.

Sign up for Margaret's newsletter at theknitwit.org/news

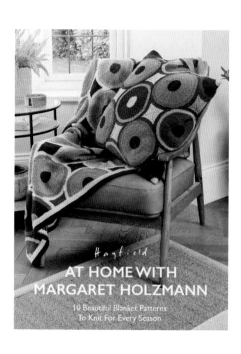